Blow the Bugle, Draw the Sword

The Wars, Campaigns, Regiments and
Soldiers of the British & Indian Armies
During the Victorian Era, 1839-1898

W. H. G. Kingston

CW00550397

LEONAUR

Blow the Bugle, Draw the Sword: the Wars, Campaigns, Regiments and Soldiers of the British & Indian Armies During the Victorian Era, 1839-1898
by W. H. G. Kingston

Published by Leonaur Ltd in 2007

Originally published under the title
Our Soldiers

Text in this form and material original to this edition
copyright © 2007 Leonaur Ltd

ISBN: 978-1-84677-265-8 (hardcover)
ISBN: 978-1-84677-266-5 (softcover)

http://www.leonaur.com

Publisher's Notes

Blow the Bugle, Draw the Sword

Contents

Ford o' Kabul River

Kabul town's by Kabul river—
Blow the bugle, draw the sword—
There I lef' my mate for ever,
Wet an' drippin' by the ford.
Ford, ford, ford o' Kabul river,
Ford o' Kabul river in the dark!
There's the river up and brimmin',
   an' there's 'arf a squadron swimmin'
'Cross the ford o' Kabul river in the dark.

Kabul town's a blasted place—
Blow the bugle, draw the sword—
'Strewth I shan't forget 'is face
Wet an' drippin' by the ford!
Ford, ford, ford o' Kabul river,
Ford o' Kabul river in the dark!
Keep the crossing-stakes beside you,
   an' they will surely guide you
'Cross the ford o' Kabul river in the dark.

Kabul town is sun and dust—
Blow the bugle, draw the sword—
I'd ha' sooner drownded fust
'Stead of 'im beside the ford.
Ford, ford, ford o' Kabul river,
Ford o' Kabul river in the dark!
You can 'ear the 'orses threshin',
   you can 'ear the men a-splashin',
'Cross the ford o' Kabul river in the dark.

Kabul town was ours to take—
Blow the bugle, draw the sword—
I'd ha' left it for 'is sake—
'Im that left me by the ford.
Ford, ford, ford o' Kabul river,
Ford o' Kabul river in the dark!
It's none so bloomin' dry there;
 ain't you never comin' nigh there,
'Cross the ford o' Kabul river in the dark?

Kabul town'll go to hell—
Blow the bugle, draw the sword—
'Fore I see him 'live an' well—
'Im—the best beside the ford.
Ford, ford, ford o' Kabul river,
Ford o' Kabul river in the dark!
Gawd 'elp 'em if they blunder,
 for their boots'll pull 'em under,
By the ford o' Kabul river in the dark.

Turn your 'orse from Kabul town—
Blow the bugle, draw the sword—
'Im an' 'arf my troop is down,
Down an' drownded by the ford.
Ford, ford, ford o' Kabul river,
Ford o' Kabul river in the dark!
There's the river low an' fallin',
 but it ain't no use o' callin'
'Cross the ford o' Kabul river in the dark.

Rudyard Kipling

The Afghan Campaigns
1839–42

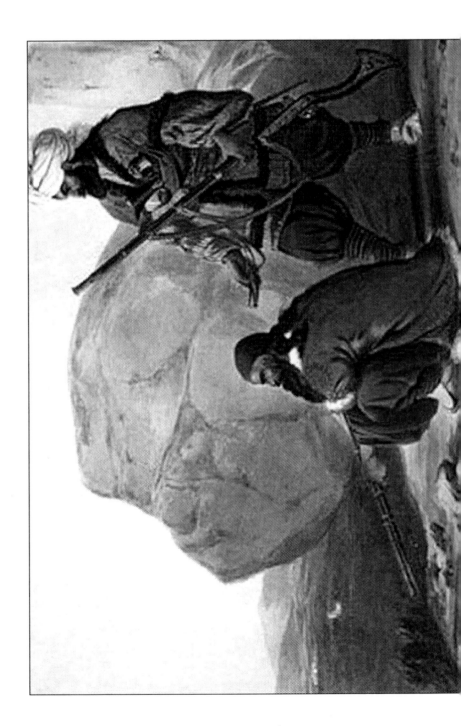

The Afghan Campaigns
1839-42

In 1809 the reigning Ameer of Afghanistan, Shah Soo-jah-ul-Moolk, was dispossessed of his throne and an exile. Runjeet Singh, the Sikh ruler of Punjab, plundered and imprisoned him at Lahore, and obtained from him the famous Kohinoor, the great diamond which is now among the crown jewels of Great Britain. Eventually Soojah escaped from Lahore and became a pensioner of the East India Company. For many years after the fall of Shah Soojah, anarchy ruled in Afghanistan, until in 1826 Dost Mahomed established himself upon the throne at Cabul.

Meantime Shah Soojah never ceased to plot for his restoration, and in 1832 came to an agreement with Runjeet Singh, in pursuance of which the latter undertook to assist him in an armed attempt to oust Dost Mahomed. The Indian Government, while professing neutrality, indirectly assisted Shah Soojah by paying his pension in advance.

In 1833 Shah Soojah's army was thoroughly beaten by Dost Mahomed before Candahar, though he himself escaped. But Runjeet Singh was more successful; he drove the Afghans back into the Khyber Pass and occupied Peshawar, which province he held against all the attempts of the Afghan Ameer to expel him.

In 1837 the Shah of Persia, under the instigation of and with assistance from, Russia, and in spite of strong remonstrances by the British, made war upon Afghanistan and marched upon Herat.

ELDRED POTTINGER AT HERAT

The siege of this place commenced on the 23rd of November 1837, and lasted over nine months, when it utterly collapsed, owing mainly to the determination and courage of Lieutenant Pottinger, who had arrived in the city just before, and assisted the Afghans in the defence. Notwithstanding the assistance of Russian volunteers the Persian attack was but feebly delivered; still, but for the presence of Pottinger and the courage given by his example, the Afghan defence would have been equally spiritless. At length, after some days' bombardment, a general assault was made on the 23rd of June 1838, and repulsed by Pottinger with heavy loss. Soon after the Shah, hearing that a British expedition had been sent up the Persian Gulf to force him to retire, raised the siege and left Herat, which has remained up to the present in the hands of the Afghans—a fact which may be said to be in the first instance due to the heroic achievements of one young British officer, Lieutenant Eldred Pottinger.

THE AFGHAN WAR

The Indian Government had now determined, for reasons into which it is not our province to inquire, to make war upon Dost Mahomed and to replace Shah Soojah upon the throne.

This war, which ended so disastrously to our arms and prestige, seems at this time, when it is possible to take an impartial view of the question, to have been one of wanton aggression against a prince well disposed towards our Government—and who, with whatever faults he had, was a strong and wise ruler, and accepted by his people—in order to force upon the Afghans a mere nominee of the British, and one whose authority could only be supported by the bayonets of an alien race. Such an enterprise was as discreditable to our councillors as it proved to be disastrous to our soldiers.

The army collected for this purpose consisted of the Bengal contingent, which, after leaving a division in reserve at Ferozepore, was 9500 strong, under the command of Sir Willoughby Cotton, and the Bombay contingent, consisting of another 6000, the whole being under the command of Sir John Keane.

At the same time, another force, nominally under the command of Shah Soojah, was to be raised in the Company's territories, to accompany him into Afghanistan. This army crossed the Indus near the fortress of Bukkur, entering territories famous from their association with the operations of Alexander the Great, and which had never before been traversed by British troops.

Marching from Shikapore, the army advanced for fifty miles through the dark defiles of the Bolan Pass, lofty mountains covered with snow towering above their heads. It now entered a desert region, where provisions were not to be procured, and where on every side the troops were assailed by the fierce Beloochees, who attacked foraging parties and camp followers, and plundered the baggage left in the rear. Early in April, the troops marched through the vale of Shawl, forded many rivers, and passed the heights of Kozak, over which the artillery was dragged by the men with ropes, till at length, surmounting all difficulties, the army reached Candahar on the 27th of April 1839.

On the 27th of June the march was resumed, but it was necessary to leave a strong garrison at Candahar, and, strange to say, probably owing to the difficulties of transport, the siege-guns which had been dragged with so much toil through the passes were left behind, while supplies were so short that the army had to proceed on half rations.

Capture of Ghuznee, 23rd July

On the 21st of July the army arrived before the famous fortress of Ghuznee, which was considered impregnable by the Afghans.

13

The city of Ghuznee lies between Candahar and Cabul, about 230 miles distant from the former, and 90 from the latter place. It stands on the extreme points of a range of hills, which slope upwards and command the north-east angle of the Balla Hissar. As the British advanced on it, and observed its strong fortifications rising up before them on the side of a hill, they saw that the place could not be reduced by artillery for want of the siege-guns left at Candahar, and at the same time a high wall with a wet ditch in front made operations with scaling-ladders or mining equally impossible.

It was discovered, however, by Captain Thomson, who made an inspection under heavy fire from the walls, that though the gates had been built up the Cabul gate still existed, and he reported that this one, though at great risk, could be blown up, and so an attempt to take the place by storm could be made. The want of supplies made it absolutely necessary to take the place, and therefore Sir John Keane gladly accepted Captain Thomson's proposal.

The morning of the 23rd of July, just before daybreak, was the time fixed for the assault. The regiments told off for the service were the 2nd, 13th, and 17th (Queen's), and the Company's European regiment, under Major Caruthers, Lieutenant-Colonel Orchard, Colonel Croker, and Major Tronson. The advance consisted of the light companies of these four regiments. The night and morning were unusually stormy. The advance was placed under the command of Colonel Dennie of the 13th Light Infantry, and the main column under Brigadier Sale. The explosion party was directed by Captain Thomson, who had under him Lieutenants Durand and Macleod of the Bengal, and Captain Peat of the Bombay corps. Under cover of the darkness, the noise the men might make being overpowered by the roaring of the wind, the storming column advanced along the Cabul road, while the engineers carried up their powder-bags to the gate. Meantime the General filled the gardens near the city walls with the sepoys, who kept up a sharp fire on the wall, while the light batteries opened hotly upon the works.

This demonstration fixed the attention of the enemy, and called forth a responsive fire. Suddenly a row of blue lights appeared along the walls, illuminating the place, and showing that the Afghans were manning them in expectation of an escalade. All this time the British engineers were quietly piling their powder-bags at the Cabul gate. It was a work that required great courage, and it was done well; but at first the powder failed to ignite, and Lieutenant Durand was obliged to scrape the hose with his finger-nails. Again the port-fire was applied. The powder exploded. The noise of the explosion was almost overpowered by the roaring of the guns and the rushing of the wind. Still, many an Afghan trembled at the ominous sound. Mighty indeed was the effect. Down with a crash came heavy masses of masonry and shivered beams in awful ruin and confusion. Now occurred a slight delay. It had been agreed that the signal for the storming party should be the bugle-call "Advance," but the bugler had fallen, and so Durand had to rush back to the nearest party he could find. At length the signal was given. The advance was sounded. Colonel Dennie at the head of his brave band rushed forward through the breach, amid clouds of smoke and dust, and soon the bayonets of his light companies were crossing the swords of the enemy, who had rushed down to the point of attack. A few moments of darkness and confusion, and then the foremost soldiers caught a glimpse of the morning sky, and pushing gallantly on, were soon established in the fortress.

Three hearty, animating cheers, so loud and clear that they were heard throughout the general camp, announced to their excited comrades below that Dennie and his stormers had entered Ghuznee.

Colonel Sale was pressing on to support Dennie, when, deceived by a false report that the latter had failed to enter the breach, he halted his column. There was a pause of painful doubt; but the true state of affairs was soon ascertained. Again the cheering notes of the bugle sounded the advance, and the British troops pushed on. But the enemy had profited by the pause, and numbers crowded to the breach. One of their number, rushing over the ruins, brought down the gallant Sale by a cut on the face with his sharp sabre. The Afghan repeated his blow as his opponent was falling; but the pommel, not the edge of his sword, this time took effect, though with stunning violence. He lost his footing, however, in the effort, and both rolled down together amid the fractured timbers of the gate. Sale now made an effort to master the weapon of his opponent. He snatched at it, but one of his fingers met the edge of the sharp blade. He quickly withdrew his wounded hand, and placed it over that of his adversary, so as to keep fast hold of the hilt; but the Afghan was active and powerful, and he was himself faint from loss of blood. Happily, at that moment Captain Kershaw, of the 13th, approached the scene of conflict. The wounded leader called to him by name for aid. He gave it effectually by passing his sabre through the body of the Afghan; who, however, continued to struggle gallantly. At length the Brigadier for a moment got the uppermost. Still retaining in his left hand the weapon of his enemy, he dealt him with his right a cut from his own sabre, which cleft his skull from his crown to the eyebrows. The Mohammedan once shouted *"Ne Ullah!"* (O God!) and never moved or spoke again.

At length the enemy gave way. The British pushed on. The support, under Colonel Croker, advanced, and the reserve speedily followed; and soon the colours of the 13th Regiment, planted by the brave young Ensign Frere, as well as those of the 17th, were flying out in the morning breeze from the ramparts of Ghuznee.

The struggle within the fort, for a considerable time, was most desperate. In addition to a heavy fire kept up on them, the British troops were assailed by the enemy sword in hand, as well as with daggers, pistols, and other arms; but British courage, perseverance, and fortitude overcame all opposition, and the enemy were soon to be seen abandoning their guns, running in all directions, throwing themselves down from immense heights, and endeavouring to make their escape over the walls. By five o'clock the capture of the Afghans' last stronghold was complete. But there was much hard fighting within the walls. In the frenzy of despair the Afghans rushed out from their hiding-places, plying their sabres with terrible effect, though only to meet with an awful retribution from the musketry or bayonets of the British infantry. Some, in their frantic efforts to escape by the gateway, stumbled over the burning timbers, wounded and exhausted, and were slowly burnt to death. Some were bayoneted on the ground, and others hunted into corners and shot down like dogs; but though many an Afghan sold his life dearly, and cut to the last at his hated enemy, the appeals of the helpless for mercy were never made in vain. And when resistance ceased, not a conquered enemy was injured.

So Ghuznee fell to the British army, and was made over to Shah Soojah. It cost the victors only 17 killed, and 165 wounded; of these last, 18 were officers.

Upwards of 500 of the garrison were buried by the victors; many more fell beyond the walls under the sabres of the British horsemen. Sixteen hundred prisoners were taken, and large stores of grain and flour fell into the hands of the conquerors.

The fall of Ghuznee—a fortress hitherto deemed by the Afghans impregnable—astonished Dost Mahomed, and was the cause of the ruin which soon afterwards overtook him.

Capture of Khelat, 13th November

In the northern part of Beloochistan stands the strong mountain fortress of Khelat. The chief, Mehrab Khan, had offended the British, and it was resolved to annex his territories to the kingdom of Shah Soojah. Khelat is a place of commanding strength. The citadel rises high above the buildings of the town, and frowns down menacingly on its assailants. On the north-west of the fort are three heights. On these the Khan had posted his infantry, supported by five guns in position. General Willshire was sent to capture it, with the 2nd and 17th Queen's Regiments, the 31st Bengal Native Infantry, with two howitzers, four of the Shah's 6-pounder guns, and a detachment of local horse. On the morning of the 13th of November he found himself before the place. The Engineer officers reported that until the heights were carried it would be impossible to proceed against the fortress; accordingly orders were issued for the attack. It was Willshire's hope that the enemy might be driven down to the gate of the fortress, and that the stormers might rush in with them. Gallantly our brave soldiers made their way up the heights—gallantly they were carried, and right nobly the guns were captured.

The shrapnel shot from Stephenson's batteries fell with too deadly an aim among the Beloochee footmen for them to hold their position on the hills. They fled towards the walls of their fortress, and the British infantry pushed hotly after them; but, in spite of all their exertions, our brave soldiers were not in time to secure an entrance—the gates were closed against their advance. The enemy's artillery, planted on the walls, was now brought into play. The British infantry were compelled to find shelter behind some ruined buildings, while our batteries, planted on the heights, opened upon the gate and the neighbouring defences. Two of Cooper's guns were brought within 200 yards of the walls. The gunners suffered much from the matchlocks of the enemy, but undauntedly continued to fire full upon the gate. At length it gave way. Pointing his hand towards the gateway, Willshire boldly rode down to show the infantry that an entrance was ready for them. Rising at once from their cover, with a loud hurrah they rushed on. Pennycuick and his men were the first to enter. The other companies eagerly followed, till the whole of the storming column were within the walls of Khelat.

Onward they struggled manfully towards the citadel. Every inch of ground was obstinately disputed. The citadel was reached, but there was here a desperate resistance. Sword in hand, Mehrab Khan and some of his principal chiefs stood to give battle to their enemies. The Khan himself fell dead with a musket-ball through his breast. Eight of his principal sirdars fell beside him. Heaps of dead lay around,—many fine-looking men,—their shields shot through and broken, swords and matchlocks scattered about in every direction, telling of the fierce fight. A small party held out in an inner apartment; there was no reaching them, except by a narrow passage which admitted but of one at a time. Three or four attempted it, and were instantly shot dead. The little band of Beloochees would not trust the British. At length Lieutenant Loveday was sent up to them alone. It was a critical moment for him; but they listened to his proposals, and surrendered. And Khelat was won, the British loss being 138 killed and wounded.

These defeats had a very depressing effect upon the followers of Dost Mahomed, who, although still at the head of an army of 14,000 men, found that there was no courage in his faint-hearted followers, and that they could not be trusted even to be true to himself. His position being thus hopeless, Dost Mahomed fled from Cabul on the 2nd of August, and that city was entered in state by Shah Soojah, who then, though for a short time, was restored to the throne which he had lost thirty years before.

The army now ceased to be an expeditionary force, and became settled as an army of occupation. The officers sent for their wives and families, and for a time English society and English amusements may be said to have been established in Cabul. Still Shah Soojah was not accepted by the people, his rule was exacting and cruel, and disaffection was rife in the country, which was rapidly preparing to rise.

In the meantime, Dost Mahomed was still to be reckoned with. After his flight from Cabul he and his son Akbar had gone to Bokhara, where for a time they were in captivity.

Escaping thence, they reached Khartoum, where the Dost's family were under the protection of his brother Jubbar Khan. Here he found the tribes strongly in his favour, and soon gathered force wherewith to oppose the British who were concentrating at Bamian, where a small force under Colonel Dennie arrived on the 14th of September 1840.

THE BATTLE OF BAMIAN

On the 18th of September Colonel Dennie moved out with a detachment to drive a force of the enemy out of a valley near Bamian. Soon after eight o'clock, two horse artillery guns, under Lieutenant Murray Mackenzie, two companies of the 35th Native Infantry, two companies of the Goorkha corps, and about four hundred Afghan horse, marched out to meet the enemy. About half an hour afterwards, Dennie, with two more companies of the native infantry regiment, and two also of the Goorkha corps, followed, in support of the advanced detachment. Instead of coming merely upon the advance of the enemy, the Brigadier found an army in his front; but, in spite of the slender force at his command, and the apparently overwhelming numbers of the enemy, he did not hesitate for a moment. His men were eager to advance, and he himself was full of confidence and courage. The enemy had got possession of a chain of forts reaching to the mouth of the defile, and were collected in bodies round the several forts, and upon the hills on either side of the valley. Mackenzie's guns began to play upon them. For some short time the Oosbegs, forming part of the Dost's force, stood the fire, but the guns were ably served, and the shrapnel practice told with terrific effect on dense bodies of men, who had nothing to give back in return.

The Oosbegs retreated; the British guns were pushed forward, opening a destructive fire, first from one distance, then from another, upon the wavering enemy. The Dost's army was soon broken to pieces, and the British cavalry were then let slip in pursuit. Following the disordered masses of the enemy for some miles along the defile, they cut down large numbers, and dispersed them in all directions. The defeat of the Dost's army was complete, and he and his son owed their lives to the fleetness of their steeds.

Dost Mahomed's Last Charge

Notwithstanding all this, Dost Mahomed, not yet beaten, was soon once more in command of a respectable force. The force which had been pursuing him under Sir Robert Sale came up with him on the 2nd of November. As our cavalry advanced upon him, Dost Mahomed, at the head of a small band of horsemen, strong, sturdy Afghans, but badly mounted, prepared to meet his assailants. Beside him rode the bearer of the blue standard, which marked his place in the battle. He pointed to it, and reined in his horse, then snatching the white *lunghi* from his head, stood up in his stirrups uncovered before his followers, and called upon them in the name of God and the Prophet to drive the cursed Kaffirs from the country of the faithful. "Follow me," he cried aloud, "or I am a lost man!" Slowly, but steadily, the Afghan horsemen advanced. The English officers who led our cavalry to the attack covered themselves with glory; but the native troopers, those vaunting horsemen, treacherous not for the first time even now, and who were in after years to prove traitors of the darkest dye, fled like sheep. Emboldened by the dastardly conduct of the men of the 2nd Light Cavalry, the Afghan horsemen dashed on, driving their enemy before them, and not stopping till they were almost within reach of the British guns.

The British officers unsupported by their men met the full force of the Afghan charge, and fought bravely to the last. Lieutenants Broadfoot and Crispin were killed, while Captains Fraser and Ponsonby, though badly wounded, broke through their assailants.

The next evening poor gallant Dost Mahomed, seeing his cause was hopeless, gave himself up to the British at Cabul, and shortly after was sent to British India.

NEAR SOORKHAB, NOVEMBER 1841

The chiefs of certain hill tribes, Kuzzilbashs, Ghilzyes, and other robbers and bandits by profession, had been accustomed to receive subsidies to induce them to refrain from robbing any caravans or parties travelling in the neighbourhood of their territories. The expenses of the war in Afghanistan had been enormous; and it becoming necessary to retrench, it was unwisely determined to begin by cutting off the pay of these chiefs. They resented the measure, and assembling in vast numbers, took every opportunity of attacking the British troops passing through the defiles of their mountainous country. Sale's brigade had reached Jugdulluck with little opposition; but on the next march it was seen that the heights were bristling with armed men, and a heavy fire was poured in with terrible effect from all the salient points on which the mountaineers had posted themselves. Sale threw out his flanking parties, and the light troops, skirmishing well up the hillsides, dislodged the enemy, whilst a party under Captain Wilkinson, pushing through the defile, found that the main outlet had not been guarded, and that the passage was clear. The march was resumed, but the enemy were not yet weary of the contest. Reappearing in great numbers, they fell furiously upon the British rearguard, and for a time the men thus suddenly assailed were in a state of terrible disorder. The energetic efforts of the officers, however, brought them back to a sense of their duty. Broadfoot, Backhouse, and Fenwick rallied and reanimated them. But the British loss was heavy; upwards of 100 were killed and wounded, and among them fell the gallant Captain Wyndham, of the 35th Native Infantry. Although lame from a hurt, at the moment of peril he had dismounted to save the life of a wounded soldier, by bearing him from the combat on his charger. When the rearguard broke before the onset of the Ghilzyes, unable to keep pace with the pursued, he turned, fought, and, overpowered by numbers, fell beneath the swords and knives of an unsparing foe. The force halted at Gundamuck. The political managers of affairs in Afghanistan fancied that this would prove the termination of disturbances in that country. Unhappily the storm which was to break with such fearful violence was only now gathering.

Retreat from Cabul, 6th January 1842

The British army had, as we have seen, advanced on Cabul, the capital of Afghanistan, in August 1839. Since that period it had been placed in cantonments outside the city. Major-General Sir V. Cotton had at first commanded in Afghanistan. He was succeeded by Major-General Elphinstone, who assumed the command in April 1841. On the morning of the 2nd of November 1841, the inhabitants of Cabul broke out in rebellion, and murdered Sir A. Burnes, the political agent, as well as his brother and Lieutenant Broadfoot, who sold their lives dearly. The rebellion extended rapidly through the country; supplies were cut off, and it was resolved to retreat from Cabul.

The amount of the British force was 4500 fighting men: the camp followers were about 12,000 men, besides women and children. The retreat commenced at 9 a.m. on the 6th of January 1842. It was as disastrous as any in the pages of history. A revengeful, active enemy, bitter cold and driving snow overwhelmed them; and of that great multitude, only one officer, Dr. Brydon, reached Jellalabad in safety. All the rest had died from cold or the sword of the enemy—except those who had been delivered as hostages at the commencement of the retreat, or who had been taken prisoners; an account of whose release will be hereafter given.

DEFENCE OF JELLALABAD
OCTOBER 1841 TO APRIL 1842

Before it was suspected to what extent the insurrection in Afghanistan would reach, Sir Robert Sale was placed in command of a brigade which was ordered to return to Hindostan. His road led through the Ghilzye defiles. Here, for several days, he was attacked by the mountaineers, but fighting his onward way, he reached Gundamuck. Here he heard of the outbreak at Cabul. Deeming it important to push on, he left a considerable portion of his camp equipage at Gundamuck, under charge of some Afghan levies; but they proved traitors, plundered the baggage, and set fire to the cantonment. Captain Burn and the other European officers were pursued by the insurgents, but succeeded in reaching the British camp.

Sir Robert Sale renewed his march the next morning, but already the whole armed population of the district was on the alert. The Afghans crowned each height as soon as our pickets were withdrawn, swarmed like hornets round the camp, and were repelled only by the most strenuous efforts. They permitted the advanced guard and the main body to pass through the town of Futtehabad without interruption. Bodies of them even came in guise of unarmed suppliants to beg for protection. But no sooner had the rearguard passed the houses and fort of this town, than a destructive fire was opened upon it. Captain Broadfoot and his sappers turned fiercely round more than once, and inflicted vengeance for this treachery; and Colonel Dennie, in the end, dexterously decoyed the enemy away from their walls into the open plain, and then the cavalry, under Captain Oldfield and Lieutenant Mayne, charging among them with headlong valour, strewed the ground with 150 slain. That night the force encamped under the walls of Jellalabad, and took possession of it next morning, the 12th of November. It was a most important object to occupy this place, in order to establish a post on which the corps at Cabul might retreat it necessary, and then form a link in the chain of communication with India. A glance at the map will show the immense distance which the British forces were from all support, with intricate passes, lofty mountains, deserts, and broad rivers intervening between them and India; while on every side swarmed hostile tribes, accustomed to warfare, and sworn to destroy them.

Jellalabad was the winter residence of the rulers of Cabul, and inferior only to that city and Candahar. The walls were, however, in a state which might have justified despair as to the possibility of defending them. They were also far too extensive for our small force, embracing a circumference of upwards of 2300 yards. There was no parapet, except for a few hundred yards. In many places the walls were not more than two feet high, while rubbish had accumulated to such an extent that there were roads over them into the country.

The population within was disaffected, and without were ruined forts, walls, mosques, tombs, and gardens, from which a fire could be opened at 20 or 30 yards. Captains Broadfoot and Havelock and Colonel Dennie assured the General that the works might be restored by adequate exertions, and it was therefore resolved to occupy the town.

The brigade was scarcely within the walls, when the plain was darkened by masses of the enemy. They had expected that the British troops would continue their progress towards India, and looked for a rich harvest of plunder of their baggage between Jellalabad and Peshawar. It was determined to read them a salutary lesson, and Colonel Monteith was ordered to drive them away. He issued from the gate on the morning of the 14th of November, with horse, foot, and artillery, 1100 in number, of whom 300 were Europeans, and fell on the enemy with such vigour and skill, that the masses broke up and fled, leaving 200 dead on the field. At noon not an Afghan remained, and all molestation ceased for fourteen days. On the 15th, the work of clearing away the ruins and restoring the fortifications was commenced, under the direction of Captain Broadfoot. The day was spent by him in superintending the work, the evening was devoted to his plans and calculations. Working parties were told off, who laboured from dawn to dusk—officers and men worked with emulation; and in a few weeks the ramparts were ready to receive the guns, and everything around the town that could afford cover to the enemy was, as far as possible, cleared away. The chief cause of anxiety to Sir Robert Sale was the deficiency of ammunition, which a single prolonged engagement would go nigh to exhaust. The men were therefore ordered not to expend a single shot uselessly.

On the 29th of November, large bodies of Afghans poured down upon the plains from the surrounding valleys, and opened a desultory fire on the town. As they interrupted the workmen on the fortifications, Colonel Dennie sallied out of the gates soon after midday on the 1st of December, with 300 men from each regiment, to disperse them. The Afghans fired a volley and fled—the troops followed. The guns dealt destruction among the fugitives; the cavalry, galloping in pursuit, drove some into the river, and cut down others, till 150 bodies strewed the plain. The garrison enjoyed a long period of repose in consequence of this spirited repulse of the enemy. At length news reached the gallant band of the disasters at Cabul; and Dr. Brydon arriving in the city, confirmed the sad news. Councils of war were held, and there was some talk of evacuating Jellalabad; but there were brave spirits among the garrison, who saw, and loudly spoke, not only of the disgrace, but of the suicidal folly of such a measure. Their bolder counsels prevailed, and it was determined to hold out to the last extremity. There was Havelock, whose name was afterwards to be in the mouth of every British soldier, as one to be loved and imitated; there were Broadfoot and Dennie, true heroes of the noblest stamp.

On the 19th of February a letter was received from General Pollock, who had arrived in Peshawar, approving of their resolution to hold out, and promising to advance as soon as possible to their aid. Sir Robert replied that the whole of the horses of his cavalry and artillery must perish in another month if he was not succoured before that time, and that then a retreat even on a force advancing to his relief would be impossible.

Major Havelock and Captain Wade were seated by Sir Robert's side, the former writing the reply to General Pollock, when the house began to shake violently. A fearful earthquake was taking place. The shocks continued, without intermission, with frightful violence—a confused, rumbling sound wildly mingled with the crash of falling houses and the outcries of the inhabitants. The earth was so uplifted that it was scarcely possible for the people to keep their feet. But the destruction of the defences was most appalling. All the parapets were shaken down, several of the bastions were injured, all the guard-houses were cast to the ground, a third of the town was demolished, and a considerable break made in the ramparts of a curtain in the Peshawar face, while the Cabul gate was reduced to a shapeless mass of ruins.

The garrison did not lose heart even under these appalling circumstances. The camp of the enemy they knew was only seven miles off, and he might be upon them in a few hours. It was also necessary to guard against a rush which any parties of the enemy concealed in the neighbourhood might make against the ruined walls. At the sound of the bugle the troops assembled on the ramparts. When it was ascertained that no enemy was near, they piled their arms, and set to work with brave determination to restore the defences. Temporary parapets of loose clods were thrown up, the earth was cleared out of the ditch, gabions were filled to block up the main breaches, and palisades fixed to impede the progress of assailants through others. In a few hours the walls wore a more encouraging aspect. The Afghans, when a few days afterwards they approached the fortress and saw the wonderful state of repair in which it had been placed, believed that it had escaped through the power of English witchcraft. The difficulties of the garrison, however, increased great anxiety was felt for the subsistence of the cavalry and artillery horses. Foraging parties were sent out daily under an escort, and were constantly attacked by the enemy; and the close investment of the place by Akbar Khan made it impossible for them to get in the needed supplies.

At length, on the 11th of March, the Afghans approached so near the walls, that it was suspected that they purposed undermining them. To prevent this Colonel Dennie made a vigorous sally with 800 men, and ascertained that they had commenced no operation of the sort. Akbar Khan then advanced on the city with his whole force. It was a critical moment, but the hearts of none of the garrison failed them. He was received with so hot a fire from the ramparts, while horse and foot attacked him with such heroic courage, that he was compelled to fly, leaving more than 100 dead on the field.

Starvation now threatened the garrison. For many days the European regiments had been on half rations of salt beef, without vegetables, while the native troops subsisted mainly on flour; and it was doubtful whether this allowance would be continued beyond the second week in April. When, however, they were almost reduced to despair that help would come in time to preserve their lives, some large flocks of sheep were seen grazing on the plains before them. At first it was believed that they were placed there to lure them out to destruction, but the desire to capture them at all hazards became too strong to be resisted. About 200 men of the 13th, and the same number of the 35th, with some sappers and miners, were allowed to sally out to bring in the prey. They succeeded beyond their most sanguine expectations, and 500 sheep and goats were captured and brought in amid shouts of laughter by the men. This success raised the spirits of the whole garrison, and made them more than ever determined to hold the fort until rescue should come.

On the 6th of April the situation again changed and the fortunes of the garrison once more seemed desperate. Spies had brought in rumours of a serious check inflicted upon General Pollock by the enemy at Ali-Musjid, and Akbar Khan had salutes fired in honour of this supposed victory.

Few of the officers believed these reports, but they were only the more eager to attack Akbar in force, and so, it victorious, effect their own relief, and support General Pollock if the report should turn out to be true. This plan of action was especially urged by Havelock upon the General, and though at first Sir Robert Sale, brave as he was, shrank from the responsibility of ordering so daring an effort, he in the end agreed. On the 7th of April the infantry marched out in three columns. The centre, under Colonel Dennie, consisted of the 13th, 500 strong; the left, of the 35th, under Colonel Monteith, mustering the same number of bayonets; and the right, under Captain Havelock, composed of one company of the 13th, another of the 35th, and the detachment of sappers under Lieutenant Orr, the whole amounting to 360. Captain Broadfoot lay on his couch, suffering from a dangerous wound received in a sortie on the 24th of March.

It was at this time reported in the town that Akbar Khan was preparing to retreat.

Without sound of bugle or drum, at early dawn the troops fell into their ranks and marched out of Jellalabad. Notwithstanding the report of his flight, Akbar Khan's troops, 6000 in number, were found drawn up in front of his camp, his left resting on the Cabul river. Havelock moved on rapidly in advance with his column, and driving the skirmishers before him, pushed on towards the enemy's camp, the other columns following. Sir Robert Sale was with the centre column. At about three-quarters of a mile from Jellalabad, a flanking fire was opened from one of the forts on that column, and Sir Robert ordered Colonel Dennie to storm it. Accordingly, rushing on with his men of the gallant 13th, he passed the outer wall through an opening, but found himself exposed to a murderous fire from the inner keep. Here fell the brave Colonel Dennie, mortally wounded by an Afghan marksman. He was acknowledged by all to be one of the most gallant soldiers in the British army. This false move nearly produced disastrous consequences. Akbar Khan, seeing Havelock, who was much in advance, unsupported, brought down a body of 15,000 cavalry on his feeble column. Havelock posted the company of the 13th in a walled enclosure on his right, to pour a flanking fire on the enemy, and formed the rest into square. That he might be able to command both parties, he himself remained outside the square till the horsemen were close upon them. His horse rearing, he was thrown, and the animal galloped back riderless to the town. He would have been killed by the Afghans had not a sapper and two men of the 13th rushed forward and rescued him. The enemy's horse, charging with much resolution, approached within 30 yards; but their leader was shot, and, exposed to a heavy fire in front and flank, they retired in confusion. Again Havelock's column advanced, and once more the Afghan horse charged it. Thrown into one square, it awaited the attack, which was more easily repulsed than the first. Sir Robert then sent Backhouse's guns to Havelock's assistance. The column, cheering them as they came on, advanced against the enemy's encampment and penetrated it, driving the Afghans headlong into the river. The other columns now came up, the camp was attacked on three points, and in a short time the enemy were dislodged from every part of their position, their cannon taken, and their camp burnt. Four guns, lost by the Cabul and Gundamuck forces, were recaptured, and a great quantity of ordnance stores and *materiel* was taken or destroyed. The field was strewed with the bodies of the Afghans, while the loss on the side of the victors amounted to only 10 killed and 50 wounded.

Thus the garrison of Jellalabad, after having been isolated in a hostile country for five months, surrounded by enemies, and constantly threatened with destruction, achieved its own relief. The peasantry now brought in ample supplies of provisions, and on the 16th of April the relieving force under General Pollock, having gallantly fought its way through the Khyber Pass, routing the Afridis who guarded it, approached the long beleaguered city, an exploit second to none in the annals of warfare; and thus was accomplished the successful defence of Jellalabad.

Forcing the Khyber Pass, 5th April 1842

Meanwhile, when the news reached India that a British army had been destroyed in Afghanistan, and that General Sale, with another, was closely besieged in Jellalabad, a strong force was despatched under General Pollock to his relief. General Pollock had to encounter many difficulties in his march, but the greatest was forcing the Khyber Pass, which was known to be guarded by a numerous, active, and daring enemy. The troops had arrived at Jumrood, on the east end of the pass—on the west end was Ali-Musjid. The hills on either side of the pass were rocky and precipitous, presenting great obstacles to troops, guarded as they were by numerous bodies of Afridis, long accustomed to warfare. The difficulties were great, but they were known, and General Pollock prepared to surmount them. Brigadier Wild was in command of the advance guard, and General McCaskill of the rear.

Before dawn on the 5th of April Pollock's force set out from Jumrood to the entrance of the Khyber Pass. It was formed of eight regiments of infantry, among whom were the 9th Queen's Regiment, three cavalry corps, including two squadrons of the 3rd Dragoons, artillery, and sappers, in all some 8000 men. Brigadier Wild was in command of the advance guard and General McCaskill of the rear. The arrangement of the march was that the heights on either side should be occupied by infantry, the right being under the command of Colonel Taylor, and the left of Colonel Morley; and while these advanced along the heights the main column was to advance through the pass.

At three o'clock in the morning the army commenced its march. It moved off in the dim twilight without beat of drum or sound of bugle. The crowning columns moved off to the right and left, and commenced in silence to climb the heights, which were covered with the enemy; but so little did they expect that mode of attack, that the flankers had ascended a considerable distance before the Khyberees were aware of their advance. Daylight soon revealed the respective positions of the contending forces, and the struggle commenced.

The hill men had thrown up across the pass a formidable barricade, composed of stones, mud, and branches of trees. Behind this barrier the enemy were gathered in force, waiting the opportunity to attack the main column when it should attempt the pass. But this opportunity did not come, for the main column on entering the pass halted in battle array, while the infantry on the hills performed the duty assigned to them of clearing the heights.

The left column was soon actively engaged; the right could not at first surmount the heights, from their precipitous character; but Colonel Taylor and his men, not to be defeated, stole round the base of the mountain unseen, and found a more practicable ascent than that they had at first tried. "Then on both sides the British infantry were soon hotly engaged with the mountaineers, clambering up the precipitous peaks, and pouring down a hot and destructive fire upon the surprised and disconcerted Khyberees, who had not expected that our disciplined troops would be more than a match for them on their native hills. But so it was. Our infantry, native and British, were beating them in every direction, and everywhere the white dresses of the Khyberees were seen as they fled across the hills."

Now was the time for Pollock to advance. The centre column did not attempt to move forward until the flankers had fought their way to the rear of the mouth of the pass. But when he had fairly turned the enemy's position, he began to destroy the barriers, and prepared to advance into the pass. The enemy had assembled in large numbers at the mouth; but finding themselves outflanked, they gradually withdrew, and without opposition Pollock now cleared his way through the barricade, and pushed into the pass with his long string of baggage. The great extent of his convoy was his chief difficulty for the rest of the day.

The march to Ali-Musjid occupied the greater part of the day. The heat was intense. The troops suffered greatly from thirst, but they all did their duty well. During the night, in spite of the bitter cold, the heights were held, and the enemy, who were constantly firing on the troops, kept in check. From thence the march was without incident, and the head of the column marched into Jellalabad unresisted on the 13th, a fortnight after the gallant sortie by which the garrison had freed themselves of Akbar Khan and his army.

Occupation of Cabul, 1842

Victory had once more settled on the standards of the British army. On the 8th of September the first division of General Pollock's army approached the hills which overlook the pass of Jugdulluck. The Afghans attempted to oppose their invaders, but were driven back like sheep from hill to hill by the soldiers of the 13th, many of them the raw recruits whom Havelock had brought up from Calcutta the preceding year, and whom five months of hard service at Jellalabad had turned into veterans.

Akbar Khan's last stand was made at Tzeen, a valley surrounded by hills; but these were gallantly stormed, and the enemy, as before, driven from crag to crag, fighting with all the fury of despair; but they were ultimately put to flight, and two days afterwards General Pollock's force was encamped at Cabul. One of the first results of this victory was the rescue of Lady Sale and the other prisoners who had been carried off by Akbar Khan.

Among the officers rescued with Lady Sale was Lieutenant Mein, of Her Majesty's 13th Light Infantry, who had distinguished himself by his gallantry in the retreat from Cabul, before he was taken prisoner. Lieutenant Eyre gives us an account of him:—"Sir Robert Sale's son-in-law, Lieutenant Sturt, had nearly cleared the defile, when he received his wound, and would have been left on the ground to be hacked to pieces by the Ghazees, who followed in the rear to complete the work of slaughter, but for the generous intrepidity of Lieutenant Mein, of Her Majesty's 13th Light Infantry, who, on learning what had befallen him, went back to his succour, and stood by him for several minutes, at the imminent risk of his own life, vainly entreating aid from the passers-by. He was at length joined by Sergeant Deane of the sappers, with whose assistance he dragged his friend on a quilt through the remainder of the pass, when he succeeded in mounting him on a miserable pony, and conducted him in safety to the camp, where the unfortunate officer lingered till the next morning, and was the only man of the whole force who received Christian burial. Lieutenant Mein was himself suffering from a dangerous wound in the head, received in the previous October." His heroic disregard of self, and fidelity to his friend in the hour of danger, are well deserving of a record in the annals of British valour and virtue. Besides the officers and ladies, 36 non-commissioned officers and men of the 44th Regiment were rescued, making 105 in all, who, with Dr. Brydon, formed all that remained of the troops who left Cabul in 1841.

The British avenging army arrived at Cabul on the 15th of September 1842, and encamped on the racecourse.

The following morning the British colours were hoisted on the most lofty pinnacle of the battlements of the Balar Hissar, where they could be seen from all parts of the city.

A royal salute was fired, the national anthem was played, and the troops gave three cheers. The colours were hoisted regularly every day on the Balar Hissar as long as the troops remained at Cabul.

DEFENCE OF CANDAHAR, 1842

Major-General Sir William Nott, with the 40th Regiment, and other troops, was stationed at Candahar when the Afghan insurrection broke out. On the morning of the 12th of January 1842, a large force of the insurgents, under two powerful chiefs, approaching within eight miles of the city, Sir William Nott, with his troops, the 40th Regiment forming the advance, went out to meet them. Although the Afghans were strongly posted, they were quickly put to flight. From this period up to the 7th of March the troops remained all night long accoutred and ready for action. In consequence of the severity of the weather, the British could not again quit the city to punish the enemy, who swarmed around and plundered the neighbouring villages. At length the position became so dangerous, that early in March every Afghan was expelled from the city, and then the General, leaving a small garrison in the city, marched on to attack the enemy. As he advanced the Afghans retired, and so gradually drew him away from the city. Suddenly, on the night of the 10th, a large force doubled back on Candahar and made a furious attack on the gates, one of which they set on fire and tore down. The garrison were hard-pressed, but fought valiantly for three hours behind an improvised rampart, and eventually drove off the enemy. Nott was not able to return to Candahar till the 12th, but it was now free from the enemy. Here he had to stay waiting for ammunition and supplies, which eventually reached him, escorted by a force under Sir R. England, and on the 10th of August he marched to Cabul, passing on the way the fort of Ghuznee. This, it will be remembered, had been valiantly taken by storm by our troops three years before, now it was again in Afghan hands. For after a siege of three and a half months in the preceding December, the enemy, aided by treachery, found a way in, and the garrison, few in number, retired to the citadel. On the 6th of March they at length surrendered, under a promise of safe-conduct with colours and arms and the honours of war to Peshawar, and, as was customary at this date, fell victims to Afghan treachery, and were massacred or made prisoners.

On the march to Ghuznee, General Nott on the 30th of August came up with an army of 12,000 men, and after a severe fight utterly defeated them. On the 5th of September Ghuznee was once again occupied by our troops, and on the 17th Cabul was reached, just two days after Pollock had entered.

The grand bazaar in Cabul, in which the remains of the British Envoy had been exposed to insult, having been destroyed on the 12th of October, the army commenced its return to India. On the way the fortifications of Jellalabad were blown up; and on the 17th of December, the brave garrison of that place marching in advance, and wearing the medals granted to them, the whole army made a triumphal entrance into Ferozepore.

The 13th Light Infantry have "Jellalabad"; the 40th and 41st, "Candahar and Ghuznee"; and the 3rd Light Dragoons, 9th, 13th, 31st, 40th, and 41st, "Cabul, 1842." Thus ended the Second Afghan Campaign.

The Conquest of Scinde
1843

The Battle of Meeanee

The Conquest of Scinde
1843

BATTLE OF MEEANEE, 17TH FEBRUARY 1843

Scinde is a large province, through the western portion of which the river Indus flows before it reaches the Indian Ocean. Hyderabad is the capital, situated on the banks of the Indus. This country was ruled by a number of chiefs or princes, who held the title of Ameer. They were a lawless and rapacious set, and tyrannised over their subjects with the most barbarous cruelty. When, however, it was resolved (in 1831) to open up the Indus for the navigation of our merchant vessels, it became important to secure their friendship; and to effect that object, Colonel Pottinger was despatched by Lord William Bentinck, and succeeded in forming with them a treaty, by which they guaranteed all the objects desired by the British Government. For some years, while they believed that it was their interest to be honest, they remained tolerably faithful to the English; when, however, they fancied, from our disasters in Afghanistan, that the British power was on the wane, they instantly began to plot with our enemies for our overthrow. To put a stop to these proceedings, Lord Ellenborough, the Governor-General of India, despatched General Sir Charles Napier with an army into Scinde, and gave him the following instructions:—"Should any Ameer or chief, with whom we have a treaty of alliance and friendship, have evinced hostile intentions against us during the late events, which may have induced them to doubt the continuance of our power, it is the present intention of the Governor-General to inflict on the treachery of such an ally and friend so signal a punishment as shall effectually deter others from similar conduct." Sir Charles, who was encamped at Sukkur, in upper Scinde, on the right bank of the Indus, soon obtained ample proof of the treachery and hostility of the Ameers, and prepared for war by disciplining and organising his troops, who were composed chiefly of raw levies with little experience. On the same side of the Indus as Sukkur, and about twenty miles from the river, was Shikarpoor, with Roree on the left bank, and the fortress of Bukkur between them.

One of the principal Ameers was Roostum, and an arch traitor. He had already induced a large number of Beloochees, a warlike race from Beloochistan, to prepare for battle. Many also remained in their homes, ready for the signal to flock to his standard. He and the other chiefs did not delay long in raising that standard, and a force of 60,000 men was soon collected near the capital of Hyderabad, at a spot afterwards to become famous, called Meeanee. Sir Charles had led his forces down the left bank of the Indus, several steamers accompanying his progress. On the 16th of February the British army had reached Muttaree, about sixteen miles from Hyderabad, when Sir Charles heard that 20,000 Beloochees had suddenly crossed the Indus, and that not less than 36,000 men were really in order of battle. In consequence of the garrisons he had been compelled to leave in his rear, his own army consisted at this time of only 2600 men of all arms fit for duty. Still his resolution remained unshaken. He well knew what discipline could do against untrained hordes, however brave, and he was also well aware of the danger of retreating before a barbarian enemy. He was informed that the enemy's cavalry was 10,000 strong, and that they were posted on a vast plain of smooth hard clay or sand, while his whole cavalry force numbered but 800. Marching on the night of the 16th, his advanced guard discovered the enemy at eight o'clock next morning, and at nine o'clock the British line of battle was formed. The enemy, 36,000 strong, were posted along the dry bed of the river Fullaillee, which falls into the Indus. Its high bank, sloping towards the plain in front, formed a rampart. Their position was about 1200 yards wide. Eighteen guns, massed on the flank in advance of the bank, poured their shot on the British troops while forming the line, and the Beloochee wings rested on *shikargahs* (copses or woods), which lined the plain so far as to flank the advance on both sides. They were very large and dense, and that on the Beloochee right intersected with *nullahs* (water-courses) of different sizes, but all deep, carefully scarped, and defended by matchlock-men. Behind the shikargahs, the Fullaillee made a sudden bend to the rear, forming a loop, in which the Ameer's cavalry was placed.

The shikargah on the enemy's left was more extensive, and, though free from nullahs, very strong. It was covered towards the plain by a wall, having one opening, not very wide, about half-way between the two armies. Behind this wall 5000 or 6000 men were posted, evidently designed to rush out through the opening upon the flank and rear of the British when the latter advanced. Some matchlock-men were seen astride on this wall, which was ten feet high, but they soon disappeared; and the General, discovering that there were no loopholes or scaffolding to the wall, ordered Captain Tew, with a company of the 22nd, to occupy and defend it to the last. It was another Thermopylae. The gallant Tew died in the gap, but the post was maintained, and thus 6000 enemies were paralysed by only 80.

As the British army advanced—the baggage, cast into a circle, was left close in the rear, surrounded by camels, which were made to lie down with their heads inwards, and their bales placed within them for their armed followers to fire over, thus forming a fortress not very easy to storm. Two hundred and fifty Poona horsemen, and four companies of infantry under Captain Tait, were the only force which could be spared for its protection.

The order of battle was thus formed:—

Twelve guns, under Major Lloyd, flanked by 50 Madras sappers, under Captain Henderson, were on the right. On Lloyd's left stood the 22nd Queen's Regiment, under Colonel Pennefather, not 500 strong, half Irishmen, strong of body, high-blooded soldiers, who saw nothing but victory. On the left were the swarthy sepoys of the 22nd Bombay Native Infantry; then the 12th, under Major Reid, and the 1st Grenadiers, led by Major Clibborne; the whole in the echelon order of battle. Closing the extreme left, but somewhat held back, rode the 9th Bengal Cavalry, under Colonel Pattle. In front of the right infantry, skirmishers were thrown out, and on the left the Scinde horsemen, under Captain Jacob, fierce Eastern troops, were pushed forward. Between the two armies there was a plain of about 1000 yards, covered for the first 700 with a low jungle, which impeded the march of the British troops. For 300 yards, however, in front of the Beloochee line, it had been cleared to give free play for their matchlocks, with which they fired long shots at times without showing themselves.

The order to advance was given, and the General and his staff rode forward in face of the heavy fire from the Beloochee guns. The enemy's right was strongly protected by the village of Kottree, now filled with matchlock-men. The main body of the British advanced in columns of regiments, the right passing securely under the wall of the enclosure, where Tew's gallant company, now reinforced by a gun, were with a rattling fire of musketry keeping their host of foes in check. Onward marched the main body of the British army, while Clibborne's grenadiers were storming the village of Kottree on the left. The level was all the time swept by the Beloochee guns and matchlocks, answered at times by Lloyd's battery, but nothing stopped the progress of the gallant band. When within 100 yards of the Fullaillee, the 22nd opened into line, and all the columns formed in succession, each company as it arrived throwing its fire at the top of the bank, where the faces of the Beloochees could be seen bending with fiery glances over their levelled matchlocks.

The British front was still incomplete, when the voice of the General, loud and clear, was heard commanding the charge. The order was answered by a hearty British cheer. Four guns were run forward, and the infantry, at full speed, dashed on towards the river, and rushed up the sloping bank. The stern Beloochees, with matchlocks resting on the summit, let their assailants come within 15 yards before they delivered their fire; but the steepness of the slope inside, which rendered their footing unsteady, and the rapid pace of the British, spoilt their aim, and the execution done was not great.

The next moment the 22nd were on the top of the bank, thinking to bear all down before them; but even they staggered back at the forest of swords waving in their front. Thick as standing corn, and gorgeous as a field of tulips, were the Beloochees in their many-coloured garments and turbans. They filled the broad, deep bed of the now dry Fullaillee; they were clustered on both banks, and covered the plain beyond. Guarding their heads with their large dark shields, they shook their sharp swords, gleaming in the sun, and their shouts rolled like a peal of thunder, as, with frantic might and gestures, they dashed against the front of the 22nd. But with shrieks as wild and fierce, and hearts as big, and arms as strong, the British soldiers met them with the bayonet, which they used with terrible effect against their foremost warriors. At the same time the few guns that could be placed in position on the right of the 22nd, flanked by Henderson's small band of Madras sappers, swept diagonally the bed of the river, tearing the rushing masses with a horrible carnage. Soon the sepoy regiments, 12th and 25th, prolonged the line of fire to the left, coming into action successively in the same terrible manner.

Now the Beloochees closed in denser masses, and the dreadful rush of their swordsmen was felt, and their shouts answered by the pealing musketry, and such a fight ensued as has seldom been recorded in the annals of warfare. Over and over again those wild, fierce warriors, with shields held high and blades drawn back, strove with strength and courage to break through the British ranks. No fire of small-arms, no sweeping discharge of grape, no push of bayonets could drive them back; they gave their breasts to the shot, their shields to the bayonet, and, leaping at the guns, were blown away by twenties at a time: their dead rolled down the steep slope by hundreds, but the gaps were continually filled from the rear; the survivors pressed forward with unabated fury, and the bayonet and sword clashed in full and frequent conflict.

Thus they fought—never more than five yards apart, often intermingled, and several times the different regiments were forced backwards, but their General was always there to rally and cheer them. At his voice their strength returned, and they recovered ground, though soon in the dreadful conflict nearly all their regimental leaders were killed or wounded.

Major Teasdale, animating the sepoys of the 25th Regiment, rode violently down a gap in the Beloochees, and was there killed by shot and sabre.

Major Jackson, of the 12th, coming up with his regiment, the next in line, followed the same heroic example. Two brave havildars kept close to him, all three in advance of their regiment, and all fell dead together, but not till several of the fiercest of the Beloochee swordsmen were seen to sink beneath the brave Jackson's strong arm and whirling blade. Here also fell Captains Cookson and Meade, and Lieutenant Wood, nobly cheering on their men to the attack, while Tew had died at his post at the entrance of the shikargah. Many more were desperately wounded: Colonel

Pennefather and Major Wylie; Captains Tucker, Smith, Conway; Lieutenants Plowden, Harding, Thayre, Bourdillon; Ensigns Firth, Pennefather, Bowden, Holbrow.

Lieutenant Harding, of the 22nd, was the first to leap upon the bank. His legs were cut by the swordsmen, and he fell, but rose again instantly, and, waving his cap, cheered his men to the charge. Receiving another sword-cut, his right hand was maimed; yet still he urged the men forward, till at length a shot went through his lungs, and again he fell, and was carried out of the fight.

Lieutenant McMurdo, a young staff-officer, rode, like Teasdale and Jackson, into the bed of the Fullaillee, and his horse being killed, he fell. Regaining his feet, he met and slew Jehan Mohamed, a great chief and a hardy warrior, in the midst of his tribe. Several of Jehan's followers then engaged him in front, while one struck at him fiercely from behind, but being at that moment struck down by a sergeant of the 22nd, the blow fell harmless. McMurdo turned and repaid the service by cleaving to the brow a swordsman who was aiming at his preserver's back; another fell beneath his weapon, and then he and the sergeant fought their way out from among the crowds of foes pressing fiercely round them.

Several times the sepoys, when their leaders were killed or disabled, slowly receded; but the General was always at the point of the greatest danger, and then manfully his swarthy soldiers recovered their ground.

Once he was assailed by a chief, and his danger was great, for his right hand had been maimed before the battle. At the moment that the fierce warrior was about to cut him down, Lieutenant Marston, of the 25th Native Infantry, sprang to his side, killed the sirdar, and saved his General. At another period Sir Charles Napier was alone for some moments in the midst of his enemies, who stalked round him with raised shields and scowling eyes; but, from some superstitious feeling possibly, to which the Beloochees are very prone, not one attempted his destruction, which they might easily have accomplished.

When the soldiers of the 22nd saw him emerge unharmed from his perilous position, they gave vent to their feelings in a loud and hearty cheer, heard above the din of battle.

For more than three hours did this storm of war continue, and still the Beloochees, undismayed, pressed onwards with furious force, their numbers to all appearance increasing instead of being diminished by those who had been struck down. Now came the critical point in every battle. Except the cavalry, there was no reserve to bring forward. In vain the brave Jacob had previously endeavoured to turn the village of Kottree with the Scinde Horse, and to gain the flank of the enemy's position.

So heavily pressed by the Beloochees on the right, and so exhausted were his men, that he could not quit that point; but his quick eye saw that the enemy's right could be turned, and he sent orders to Colonel Pattle to charge with the whole body of the Bengal and Scinde horsemen on the enemy's right. Never was an order more promptly obeyed. Spurring hard after their brave leaders, the Eastern horsemen passed the matchlock—men in the village of Kottree, and galloped unchecked across the small nullahs and ditches about it, which were, however, so numerous and difficult, that 50 of the troopers were cast from their saddles at once by the leaps. But dashing through the Beloochee guns on that flank, and riding over the high bank of the Fullaillee, the main body crossed the deep bed, gained the plain beyond, and charged with irresistible fury. Major Story, with his Bengal troopers, turning to his left, fell on the enemy's infantry in the loop of the upper Fullaillee, while the Scindian Horse, led by Lieutenant Fitzgerald, wheeling to their right, fell on the camp, thus spreading confusion along the rear of the masses opposed to the British infantry. In this gallant charge three or four Beloochees had fallen before his whirling blade, when one, crouching, as is their custom, beneath a broad shield, suddenly stepped up on the bridle-hand, and with a single stroke brought down the horse. Fitzgerald's leg was under the animal, and twice the barbarian drove his keen weapon at the prostrate officer, but each time the blow was parried; and at length, clearing himself from the dead horse, the strong man rose. The barbarian, warned by the Herculean form and threatening countenance of his opponent, instantly cast his shield over a thickly rolled turban of many folds, but the descending weapon went through all, and cleft his skull. On charged the cavalry. The fierce Beloochees, whose fury could before scarcely be resisted, slackened their onslaught, and looked behind them. The 22nd, perceiving this, leaped forward with a shout of victory, and pushed them back into the deep ravine, where again they closed in combat. The Madras sappers and the other sepoys followed the glorious example. At length the 6000 Beloochees who had been posted in the shikargah abandoned that cover to join the fight in the Fullaillee, but this did not avail them. Both sides fought as fiercely as ever. A soldier of the 22nd Regiment, bounding forward, drove his bayonet into the breast of a Beloochee; instead of falling, the rugged warrior cast away his shield, seized the musket with his left hand, writhed his body forward on the bayonet, and with one sweep of his keen blade avenged himself. Both combatants fell dead together. The whole front of the battle was indeed a chain of single combats. No quarter was asked for, none given. The ferocity was unbounded; the carnage terrible.

The Ameers had now lost the day. Slowly the fierce Beloochees retired in heavy masses, their broad shields slung over their backs, their heads half turned, and their eyes glaring with fury. The victors followed closely, pouring in volley after volley; yet the vanquished still preserved their habitual swinging stride, and would not quicken it to a run though death was at their heels! Two or three thousand on the extreme right, who had been passed by the cavalry, kept their position, and seemed disposed to make another rush; but the whole of the British guns were turned upon them with such heavy discharges of grape and shells that they also went off. All were now in retreat; but so doggedly did they move, and so inclined did they appear to renew the conflict on the level ground, where the British flanks were unprotected, that the General recalled his cavalry, and formed a large square, placing his baggage and followers in the centre. Such was the battle of Meeanee, fought with 2000 men against 36,000. Six officers were killed and 14 wounded, and about 50 sergeants and rank and file were killed, and 200 wounded—a large proportion of the few actually engaged. Of the enemy, upwards of 6000 were killed: 1500 bodies and more lay in heaps in the bed of the Fullaillee alone.

The next morning, six of the principal Ameers presented themselves on horseback at the camp, offering their swords, and promising to deliver up Hyderabad to the victor. To Hyderabad he accordingly marched, and took possession of that city.

There was another powerful chief still in arms with 10,000 men, about six miles off, and it is asserted that, had Sir Charles at once marched against this chief, Shere Mahomed of Meerpore, he might have defeated him without loss of time; but at the same time it is evident that it was most important in the first place to secure the capital, and to give his troops refreshment after so desperate a fight.

For the first time in English despatches, the names of private soldiers who had distinguished themselves were made known—an innovation which still more endeared him to those under his command, and which was hailed with satisfaction by thousands who never saw him.

The men of the 22nd Regiment all fought most bravely, but Private James O'Neil, of the light company, was especially noticed for taking a standard while the regiment was hotly engaged with the enemy; and Drummer Martin Delany, who shot, bayoneted, and captured the arms of a chief, Meer Whulle Mohamed Khan, who was mounted, and directing the enemy in the hottest part of the engagement.

Lieutenant Johnstone, of the 1st Grenadiers, Native Infantry, cut down a Beloochee, and saved the life of a sepoy who had bayoneted the Beloochee, but was overpowered in the struggle. The names of a considerable number of the native regiments were also mentioned as conspicuous for their gallantry, as well as those of Lieutenant Fitzgerald and Lieutenant Russell, whose steady, cool, and daring conduct kept the men together in the desperate charge over the nullahs, under a heavy fire, made by the corps to get on the flank of the enemy—a manoeuvre which so mainly contributed to secure the victory to the British army.

BATTLE OF HYDERABAD, 24TH MARCH 1843

After the battle of Meeanee, the victorious army of Sir Charles Napier entered Hyderabad in triumph. He had not been there long when he heard that Shere Mahomed, or the *Lion*, one of the most powerful of the Ameers of Scinde, was in arms at the head of a large force, hoping to retrieve the losses of his brother chieftains. Considerable reinforcements for the British army were expected—some from Sukkur down the Indus, and others from Kurrachee.

Approaching Hyderabad, the haughty Ameer sent an envoy as herald to the British camp, with an insolent offer of terms, saying, "Quit this land, and, provided you restore all you have taken, your life shall be spared."

Just then the evening gun fired. "You hear that sound? It is my answer to your chief. Begone!" said Sir Charles, turning his back on the envoy.

On the 21st a column, under Major Stack, reached Muttaree—a long march from Hyderabad. The fortress of Hyderabad was by this time repaired, and the entrenched camp was complete; and, on the 16th, recruits and provisions came up from Kurrachee, and the 21st Regiment of Sepoys arrived from Sukkur, down the Indus. When the Lion had notice of Major Stack's approach, he moved with his whole army to Dubba, intending to fall on him on the following day. The General's plans were soon laid. His first care was to save Major Stack's column. He accordingly sent out Captain McMurdo with 250 Poona horsemen, to meet Stack, and to order him to advance after he had ascertained the Lion's position. The next morning, Jacob was despatched with the Scinde horsemen along the same road, and he himself followed, at a short distance, with the Bengal Cavalry and some guns, supported by all the infantry, who moved a short distance behind. Meantime Major Stack had advanced, leaving his baggage unprotected. It was attacked by a body of Beloochee matchlock-men; but Captain McMurdo, with only six Poona Horse, kept them at bay till some troops he sent for came up to his assistance. The Beloochees were ultimately driven back, and the force reached Hyderabad. Sir Charles had now 5000 men of all arms, 1100 being cavalry, with 19 guns. Leaving two guns to guard the camp, at break of day on the 24th he marched from Hyderabad upon Dubba, which was eight miles north-west of that city. The infantry and guns moved forward in a compact mass, the cavalry scouting ahead and on the flank; for so thickly covered was the whole country with houses, gardens, shikargahs, and nullahs, that 50,000 men might be in position without being discovered at half a mile distance.

Ten miles were passed over, and still the exact position of the enemy was unknown, when a scout came in with the information that the Lion was with his whole force two miles to the left.

The General, at the head of the irregular horse, galloped forward, and in a quarter of an hour found himself on a plain, in front of the whole Beloochee army. The whole plain was swarming with cavalry and infantry; the right wing resting on the Fullaillee, with a large pond of mud protecting the flank, while the left rested on a succession of nullahs and a dense wood. No distinct view could be obtained of the order of battle, but 26,000 men were before him, and they had 15 guns—11 being in battery, while two lines of infantry were entrenched, and a heavy mass of cavalry was in reserve.

The front was covered with a nullah 20 feet wide and 8 feet deep, with the usual high banks, which were scarped so as to form a parapet. Behind this the first line of infantry was posted, extending for a mile in a direction perpendicular to the Fullaillee; while behind the right wing, close to the Fullaillee, was the village of Dubba, filled with men, and prepared for resistance by cuts and loopholes in the houses.

There were other nullahs, behind which the rest of the Beloochee army was posted, with one gun on a height to the right, and the remainder behind the third line. Altogether, no position could have been better chosen or more formidable.

The march of the British force was diagonal to the front of the Beloochee army, and this brought the head of the column left in front near the right of the enemy, and the line was immediately formed on the same slant; the cavalry being drawn up on the wings, and the artillery in the intervals between the regiments.

When the line was formed, the left, being advanced, was under the enemy's cannon. One shot nearly grazed the General's leg, and several men were killed. Still the enemy's position could not be clearly made out, and to ascertain it more exactly, Captain Waddington of the Engineers, and Lieutenants Brown and Hill, rode straight to the centre of the Beloochee lines, and then, under a sharp fire of matchlocks, along the front to the junction of the centre with the left. A thick wood on the right gave the General some anxiety, as it was supposed to be filled with Beloochees, ready to rush out and attack the British rear when they were hotly engaged. To watch it, he placed the Scindian horsemen and 3rd Bombay Cavalry under Major Stack, with orders to oppose whatever enemy appeared. The battle commenced at nine o'clock. Leslie's horse artillery pushed forward, followed by the rest of the artillery in batteries, and all obtained positions where their fire crossed, and with terrible effect they raked the enemy. Lieutenant Smith, eager to discover a place where his artillery could cross a deep nullah, bravely rode up to it alone. He ascended the bank, and instantly fell, pierced by a hundred wounds. It was full of Beloochees. The gallant 22nd was again first in action, and, as they advanced under a terrific fire from the gun on the hillock, and from the matchlock-men, with whom were some of the bravest chiefs posted in the first nullah, nearly half the light company were struck down.

Beyond the first nullah, a second and greater one was seen, lined still more strongly with men, while the village became suddenly alive with warriors, whose matchlocks could also reach the advancing line. While about to lead the gallant 22nd to the charge, the General observed the cavalry on the right making a headlong dash at the enemy's left wing, in consequence of having seen some of them moving in apparent confusion towards the centre. The right flank of the British army was thus left uncovered; and had the wood been filled with Beloochees, the consequences might have been serious.

> The whole body of cavalry was at full speed dashing across the smaller nullahs, the spurs deep in the horses' sides, the riders pealing their different war-cries, and whirling their swords in gleaming circles. There the fiery Delamain led the gorgeous troopers of the 3rd Cavalry; there the terrible Fitzgerald careered with the wild Scindian horsemen, their red turbans streaming amid the smoke and dust of the splendid turmoil.

Conquest of Scinde, by Sir W. Napier

No enemy appearing from the wood, the heroic General hurried back and regained the 22nd at the moment it was rushing to storm the first nullah. Riding to the first rank, he raised that clear, high-pitched cry of war which had at Meeanee sent the same fiery soldiers to the charge. It was responded to with ardour, led by Major Poole, who commanded the brigade, and Captain George, who commanded the corps. They marched up till within forty paces of the entrenchment, and then stormed it like British soldiers. The regiments were well supported by the batteries commanded by Captains Willoughby and Hutt, which crossed their fire with that of Major Leslie. The second brigade, under Major Woodburn, consisting of the 25th, 21st, and 12th Regiments, under Captains Jackson, Stevens, and Fisher respectively, bore down into action with excellent coolness. They were strongly sustained by the fire of Captain Whitley's battery. On the right of it again were the 8th and 1st Regiments, under Majors Browne and Clibborne, which advanced with the regularity of a review up to the entrenchments. Lieutenant Coote, of the 22nd, was the first to gain the summit of the bank, where, wresting a Beloochee standard from its bearer, he waved it in triumph, while he hurried along the narrow ledge, staggering from a deep wound in his side. Then, with a deafening shout, the soldiers leaped down into the midst of the savage warriors. At that point a black champion, once an African slave, and other barbarian chiefs, fell, desperately fighting to the last.

Onward the brave 22nd fought its bloody way amid the dense masses of the enemy, ably supported by the 25th Native Infantry; and now the British line began to overlap the village of Dubba, while Stack's cavalry were completely victorious on the right, and Leslie's horse artillery, crossing the nullahs with sweeping discharges, committed fearful havoc among the dense masses of the Beloochee army. The other regiments, bringing up their right shoulders, continued the circle from the position of the 25th, and lapped still farther round the village. In this charge the 21st Sepoys stabbed every Beloochee they came up with, whole or wounded, calling out "Innes! Innes!" at every stroke of death they dealt.

In consequence of the rapidity of this charge, some confusion ensued, and while the General was endeavouring to restore order, a Beloochee field-magazine exploding, killed all near him, broke his sword, and wounded him in the hand. Still the enemy fought on fiercely; surprising feats of personal prowess were displayed. Four or five of the foe fell beneath the iron hand of Fitzgerald, whose matchless strength renders credible the wildest tales of the days of chivalry. McMurdo was engaged in three successive hand-to-hand combats, his opponents having the advantage of shields to aid their swordsmanship. He killed two in succession, but the third, with an upward stroke, cut him from the belly to the shoulder, and would have killed him, had he not cleft the man to the brows, and thus lessened the force of the blow. As it was, he received a desperate wound. Three other officers also performed surprising deeds of personal prowess. The General proved that he possessed humanity, as well as courage of the most heroic order. Near the village, a chief, retiring with that deliberate rolling stride and fierce look which all those intrepid fatalists displayed in both battles, passed near the General, who covered him with a pistol; but then remembering Meeanee, when in the midst of their warriors no hand had been raised against him, he held his finger. His generosity was fruitless, for a sepoy plunged his bayonet into the man with the terrible cry of "Blood! blood!"

Much to the General's satisfaction, 16 wounded prisoners were taken, whereas at Meeanee the lives of only 3 had been saved.

Slowly and sullenly the enemy retired, some going off with their leader to the desert, others towards the Indus; but the latter were intercepted by the victorious cavalry of the right wing, and driven in masses after their companions into the wilderness. Meanwhile the General in person led the Bengal and Poona Horse, under Major Story and Captain Tait, through the valley of Dubba against the retreating masses, putting them to the sword for several miles, but not without resistance, in consequence of which the brave Captain Garrett and others fell. The Lion himself was seen, and very nearly captured by Fitzgerald and Delamain, as he was escaping on his elephant.

On his return with the cavalry, the General was received with three hearty cheers by his troops. In this bloody battle, which lasted three hours, the British lost 270 men and officers, of which number 147 were of the gallant 22nd Regiment, who had sustained the brunt of the fight. Though fought near Dubba, this battle is best known as that of Hyderabad, which name is inscribed on the colours and medals of the soldiers by whom it was won.

Sir Charles Napier had resolved to make the battle a decisive one. Having arranged for sending his wounded to Hyderabad, reorganised his army, and ascertained that the enemy had retreated towards Meerpoor, in eight hours he was again marching in pursuit. During the battle the thermometer stood at no degrees, and the heat was daily increasing. On that day his troops had marched twelve miles to find the enemy, fought for three hours, and had been employed for eight in collecting the wounded, burying the dead, and cooking, rather than in resting; but all were eager for a fresh fight; as evidence of which, several of the 22nd Regiment concealed their wounds, that they might take part in it, instead of being sent back to Hyderabad.

Their names are recorded—John Durr, John Muldowney, Robert Young, Henry Lines, Patrick Gill, James Andrews, not severely hurt; Sergeant Haney, wound rather severe; Thomas Middleton, James Mulvey, severely wounded in the legs; Silvester Day, ball in the foot. It was only discovered that they were wounded on the march, when, overcome by thirst, they fell fainting to the ground. Captain Garrett and Lieutenant Smith were killed in the battle; and Lieutenants Pownoll, Tait, Chute, Coote, Evans, Brennan, Bur, Wilkinson, McMurdo, and Ensign Pennefather were wounded.

The next day the Poona Horse were at the gates of Meerpoor. The Lion fled with his family and treasure to Omercote, and the gates of the capital were at once gladly opened to the victors. While the General remained at Meerpoor, he sent forward the camel battery of Captain Whitley, supported by the 25th Sepoy Infantry, under Major Woodburn. There was but little water, and a risk of the Indus rising, so that it would have been dangerous to have gone with the whole army. He promised the Lion terms if he would surrender at once. News was brought him that the Indus was rising. He despatched orders to Captain Whitley to return. That officer had just received information that the Ameers had again fled, and that Omercote might be captured. He was then distant 20 miles from that place, and 40 from Meerpoor. A young officer, Lieutenant Brown, who had already distinguished himself, undertook to ride these 40 miles to obtain fresh instructions. He reached Meerpoor without a stop, and borrowing one of the General's horses, rode back again under a sun whose beams fell like flakes of fire, for the thermometer stood at above 130 degrees. He bore orders to attack Omercote. The little band pushed forward, and, on the 24th, Omercote opened its gates.

Thus was this important place reduced ten days after the battle of Hyderabad, though 100 miles distant, and in the heart of the desert. This capture may be said to have completed the conquest of Scinde. The Lion was still at large, but he was finally hunted down and crushed by different columns sent against him, under Colonels Roberts, Chamberlayne, and Captain Jacob. Scinde was annexed to British India, and Sir Charles Napier was appointed its first governor, independent of the Presidencies, with directions to abolish slavery, to tranquillise the inhabitants, and to bring out the resources of the country he had so bravely acquired.

The Gwalior Campaign
1843

THE BENGAL NATIVE ARMY

The Gwalior Campaign
1843

BATTLE OF MAHARAJPOOR
29TH DECEMBER 1843

The loss of British prestige in the defiles of Afghanistan had induced many of the native princes of India to fancy that the power of England was on the wane, and that they might assume a tone of authority and independence which they would not before have ventured to exhibit. Among others, the Mahratta Court at Gwalior adopted a line of policy inimical to British interests, and contrary to the engagements into which their princes had entered.

Lord Ellenborough, foreseeing that they would make an attempt to emancipate themselves altogether from British influence, assembled an army on the frontier facing the Mahratta territory, and called it the "Army of Exercise." It was gradually increased, and placed under the command of Sir Hugh Gough. Various insulting acts having been committed by the Mahratta Government against the English, and no apology having been made, the Governor-General ordered the army to enter the Mahratta territory.

General Grey took the lead with a division of infantry and a brigade of cavalry, and, crossing the Jumna at Calpee, threatened the Gwalior territory from the south; while two divisions of infantry, and two brigades of cavalry, with the usual complement of artillery, moved down from the northward under the command of Sir Hugh Gough himself. General Grey, having advanced from Bundelcund, reached Panniar, about 12 miles from Gwalior, on the 28th of December. The enemy, estimated at about 12,000 in number, took up a strong position on the heights near the fortified village of Mangore. Although the British troops were much fatigued by their long march, the enemy were immediately attacked and driven from height to height, till the rout was completed. The British loss was 215 killed and wounded.

Sir Hugh Gough advanced, and found the enemy awaiting him at a strong post which they had selected on the evening of the 28th. It was reconnoitred; but during the night the Mahratta forces left their entrenched position, and took up another three or four miles in advance of it. The British troops numbered about 14,000 men, with 40 pieces of artillery. The Mahrattas mustered 18,000 men, including 3000 cavalry and 100 guns. The Mahratta army had under Scindia been carefully organised by European officers, and was therefore composed of well-disciplined men, equal in bravery to any of the natives of India.

On the morning of the 29th, no fresh reconnaissance having been made, the British forces found themselves in the presence of an enemy they fancied some miles off. Many ladies, on their elephants, were on the field when the action commenced by the gallant advance of Major-General Littler's column upon the enemy, in front of the village of Maharajpoor.

The enemy's guns committed severe execution as they advanced; and though the Mahrattas fought with the most desperate courage, nothing could withstand the headlong rush of the British soldiers. Her Majesty's 39th Foot, with their accustomed dash, ably supported by the 56th Native Infantry, drove the enemy from their guns into the village, bayoneting the gunners at their posts. Here a sanguinary conflict took place. The fierce Mahrattas, after discharging their matchlocks, fought sword in hand with the most determined courage. General Valiant's brigade, with equal enthusiasm, took

Maharajpoor in reverse, and 28 guns were captured by this combined movement. So desperately did the defenders of this strong position fight, that few escaped. During these operations, Brigadier Scott was opposed by a body of the enemy's cavalry on the extreme left, and made some well-executed charges with the 10th Light Cavalry, most ably supported by Captain Grant's troop of horse artillery, and the 4th Lancers, capturing some guns and taking two standards, thus threatening the right flank of the enemy.

On this, as on every occasion, Sir Henry, then Captain Havelock, distinguished himself. The 56th Native Infantry, who had been brigaded with Her Majesty's 39th, were advancing on the enemy, but at so slow a pace as to exhaust the patience of Sir Hugh Gough.

"Will no one get that sepoy regiment on?" he exclaimed.

Havelock offered to go, and riding up, inquired the name of the corps.

"It is the 56th Native Infantry."

"I don't want its number," replied he. "What is its native name?"

"Lamboorunke pultum—Lambourn's regiment."

He then took off his cap, and placing himself in their front, addressed them by that name, and in a few complimentary and cheering words reminded them that they fought under the eye of the Commander-in-Chief. He then led them up to the batteries, and afterwards remarked, that "whereas it had been difficult to get them forward before, the difficulty now was to restrain their impetuosity."

In conformity with the previous instructions, Major-general Valiant, supported by the 3rd Cavalry Brigade, moved on the right of the enemy's position at Chouda. During the advance he had to take in succession three strongly entrenched positions, where the enemy defended their guns with frantic desperation. Here Her Majesty's 40th Regiment lost two successive commanding officers, Major Stopford and Captain Coddington, who fell wounded at the very muzzles of the guns. It captured four regimental standards. This corps was ably and nobly supported by the 2nd and 16th Grenadiers, under Lieutenant-Colonels Hamilton and McLarey. Major—General Littler, with Brigadier Wright's brigade, after dispersing the right of the enemy's position at Maharajpoor, steadily advanced to fulfil his instructions to attack the main position at Chouda, and was supported most ably by Captain Grant's troop of horse artillery, and the 1st Regiment of Light Cavalry. This column had to advance under a severe fire, over very difficult ground, but when within a short distance of the enemy, the gallant 39th Regiment, as before, rushing forward, led by Major Bray, and gallantly supported by the 56th Regiment, under Major Dick, carried everything before them, and thus gained the entrenched main position of Chouda.

The battle of Maharajpoor was now virtually won. The loss on both sides had been severe. The British had 106 killed, of whom 7 were officers, and 684 wounded, and 7 missing, making a total loss of 797. The Mahrattas are supposed to have lost between 3000 and 4000 men.

In consequence of this victory and that of Panniar, the Mahratta Durbar submitted to the British Government. Lieutenant-Colonel Stubbs was appointed governor of the fort of Gwalior, which commands the city. The Mahratta troops were disbanded, and a British contingent was formed, to be maintained at the cost of the Gwalior Government, which was compelled to pay forthwith the expenses of the campaign.

The Punjab Campaigns
1845–49

The Battle of Mudki

The Punjab Campaigns
1845-1849

BATTLE OF MOODKEE, 18TH DECEMBER 1845

On the death of Runjeet Singh, the Lion of Lahore, chief of the Sikhs and ruler of the Punjab, in 1839, the throne was seized by his reputed son, Sher Singh. He was a good-natured voluptuary, and utterly unable to manage the warlike troops raised by his father. He was disposed to be friendly with the English, but being assassinated by Ajeet Singh on the 15th of September 1843, Dhuleep Singh was proclaimed Maharaja, and Heera Singh was raised to the dangerous office of vizier.

The new vizier soon found that he could, no more than his predecessor, content the army. His only chance was to give it employment, or rather induce it to engage in a contest with the British, which he hoped might terminate in its dispersion. Probably, like other rulers nearer England, he was prepared for either contingency. Should the army be successful, he would take advantage of their success; if destroyed, he would not be ill pleased. The Sikhs, indulging themselves with the idea of the conquest of British India, virtually declared war against the English on the 17th of November. They commenced crossing the Sutlej on the 11th of December; and on the 14th of that month a portion of the army took up a position a few miles from Ferozepore. The Sikhs, it should be understood, had some territory on the eastern side of the Sutlej, and it is supposed that they had from time to time sent across guns, and buried them there, to be ready for their contemplated invasion of British India. At length, on the 13th of December, the Sikh army crossed the Sutlej, and threatened Ferozepore, but were held in check by the bold front shown by the garrison of that place under Major-General Sir John Littler.

Meantime, the army of the Sutlej, under Sir Hugh Gough, was advancing on them. After a trying march of 150 miles, with little rest, and a scarcity of water, on the afternoon of the 18th of December the information was received by the British army that the Sikhs were advancing on Moodkee, which they had just reached. The troops immediately got under arms, the horse artillery and cavalry were pushed forward; the infantry, accompanied by field batteries, moving on in support. Before long the enemy, it was found, were approaching in order of battle, with 20,000 infantry, the same number of cavalry, and 40 guns. The country over which the two armies were advancing to the conflict is a dead flat, covered at short intervals with a low but thick jungle, and dotted with sandy hillocks. The enemy screened their infantry and artillery behind this jungle and such undulation as the ground afforded.

The British cavalry, under Brigadiers White, Gough, and Mactier, advanced rapidly to the front in columns of squadrons, and occupied the plain, followed by five troops of horse artillery, under Brigadier Brooke, who took up a forward position, having the cavalry on his left flank. The British infantry now forming from echelon of brigade into line, the enemy opened a severe cannonade on them, which was vigorously replied to by the batteries of horse artillery under Brigadier Brooke. A gallant charge of the 3rd Light Dragoons, the 5th Light Infantry, and 4th Lancers, turned the left of the Sikh army, put their cavalry to flight, and sweeping along the whole rear of the infantry and guns, silenced them for a time. After this, Brigadier Brooke pushed on his horse artillery, and while the cannonading was resumed on both sides, the infantry, under Major-Generals Sir Harry Smith, Gilbert, and Sir John McCaskill, attacked in echelon of lines the enemy's infantry, almost invisible among the jungle and the approaching darkness of night. The enemy made a stout resistance; but though their line far outflanked the British, that advantage was counteracted by the flank movements of the cavalry. The roll of fire from the British infantry showed the Sikhs that they had met a foe they little expected, and their whole force was driven from position after position at the point of the bayonet, with great slaughter and the loss of seventeen pieces of artillery.

Night alone saved them from worse disaster, for this stout conflict was maintained for an hour and a half in dim starlight, amidst a cloud of dust from the sandy plain, which yet more obscured every object. The victory was not, however, obtained without severe loss to the British. Sir John Mc-Caskill was shot through the chest, and killed on the field; the gallant Sir Robert Sale, the brave defender of Jellalabad, received so severe a wound in the leg that he shortly after died from its effects; many other officers and men were killed, making in all 215; and 657 were wounded. The enemy's sharpshooters had climbed into trees, and from thence killed and wounded many officers. The victorious army returned to camp at midnight, and halted on the 19th and 20th, that the wounded might be collected, the captured guns brought in, and the men refreshed.

BATTLE OF FEROZESHAH, 21ST DECEMBER 1845

The Sikhs had entrenched themselves in a camp a mile in length, and half a mile in breadth, with the village of Ferozeshah in the centre. They numbered nearly 60,000 men, and 108 pieces of cannon of heavy calibre in fixed batteries.

The Umbala and Sir John Littler's forces, having formed a junction, now arrived. The British army, thus increased, consisted of 16,700 men, and 69 guns, chiefly horse artillery. The united forces advanced at about four o'clock in the afternoon of the 21st, to attack the entrenched camp of the Sikhs. The Governor-General, Sir Henry Hardinge, had offered his services to Sir Hugh Gough as second in command, and was actively engaged in the operations of this and the following day. The divisions of Major—General Sir J. Littler, Brigadier Wallace, and Major-General Gilbert deployed into line, having the artillery in the centre, with the exception of three troops of horse artillery, one on either flank, and one in support. Major—General Sir H. Smith's division and the cavalry moved in a second line, having a brigade in reserve to cover each wing. Sir Hugh Gough directed the right wing, and Sir Henry Hardinge the left wing of the army.

The infantry advanced under a terrific storm of shot and shell from upwards of 100 Sikh guns, 40 of them of battering calibre; but nothing stopped the impetuous onset—the formidable entrenchments were carried—the men threw themselves on the guns, and with matchless gallantry wrested them from the enemy. No sooner, however, were the Sikhs' batteries won, than the enemy's infantry, drawn up behind their guns, opened so tremendous a fire on the British troops, that in spite of their most heroic efforts, a portion only of the entrenchment could be carried.

Sir Harry Smith's division advancing, captured and retained another point of the position, and Her Majesty's 3rd Light Dragoons charged and took some of the most formidable batteries; yet the enemy remained in possession of a considerable portion of the great quadrangle, whilst the British troops, actually intermingled with them, held the remainder, and finally bivouacked upon it, exhausted by their gallant efforts, greatly reduced in numbers, and suffering extremely from thirst, yet animated by that indomitable spirit which they had exhibited throughout the day. Whenever moonlight, however, exhibited the British position, the enemy's artillery never failed severely to harass them.

Sir John Littler's division, which had advanced against the strongest part of the work, suffered severely, especially Her Majesty's 62nd Regiment, which had 17 officers killed and wounded out of 23.

It was not till they had done all that men could do that they retired. The 3rd Dragoons in this desperate charge lost 10 officers, and 120 men out of 400. When the Sikhs found that Sir Harry Smith had retired from the village, they brought up some guns to bear upon the British. The fire of these guns was very destructive. When the Governor-general found this, mounting his horse, he called to the 80th Regiment, which was at the head of the column, "My lads, we shall have no sleep until we take those guns." The regiment deployed immediately, and advancing, supported by the 1st Bengal Europeans, drove a large body of Sikhs from three guns, which they captured and spiked, and then retiring, took up its position again at the head of the column, as steadily as if on parade. "Plucky dogs!" exclaimed the Governor-General; "we cannot fail to win with such men as these." His aide-de-camp, Lieutenant-Colonel R. Blucher Wood, was severely wounded in the attack. For the rest of the night the column was unmolested, but its position was one of great danger,—150 yards only from an overpowering foe, while neither the Governor-General nor Sir Hugh Gough could tell in what direction Sir John Littler and Sir Harry Smith were to be found. It was suspected, also, that the Sikh army had been greatly reinforced by Tej Singh. The two generals therefore agreed to hold their ground, and at earliest dawn to attack the enemy, taking their batteries in reverse, and to beat them, or to die honourably on the field. The whole of Sir Henry Hardinge's personal staff had been disabled, except his son, Captain A. Hardinge, who had his horse killed under him.

Of that memorable night he himself has given us a most graphic description:—"It was the most extraordinary of my life. I bivouacked with the men, without food or clothing, and our nights are bitterly cold. A burning camp in front—our brave fellows lying down under a heavy cannonade, which continued during the whole night, mingled with the wild cries of the Sikhs, our English hurrah, the tramp of men, and the groans of the dying. In this state, with a handful of men who had carried the batteries the night before, I remained till morning, taking very short intervals of rest, by lying down with various regiments in succession, to ascertain their tempers and revive their spirits. I found myself again with my old friends of the 29th, 31st, 50th, and 9th, and all in good heart. My answer to all and every man was, that we must fight it out, attack the enemy vigorously at daybreak, beat him, or die honourably on the field.

"The gallant old General, kind-hearted and heroically brave, entirely coincided with me. During the night I occasionally called on our brave English soldiers to punish the Sikhs when they came too close, and were imprudent; and when morning broke, we went at it in true English style. Gough was on the right. I placed myself, and dear little Arthur by my side, in the centre, about thirty yards in front of the men, to prevent their firing; and we drove the enemy without a halt from one extremity of the camp to the other, capturing thirty or forty guns as we went along, which fired at twenty paces from us, and were served obstinately. The brave men drew up in an excellent line, and cheered Gough and myself as we rode up the line, the regimental colours lowering to me as if on parade. The mournful part is the heavy loss I have sustained in my officers. I have lost ten aides-de-camp *hors de combat*, five killed and five wounded. The fire of grape was very heavy from one hundred pieces of cannon. The Sikh army was drilled by French officers, and the men the most warlike in India."

This letter describes the commencement of the struggle on the 22nd. The line was supported on both sides by horse artillery, while from the centre was opened a fire by such heavy guns as remained effective, aided by a flight of rockets. The

British, however, in the advance suffered much from a masked battery, which, opening on them, dismounted the guns and blew up the tumbrils. But nothing impeded the charge of the undaunted British, led on by their two heroic generals, till they were masters of the field. Their rest was short: in the course of two hours Sirdar Tej Singh, who had commanded in the last great battle, brought up from the vicinity of Fero-zepore fresh battalions, and a large field of artillery, supported by 30,000 Ghorchurras, hitherto encamped near the river. He drove in the British cavalry, and made strenuous efforts to regain the position at Ferozeshah.

Scarcely had this attempt been defeated, when more Sikh troops and artillery arrived, and a fresh combination was made against the flank of the British, with so formidable a demonstration against the captured village that it was necessary to change the whole front to the right, the enemy's guns all the time keeping up an incessant fire, while those of the British were silent for want of ammunition. Under these circumstances Sir Hugh Gough ordered the almost exhausted cavalry to threaten both flanks of the enemy at once, while the whole infantry prepared to advance. With the swoop of a whirlwind the gallant 3rd Dragoons and other cavalry regiments rushed on their foes. The Sikhs saw them coming, while the British bayonets gleamed in front. Their courage gave way; abandoning their guns, they fled from the field, retreating precipitately towards the Sutlej, and leaving large stores of grain and the *materiel* of war behind them. Thus in less than four days, 60,000 Sikh troops, supported by 150 pieces of cannon, were dislodged from their position, and severely punished for their treacherous commencement of the war.

The regiments which bear the word "Ferozeshah" on their colours are the 3rd Light Dragoons, 9th, 29th, 31st, 50th, 62nd, and 80th Regiments; while they and the 1st European Light Infantry of the Honourable East India Company's Service received the Governor—General's thanks for their courage and good conduct.

BATTLE OF ALIWAL, 28TH JANUARY 1846

While the British army were resting after the desperate encounters in which they had been engaged, and Sir Hugh Gough was watching the enemy, Sirdar Runjoor Singh Mujethea crossed from Philour, and made a movement which not only threatened the rich and populous town of Loodiana, but would have turned the right flank, and endangered the communication with Delhi. Sir Harry Smith was accordingly despatched to the relief of Loodiana. Having first captured the fort of Dhurmkote, he fought his way past the enemy to that city, where his presence restored confidence and order. This part of his duty being accomplished, and having under him 10,000 men and 24 guns, he next proceeded to attack the Sirdar Runjoor Singh, who was strongly entrenched at Aliwal, about eight miles to the westward of Loodiana, with 15,000 men and 56 guns. The Sikh force had advanced a short distance from their entrenched camp, when Sir Harry Smith, on the 28th, with his small army, advanced to meet them.

The regiments of cavalry which headed the advance of the British troops opened their glittering ranks to the right and left, and exhibited the serried battalions of infantry, and the frowning batteries of cannon.

The scene was magnificent, yet few could have failed to experience a sense of awe as the shock of battle was about to commence. The lines were not truly parallel. That of the Sikhs inclined towards and extended beyond the British right, while the other flanks were for a time comparatively distant.

It was perceived by Sir Harry Smith that the capture of the village of Aliwal was of the first importance, and the right of the infantry was led against it. The Sikh guns were keeping up a heavy fire, and Major Lawrenson, not having time to send for orders, at once galloped with his horse artillery up to within a certain distance of the enemy's guns, unlimbered, and by his fire drove the enemy's gunners from their guns.

This promptitude of the gallant officer saved many lives. The defenders of the village were chiefly hill men, who, after firing a straggling volley, fled, leaving the Sikh artillerymen to be slaughtered by the conquerors. The British cavalry of the right made at the same time a sweeping and successful charge, and one half of the opposing army was fairly broken and dispersed. The Sikhs on their own right, however, were outflanking the British, in spite of all the exertions of the infantry and artillery; for there the more regular battalions were in line, and the brave Sikhs were not easily cowed. A prompt and powerful effort was necessary, and a regiment of European lancers, supported by one of Indian cavalry, was launched against the even ranks of the Lahore infantry. The Sikhs knelt to receive the orderly but impetuous charge of the English warriors; but at that critical moment the wonted discipline of many failed them. They rose, yet they reserved their fire, and delivered it at the distance of a spear's throw, in the faces of the advancing horsemen, the saddles of many of whom were quickly emptied. Again and again the cavalry charged and rode through them, but it was not till the third charge, led by Major Bere, of the 16th Lancers, that the Sikhs dispersed; and even then, the ground was more thickly strewn with the bodies of victorious horsemen than of beaten infantry. Upwards of a hundred men of the 16th were either killed or wounded. An attempt was made by the enemy to rally behind Boondree, but all resistance was unavailing. The Sikh guns, with the exception of one, were captured, and they were driven headlong across the river. This gun was carried across the river, when Lieutenant Holmes, of the irregular cavalry, and Gunner Scott, of the horse artillery, in the most gallant way followed in pursuit, and, fording the river, overtook and spiked it.

All the munitions of war which Runjoor Singh had brought with him were captured, and the Sikh forces were thrown into the most complete dismay. The victory was decisive and complete. The loss of the British was 151 killed, and 413 wounded; that of the enemy far greater.

Sobraon, 10th February 1846

While Sir Hugh Gough was waiting for reinforcements from Delhi, as also for the arrival of Sir Charles Napier, who was moving up the left bank of the Sutlej, the Sikhs were strongly fortifying themselves at a bridge they had formed across that river at Sobraon. Their lines were encompassed by strong walls, only to be surmounted by scaling-ladders, while they afforded protection to a triple line of musketry. These formidable works were defended by 34,000 men and 70 pieces of artillery, while their position was united by a bridge of boats to a camp on the opposite side, in which was stationed a reserve of 20,000 men, and some pieces of artillery, which flanked some of the British field-works. Altogether a more formidable position could scarcely have been selected, and a Spanish officer of engineers in their service assured them that it could not be taken.

As soon as Sir Harry Smith had returned from Aliwal, and the heavy artillery had arrived from Delhi, Sir Hugh Gough determined to attack the Sikh position—his army now consisting of 6533 Europeans and 9691 natives, making a total of 16,224 rank and file, and 99 guns. On Tuesday the 10th of February, at half-past three o'clock in the morning, the British army advanced to the attack, fresh, like lions awaked out of sleep, but in perfect silence, when the battering and disposable artillery were at once placed in position, forming an extended semicircle, embracing within its fire the works of the Sikhs. A mist, however, hung over the plain and river; and it was not till half-past six, when it cleared partially away, that the whole artillery fire could be developed. Then commenced the rolling thunder, of the British guns. Nothing grander in warfare could be conceived than the effect of the batteries when they opened, as the cannonade passed along from the Sutlej to Little Sobraon in one continued roar of guns and mortars; while ever and anon the rocket, like a spirit of fire, winged its rapid flight high above the batteries in its progress towards the Sikh entrenchment. The Sikh guns were not idle, and replied with shot and shell; but neither were well-directed, nor did much damage. At first, it was believed that the whole affair was to be decided by artillery; but, notwithstanding the formidable calibre of the British guns, mortars, and howitzers, and the admirable way in which they were served, aided by a rocket battery, it could not have been expected that they could have silenced the fire of 70 pieces behind well-constructed batteries of earth, planks, and fascines, or dislodge troops covered either by re-doubts, epaulments, or within a treble line of trenches.

"For upwards of three hours this incessant play of artillery was kept up upon the mass of the enemy. The round shot exploded tumbrils, or dashed heaps of sand into the air; the hollow shells cast their fatal contents fully before them, and devious rockets sprang aloft with fury, to fall hissing among a flood of men: but all was in vain, the Sikhs stood unappalled, and flash for flash returned, and fire for fire."

It was determined, therefore, to try what the British mus-ket and bayonet could effect. The cannonade ceased, and the left division of the army, under Brigadier Stacey, supported on either flank by Captains Harford and Fordyce's batteries, and Lieutenant—Colonel Lane's troops of horse artillery, moved forward to the attack. The infantry, consisting of Her Majesty's 10th, 53rd, and 80th Regiments, with four regiments of Native Infantry, advanced steadily in line, halting only occasionally to correct when necessary, and without firing a shot; the artil-lery taking up successive positions at a gallop, until they were within 300 yards of the heavy batteries of the Sikhs. Terrific was the fire they all this time endured; and for some moments it seemed impossible that the entrenchment could be won under it. There was a temporary check; but soon persevering gallantry triumphed, and the whole army had the satisfaction of seeing the gallant Brigadier Stacey's soldiers driving the Sikhs in con-fusion before them within the area of their encampment. The check was chiefly on the extreme left, where they were exposed to the deadly fire of muskets and swivels, and enfilading artillery; but their comrades on the right of the first division, under Major-General Sir Harry Smith, headed by an old and fearless leader, Sir Robert Dick, forming themselves instinctively into masses and wedges, rushed forward, with loud shouts leaped the ditch, and swarming up, mounted the ramparts, where they stood victorious amid the captured cannon.

At this point Lieutenant Tritteon, bearing the Queen's colours, was shot through the heart, and Ensign Jones, who carried the regimental colours, was about the same time mortally wounded. The regimental colours, falling to the ground, were seized by Sergeant McCabe, and then rushing forward, he crossed the ditch and planted it on the highest point of the enemy's fortifications. There he stood under a tremendous fire, and maintained his position unhurt, though the flag was completely riddled with shot. Lieutenant Noel had seized the Queen's colours, the staff of which was shivered in his hand; and the men cheering, rushed gallantly into the works, and drove the enemy towards the river, into which they were headlong precipitated.

But for some time the Sikhs fought with steadiness and resolution, and turned several guns in the interior on their assailants. Several times the British line was driven back, and the fierce Sikhs rushing on, slaughtered without mercy all who remained wounded on the ground. Each time that with terrific slaughter the British were thus checked, with their habitual valour and discipline they rallied and returned to the charge. At length the second line moving on, the two mingled their ranks, and, supported by a body of cavalry, which, under Sir Joseph Thackwell, had been poured into the camp, everywhere effected openings in the Sikh entrenchments.

In vain the brave Sikhs held out. Each defensible position was captured, and the enemy was pressed towards the scarcely fordable river; but none offered to submit, everywhere showing a front to the victors, or stalking sullenly away, while many turned and rushed singly forth to encounter a certain death amid the hosts of the victors. The foe were now precipitated in masses over the bridge, shattered by shot, into the Sutlej, which a sudden rise had rendered hardly fordable. In their efforts to reach the right bank through the deepened waters, they suffered a dreadful carnage from the horse artillery, which poured in rapid succession volleys among them, till the river was red with the mangled bodies of men and horses; and it is supposed that fully one-third of the Sikh army perished thus or in the battle. Vast quantities of munitions of war were captured, numerous standards, and 67 guns, with 200 camel swivels. This desperate fight began at six in the morning; by nine the combatants were engaged hand to hand, and by eleven the battle was gained. Sir Robert Dick, who had commanded the 42nd Highlanders in Spain, was among the slain, as was Brigadier Taylor, C.B., the beloved colonel of the 29th Regiment, who commanded the third brigade of the second division.

The 3rd, 9th, and 16th Light Dragoons, 9th, 10th, 29th, 31st, 50th, 53rd, 62nd, and 80th Foot, received the thanks of Parliament, and have "Sobraon" on their colours. Two days after this, the British army, now joined by Sir Charles Napier, reached Lahore, and on the 22nd a brigade of troops took possession of the palace and citadel of that capital of the humbled Sikhs.

In the four battles the British lost 92 officers and 1259 men killed, and 315 officers and 4570 men wounded.

BATTLES IN THE PUNJAB, 1848

The Punjab lies between the Indus and the Sutlej, with the river Chenab in the centre. In the southern part is the province of Mooltan, governed in 1848 by Dewan Moolraj. The chief city of the province, a strongly fortified place, is also called Mooltan. A Sikh force in the Company's service was sent into the Punjab in 1847, and Lieutenant Herbert Edwardes was attached to it as political agent, and invested with a very considerable amount of authority. Young as he then was, and with little experience, either of fighting or diplomatising, he never failed to act with judgment and courage. He had soon ample exercise for both qualities. The Government determined to supersede the above-mentioned Moolraj, and to place a new Nazim, Sirdar Khan Singh, as Governor of Mooltan. This latter personage was accompanied to Mooltan by two officers—Mr. Vans Agnew, of the Civil Service, and Lieutenant Anderson, of the 1st Bombay European Fusiliers—and a considerable body of troops. Moolraj, however, had no intention of losing his government, and either prompted by his own ambition, or instigated by evil counsellors, he resolved to rebel. By bribes he won over the native troops who had accompanied the commissioners, and whom, there can be little doubt, he instigated his followers to murder. Both Mr. Agnew and Lieutenant Anderson were set upon and cruelly cut to pieces; not, however, till they had written to Lieutenant Edwardes to warn him of their danger. Lieutenant Edwardes was at that time with a small force at the distance of five days' march from Mooltan. He sent a messenger to say that he would instantly set out with all the men he could collect to their assistance, while he directed Lieutenant Taylor, who was with General Courtlandt, to join him. The heat was intense; but he pushed on, though he learned too soon that the lives of his countrymen had already been sacrificed. Moolraj was in open rebellion, collecting troops from all sides. Edwardes set to work to raise an army to oppose him, and recruiting went on actively on both sides. Edwardes did his utmost to persuade the people that it would be to their true interest to join the British. By May he had raised a force of between 5000 and 6000 men, to which were united about 1500 Sikhs, under General Courtlandt, while he was ably supported by Bhawal Khan, Nawab of Bhawulpoor, with nearly 12,000 followers. With this force, having crossed the Chenab on the 19th of June, he encountered the army of Moolraj, some 18,000 to 20,000 strong, horse and foot, and twenty guns, near the village of Kineyree. The battle began at a little after seven a.m., and was not decided till half-past four p.m. It was hotly contested, and both parties fought with desperation. Out of ten guns, the enemy succeeded in carrying only two into Mooltan, to which place they retreated, leaving 500 men dead on the field of battle. It was an important victory; but as Lieutenants Edwardes and Taylor were the only British officers present, I will not further describe it. The warning uttered to Moolraj by the murdered officers, that their countrymen would amply avenge their deaths, was about to be fulfilled.

Soon after this, Lieutenant Edwardes' force was joined by Lieutenant Lake, and other British officers. On the 1st of July was fought the battle of Suddoosam, where Dewan Moolraj, in spite of the assurances of his soothsayers that it would be an auspicious day to him, was again completely beaten, and driven up to the very walls of his capital. In this battle fell a gallant soldier, Captain Macpherson, in the service of the Nawab of Bhawulpoor, under Lieutenant Lake. The next day a serious accident happened to Lieutenant Edwardes. His pistol exploded as he was putting it into his belt, and the ball passing through his right hand, deprived him for ever of the use of it. His sufferings were great till the arrival of Dr. Cole, a young and excellent English surgeon, who won the affection of all the wounded natives he attended. The four chief leaders in these actions received the thanks of the Governor in Council, and all the credit they so fully deserved; nor was a brave Irishman, Mr. Quin, who volunteered to serve under Lieutenant Edwardes, and rendered him most efficient aid, overlooked.

There can be little doubt that, from the ill-defended condition of Mooltan, these successes might have been followed up by the capture of the city itself, had the victorious army been allowed at once to attack it; but the higher authorities decided otherwise, and Lieutenant Edwardes' force was directed to wait for the arrival of a regular army to commence the siege.

Moolraj, consequently, was allowed time to complete the defences of Mooltan, which he rendered very formidable.

No sooner had Sir Frederick Currie, the resident at Lahore, received information that Moolraj had shut himself up in Mooltan, than he despatched General Whish, with a train of heavy siege-guns, to invest it. Meantime the fort was surrounded and closely invested by the troops under Lieutenant Edwardes and the Nawab of Bhawulpoor, and had thus at their command the revenues and resources of the whole district. Lieutenant Edwardes was now joined by Lieutenant Lumsden and a young lad, Hugo James, who had come out to seek for a cadetship—a gallant boy. As he had come out to learn the art of fighting, his chief afforded him every opportunity of doing so, and "used to give him a few hundred men to take into any ugly place that wanted stopping up."

Steamers had found their way up the mighty Indus into the Chenab, and two of their officers, Captain Christopher and Mr. McLawrin, frequently joined their mess. The steamers were employed in capturing the boats, and otherwise harassing the enemy. The English leader had a great cause of anxiety from the approach of a large Sikh force, under Rajah Sher Singh, whose fidelity he had every reason to doubt. The Sikhs advanced, however, and encamped before the city, and Moolraj lost no time in endeavouring to corrupt both their leaders and common soldiers. With the latter he succeeded but too well, as the sequel will show. Meantime, Moolraj was actively recruiting, and numbers from the Sikh country flocked to his standard. Thus matters went on till the arrival of General Whish, under whom the right column of the British army encamped at Seetul-Ke-Maree, on the 18th of August 1848. Moolraj, hearing of his approach, resolved to attempt surprising him before he reached the city. Accordingly, on the night of the 16th, he sent out a strong force, accompanied by artillery horses ready harnessed, to bring away the guns they expected to capture. Now it happened that on that very day Lieutenant Edwardes, not wishing to have the Sikh force between him and General Whish, had exchanged positions with it, and both armies, according to custom, had in the evening fired a *feu de joie* on the occasion, prolonged by

General Courtlandt's gunners in honour of their approaching friends. This heavy cannonade put the British camp on the *qui vive*, and the General ordered all the tents to be struck, and the troops to get under arms, in case it should be necessary to march to Mooltan, and assist in the supposed engagement with the enemy. Scarcely had this been done than the rebel detachment reached the British camp; and instead of finding all plunged in sleep, except the usual sentries, they were received with such a rattling fire, that, after fruitlessly assailing the pickets, they fled in confusion, as many as possible mounting the artillery horses, which they had brought for so different a purpose. In the affair the British had only six men and two horses wounded, and none killed; while the enemy lost forty killed, many more wounded, and some taken prisoners. It is one of the numberless examples to be brought forward of the importance of being on the alert in the neighbourhood of an enemy. How disastrous might have been the consequences had General Whish's army not been aroused and prepared for an enemy on that occasion!

Moolraj made every attempt to destroy his enemies; and contriving to send three traitors into the camp of the irregulars, who got employed as cooks, Lieutenant Edwardes, Lake, Lumsden, Courtlandt, Hugo James, and Cole, who were dining together, were very nearly all poisoned. The wretches were shaved, flogged, and turned out of the camp, when they fled to Mooltan as fast as their legs could carry them.

SIEGE OF MOOLTAN

And now the avenging army arrived before Mooltan. General Whish's headquarters were with the right column; the left was under Brigadier Salter, and arrived on the 19th August 1848; while the heavy siege-guns, under Major Napier, with the sappers and miners, commanded by Captain H. Siddons, did not reach headquarters till the 4th of September. The European regiment attached to each column came as far as practicable by water. The irregular force under Edwardes and Lake being encamped a distance of six miles from that of General Whish, it was necessary to move it closer up to the latter, to prevent the enemy's cavalry from passing between them. The very position taken up, it was found, was within gunshot of Mooltan; but as it was an important one to hold, Lieutenant Edwardes resolved to keep it. It was not obtained without some fighting, where Lake and Pollock greatly distinguished themselves. Hugo James and Captain Wilmot Christopher accompanied Lieutenant Edwardes into the field, and greatly assisted him in carrying orders. The latter rode about with a long sea-telescope under his arm, just as composedly as if he had been on the deck of his own vessel. Encamping within shot of the enemy's walls is unheard of in regular warfare; and the irregulars soon found it anything but pleasant. One Sunday, during the service held by the Chief for the benefit of all the Christians under him, the little congregation was disturbed by about twenty shot falling round the tents in the space of a very few minutes; and when at length one found its billet, and smashed a man's thigh at the door, a general rush was made to the guns, and the whole strength of the artillery bent upon the Bloody Bastion until its fire was silenced.

On another occasion, Major Napier had one night gone over to visit Edwardes. They were sipping tea and breathing the cool night air, while Lake, exhausted with his day's work, was fast asleep in his bed, under the same awning as themselves, when, the rebel gunners seeming to awake, one shot buried itself hissing in the sand by Napier's side, and then another passed close by his friend.

A third fell at the head of Lake's bed, and his servant immediately got up, and with great carefulness turned his bed round. Lake gave a yawn, and asked sleepily, "What's the matter?"

"Nothing," replied the bearer; "it's only a cannon ball!"

Lake went to sleep again. Five minutes later another fell at his feet, when the good bearer again shifted his master's bed. Once more Lake asked, half asleep, "What's the matter *now?*" and was told in reply:

"*Another* cannon ball—nothing more!"

On which he said, "Oh!" and returned calmly to the land of dreams.

Various plans were suggested for carrying on the siege against the place, which, it was discovered, was very formidable, and not easily to be taken. Constant skirmishes took place. The European soldiers took the night duty in the trenches, to avoid the heat of the day. On the night of the 9th of September, it became necessary to dislodge the enemy from a position they had taken up among some houses and gardens in front of the trenches; and four companies of Her Majesty's 10th Regiment, a wing of the 49th Native Infantry, the rifle company of the 72nd Native Infantry, and two of General Van Courtlandt's horse artillery guns accordingly advanced, and a very sharp night-fight ensued. Ignorance of the localities, and the darkness and confusion consequent on a hastily planned night-attack, rendered the gallant efforts of the troops useless, and, after a considerable loss in killed and wounded, they were withdrawn. Lieutenant-Colonel Pattoun, of the 32nd Foot, led the attack with great gallantry. Lieutenant Richardson, adjutant of the 49th Native Infantry, an officer of Herculean frame, rushed at the barricaded door of the house most strongly occupied by the enemy, and with a mighty effort dashed it in among the rebel inmates, who threw themselves forward to oppose his entrance. Seeing that the party was too strong for him, he seized the foremost Sikh soldier in his arms, and, with his body thus shielded, backed out of the enclosure, when he hurled the half-strangled rebel back among his friends. He did not escape, however, without some severe wounds about his head and arms.

Captain Christopher had, from the first arrival of the steamers at Mooltan, shown the usual willingness of his profession to co-operate with his brother officers on shore. On the night in question he had already once conducted some reinforcements to Colonel Pattoun's assistance, but the fighting at the outposts still raged with unabated fury. Another reinforcement came up, but had no guide. "Will no one show us the way?" asked the officer of the party, looking round on the tired occupants of the trenches. "I will," replied Christopher; and putting himself at their head, he steered them with the steadiness of a pilot through ditches and gardens, under a roaring fire of musketry. Ere he reached the spot, a ball hit him on the ankle, and shivered the joint to pieces. He was borne out of the fight, but never recovered from the wound, and three weeks afterwards was numbered with the brave who fell at the siege.

The British army continued forming their approaches for the attack, and the rebels at the same time laboured without ceasing to strengthen their position. On the 12th of September, General Whish determined to clear his front. The action commenced at seven a.m. by the irregulars, under Lumsden, Lake, and Courtlandt, making an attack to distract the attention of the enemy on the left, when they expelled the enemy from an important village, and captured their magazine and hospital. Two British columns now advanced to do the real business of the day: the right, commanded by Lieutenant-Colonel Pattoun; the left, by Lieutenant-Colonel Franks; while three squadrons of cavalry, commanded by Lieutenant-Colonel Wheeler, protected the British flanks. Both the rebels and British troops fought desperately. Moolraj's entrenched position was fiercely assailed, and fiercely defended. Scarcely a man of its defenders escaped to tell their chief how calmly the young English engineer, Lieutenant Grindall, planted the scaling-ladder in their grim faces; how vainly they essayed to hurl it back; how madly rushed up the grenadiers of the 32nd; with what a yell the brave Irish of the 10th dropped down among them from the branches of the trees above; and how like the deadly conflict of the lion and tiger in a forest den, was the grapple of the pale English with the swarthy Sikhs in that little walled space the rebels thought so strong.

On this day fell Major Montizambert, of the 10th, Colonel Pattoun, Quarter—Master Taylor, Lieutenant Cubitt, and Ensign Lloyd; while Major Napier, the chief engineer, was among the wounded. Altogether, 39 men were killed, and 216 wounded. This victory of Dhurum Salah gained the besieging army a distance to the front of some eight or nine hundred yards, and brought them within battering distance of the city walls. Everybody expected that in a few hours Mooltan would be won, when the astounding news reached General Whish that Rajah Sher Singh and his whole army had gone over to the enemy. A council of war was on this immediately held, when it was decided that the siege of Mooltan should be raised, and that the British army should retire to a short distance, and there, holding a dignified attitude, wait for reinforcements. Rajah Sher Singh was, however, received with suspicion by Moolraj, and so, in a short time, he marched off to join his father and other insurgent chiefs. It was soon evident that the greater part of the Sikh population was insurgent. The only remedy for this state of things, it was agreed, was the annexation of the Punjab—Mooltan, however, must first be taken.

The interval was not passed idly. Lieutenant Taylor prepared all sorts of contrivances for facilitating siege operations; and General Courtlandt's sappers and Lieutenant Lumsden's guides prepared the enormous number of 15,000 gabions and 12,000 fascines. Moolraj was also actively employed in strengthening his defences, and in endeavouring to gain over the neighbouring chiefs to his cause. One of the most important features in the scenery round Mooltan was the Wulle Muhommud canal, which runs past the western side of the city, and the eastern of the village of Sooruj Koond. The water had been drained off by Lieutenant Glover, by damming up the mouth at the Chenab. The enemy were entrenched within this canal under the walls of the city, and General Whish determined to attack them on the 7th of November, and to drive them out at the point of the bayonet. The attack was to be made at daylight, on both sides of the canal, by a strong British brigade on the east, and by the irregular force on the west, each division carefully keeping on its own side of the canal, to prevent the friendly irregulars from being mistaken for the foe. On the very day before, some 220 men of one of General Courtlandt's regiments, called the Kuthar Mookhee, who had been placed in an advanced battery, deserted to the enemy, and endeavoured to carry off Lieutenant Pollock with them; but he was rescued by the rest of the regiment, who remained faithful; and in spite of this defection, he, assisted in a true comrade spirit by Lieutenant Bunny, of the Artillery, and Lieutenant Paton, of the Engineers, held the post with unflinching constancy till day. In consequence of this desertion, it was not deemed prudent to trust the other regiments of the same force with the posts which had been assigned to them. Lieutenant Edwardes, with his irregulars, was to supply their place; but, when all was prepared, the enemy himself attacked the British position, and the very men whose fidelity had been doubted gave such evident proof of their loyalty that they were allowed to take part in the action.

The enemy was soon repulsed, and the British advanced, as had been intended. It was at this time that a body of Rohillas irregulars, disregarding the order they had received to keep on the west side of the canal, crossed over and captured a gun on the eastern bank, when, mistaken by the sepoys for some of the Moolraj's troops, they were instantly fired on. Two had been shot down, when Private Howell, of Her Majesty's 32nd Foot, perceiving what was going on, leaped down the canal, and putting himself in front of the Rohillas, faced the British troops, and waved his shako on the end of his bayonet, as a signal to cease firing. By his presence of mind and courage many friendly lives were saved. Brigadier Markham afterwards presented Howell with fifty rupees, at the head of his regiment, sent to him by Lieutenant Edwardes. On this occasion, Lieutenants Lake and Pollock and Mr. Hugo James again distinguished themselves; and so especially did Dr. Cole, who not only attended to those who were hurt on his own side, but saved the lives of many wounded Sikhs on the field of battle—an act to be performed only by one who adds the courage of a soldier to the humanity of a physician.

Brigadier Markham led the British column. Proceeding with the force under his command across the bridges over the nullah, on the right of the allied camp in the Sooruj Koond in open column, flanking the enemy's position, they brought their shoulders forward to the left, and proceeded directly across their rear. When they had advanced sufficiently far to ensure overlapping the most distant part of their position, they wheeled into line, three guns on the right and three on the left, the whole of the cavalry (with the exception of a small party with the guns) on their right flank. The reserve, in quarter-distance column, in rear of the centre of the right brigade, advanced steadily in echelon of brigade, at fifty paces' distance from the right, under a smart fire of grape and round shot. General Markham, observing a large body of the enemy moving on his right, ordered the cavalry to attack them, to prevent them removing their guns. Major Wheeler, advancing in the most brilliant manner, charged the enemy, cutting up numbers of them, and saved the guns; then sweeping the whole British front, he re-formed speedily and in good order on the left, and moved off to cover the right. As the cavalry cleared the front, the horse artillery opened their fire, the line charged, and took the position, with the whole of the guns, on the bank of the nullah, driving the enemy across and up it with considerable loss. The action lasted about an hour. After the enemy's batteries had been destroyed, the troops returned to camp.

Never was there a more perfect triumph of discipline and good soldiership than the battle of Sooruj Koond. The British troops, who were manoeuvred as on parade, turned a large army out of a strong entrenchment, and routed them, with the loss of five guns, before they even understood the attack. The four leaders, Lieutenant-Colonels Franks and Brooks, and Major Wheeler and Brigadier Markham, were all comparatively young, and no men could have behaved with more judgment, as well as gallantry and spirit.

On the 21st of December, a Bombay division, commanded by Brigadier the Hon. H. Dundas, C.B., of Her Majesty's 60th Rifles, arrived before Mooltan, with Colonel Cheape as chief engineer, raising the army under General Whish to upwards of 15,000 men.

On the 27th of December, the united British force resumed the long-suspended siege of Mooltan.

The plan adopted was to make a regular attack upon the north-east angle of the citadel, and to expel the enemy only from so much of the suburbs as were actually required for the operations of the besiegers.

The portion of the suburbs so required consisted of some high brick-kilns; the cemetery of Moolraj's fathers, called Wuzeerabad; and Moolraj's own garden-house, Am Khas. To seize these positions was the object of the opening attack on the 27th of December. While one British column was effecting it, three others were ordered to make diversions for the purpose of distracting the enemy, with discretionary orders to follow according to the effect produced, even to the taking of the positions, if facilities offered. The third column was composed of the whole disposable force of the irregulars. Facilities did offer, and Brigadier Dundas captured, occupied, and crowned with guns some most important positions which commanded the city. The whole of the suburbs were now occupied by the British army, and it was resolved to take the city also. On this occasion Major Edwardes says that Lieutenants Lake, Pollock, Pearse, and Young all distinguished themselves, as did his writer, the brave Mr. Quin, who led on the Sooraj Mookhee regiment; but the palm was carried off by a new volunteer, Mr. McMahon, who had joined him only a few days before, and who now earned his title to be brought especially to notice by encountering in single combat the leader of the enemy's infantry, a powerful Sikh, whom he killed with one blow which divided his head.

His men at last, thinking themselves responsible for his safety, made him prisoner, and brought him back, with bent and dripping sword, to where Major Edwardes and Sir Henry Lawrence were standing directing the movements of the troops.

On the 30th of December, a shell from a mortar laid by Lieutenant Newall, of the Bengal Artillery, pierced the supposed bomb-proof dome of the Grand Mosque in the citadel, which formed the enemy's principal magazine, and descending into the combustibles below, blew the vast fabric into the air.

On the 2nd of January 1849, the breach in the Rhoonee Boorj or Bloody Bastion of the city was declared practicable, and a second at the Delhi gate was thought sufficiently good to allow of an attempt being made on it as a diversion. General Whish determined to try both; and a party from the Bengal division was told off for the Delhi gate breach, and one from the Bombay division for the breach at the Bastion. The irregular force was to assist both by a diversion on the left. The diversion was commenced at one p.m., and the assault, by a signal from the batteries, at three p.m. The storming party destined to attack the Delhi gate was led by a fine soldier, Captain Smyth, of the grenadier company of Her Majesty's 32nd Regiment. Off they started with hearts beating high; but no sooner had they emerged from the suburbs, than they found themselves on the edge of a deep intervening hollow, after crossing which, under a heavy fire of matchlocks, they discovered, to their surprise, that the city wall in front, about thirty feet in height, was unbreached and totally impracticable. This disagreeable fact had hitherto been concealed by the hollow, both from the breaching-battery and the engineers. The gallant band had therefore to retire; and without loss of time they hurried round to the breach at the Bloody Bastion, to assist their more fortunate comrades in the city.

The Bloody Bastion was assaulted by three companies of the 1st Bombay Fusiliers, under Captain Leith.

They found the breach easy to be surmounted, but it was entrenched inside, and a most bloody struggle ensued, in which the brave Captain Leith was severely wounded, and had to be carried to the rear; but his place was at once taken by Lieutenant Grey, and the redcoats pushed onwards. The first to mount was Colour-Sergeant John Bennet, of the 1st Fusiliers, who, having planted the colours of Old England on the very crest of the breach, stood beside them till the flag and staff were riddled with balls. On rushed the Fusiliers; they remembered the legends of their ancient corps, and closing with the rebels, soon made the city of Mooltan their own.

> Then arose from every crowded height and battery, whence the exciting struggle had been watched, the shouts of applauding comrades; and through the deafening roar of musketry, which pealed along the ramparts, and marked the hard-earned progress of the victorious columns through the streets, both friend and foe might distinctly hear that sound, never to be forgotten—the 'Hurrah!' of a British army after battle.

No sooner did Moolraj discover that the city was captured, than, leaving three-fourths of his army to the mercy of the victors, he retired with 3000 picked men into the citadel, intending to hold out till he could make advantageous terms for himself. The garrison who could escape made the best of their way over the city walls, and fled to their homes. Never did a city present a more awful scene of retribution than did that of Mooltan. Scarcely a roof or wall which had not been penetrated by English shells; and whole houses, scorched and blackened by the bombardment, seemed about to fall over the corpses of their defenders. The citadel itself was now closely invested, and incessantly shelled, so that there was scarcely a spot within the walls where the besieged could find shelter. In this siege the bluejackets of Old England, as well as the redcoats, took a part.

Commander Powell, of the Honourable East India Company's Navy, at the head of a body of seamen, worked one of the heavy batteries from the commencement to the termination of the siege. "It was a fine sight to see their manly faces, bronzed by long exposure to the burning sun of the Red Sea or Persian Gulf, mingling with the dark soldiers of Hindoostan, or contrasting with the fairer but not healthier occupants of the European barrack. They looked on their battery as their ship, their eighteen-pounders as so many sweethearts, and the embrasures as port-holes. 'Now, Jack, shove your head out of that port, and just hear what my little girl says to that 'ere pirate, Mol Rag' (Moolraj?), was the kind of conversation heard on board of the sailor-battery by those passing."

The citadel still held out, but by the 19th two breaches had been effected, and the assault was fixed for six a.m. on the 22nd. Before that hour the traitor sent in his submission, asking only for his own life and the honour of his women. The answer from General Whish was, that the British Government "wars not with women and children, and that they would be protected, but that he had neither authority to give Moolraj his life nor to take it." Thus Moolraj was compelled to make an unconditional surrender. This second siege of Mooltan occupied 27 days, and the British loss was 210 men killed and 982 wounded. One of the last acts of the victors was to disinter the bodies of Agnew and Anderson, and to carry them to an honoured resting-place on the summit of Moolraj's citadel, through the broad and sloping breach which had been made by the British guns in the walls of the rebellious fortress of Mooltan.

Affair at Ramnuggur, 22nd November

The Sikhs and Afghans having formed a combination against the British power, a large force was quickly assembled at Ferozepore, under the immediate orders of Lord Gough, the Commander-in-Chief, in the autumn of 1848.

Sher Singh and Chuttur Singh having effected a junction on the 21st of October, their forces amounted to 30,000. On the 21st of November, Lord Gough joined the British army assembled at Saharum. The Sikh forces were found posted at Ramnuggur. In front of this place flows the Chenab River, which has in mid-channel a small island, on which, protected by a grove of trees, was placed a battery of six guns, with some 400 men. The enemy also having boats on the river, and command of the fort, had pushed across a considerable number of infantry and cavalry. The British army having arrived in front of this strong position, a reconnaissance was made in force with cavalry and horse artillery. The Sikhs, confident in their numbers and the strength of their position, sent across their cavalry, who rode as if in defiance before the British army. A charge of the 3rd Light Dragoons, aided by light cavalry, had chastised on one point the presumption of the Sikhs. William Havelock, the colonel of the 14th, entreated to be allowed to attack another body of the enemy; and to this Colonel Cureton consented. The Commander-in-Chief also riding up, said, "If you see a favourable opportunity of charging—charge." The gallant old colonel soon made the opportunity. "Now, my lads," he exclaimed, boldly leading his dragoons to the on- set, "we shall soon see whether we can clear our front of those fellows or not." The Sikhs made a show of standing the charge, and some of them stood well. Captain Gall, while grasping a standard, had his right hand cut through by the stroke of a Sikh sword, and Lieutenant Fitzgerald's head was cleft in two by a blow from one of the enemy's weapons; but the mass of the Sikhs, opening out right and left, gave way before their victors. Colonel Cureton, however, on seeing the 14th charge, exclaimed, "That is not the body of horse I meant to have been attacked!" and, riding to the front, received in his gallant breast a matchlock ball, which killed him on the spot.

Again the trumpets of the 14th sounded, and, overturn- ing all who opposed them, onward in the direction of the island that gallant regiment took their course. The Sikh battery opened on them a heavy fire, and there was a descent of some four feet into the flat; but Havelock, disregarding all difficulties, and riding well ahead of his men, exclaimed, as he leaped down the declivity, 'Follow me, my brave lads, and never heed the cannon shot!' These were the last words he was ever heard to utter. The dragoons got among broken ground filled with Sikh marksmen, who kept up a withering fire on the tall horsemen, throwing themselves flat on their faces whenever they approached. After many bold efforts, the 14th were withdrawn from the ground, but their commander never returned from that scene of slaughter.

In this unfortunate cavalry affair, 87 men were killed, and 150 wounded.

BATTLE OF CHILIANWALA, 13TH JANUARY 1849

In January of the following year Lord Gough determined to attack the force of Sher Singh, then posted in his front at the village of Chilianwala, before he could be joined by his son, Sirdar Chuttur Singh.

The British army was marched round to take the village in the rear, and it was late in the day before they reached the ground where it was proposed they should encamp, it being Lord Cough's intention to attack early in the morning. While, however, the Quartermaster-General was in the act of taking up ground for the encampment, the enemy advanced some horse artillery, and opened a fire on the skirmishers in front of the village. Lord Gough immediately ordered them to be silenced by a few rounds from the heavy guns, which advanced to an open space in front of the village. Their fire was instantly returned by that of nearly the whole of the enemy's field-artillery, thus exposing the position of his guns, which the jungle had hitherto concealed.

It now became evident that the enemy intended to fight, and Lord Gough drew up his forces in order of battle. Sir Walter Gilbert's division was on the right, that of General Campbell on the left; the heavy guns were in the centre, under Major Horsford, which commenced the engagement by a well-directed and powerful fire on the enemy's centre. The cannonade had lasted about an hour, when Major-general Campbell's division was ordered to advance against the enemy. Part of it was victorious, but the brigade of General Pennycuick met a terrific repulse. "Its advance was daring in the extreme, but over impetuous. The order to charge was given at too great a distance from the enemy; consequently its British regiment, the gallant 24th, outstripped its native regiments, mistaking the action of their brave leaders, Brigadier Pennycuick and Lieutenant-Colonel Brookes, who waved their swords above their heads, for the signal to advance in double-quick time. The 24th, consequently, led by Colonel Brookes, rushed breathless and confused upon the enemy's batteries. Close to their position, it received a deadly shower of grape; and, while shattered by its fatal effects, was torn to pieces by a close fire poured in by the Bunno troops from behind a screen of jungle. The brigade was thrown into utter confusion. The most desperate efforts of the officers availed not to restore order. Colonel Brookes, with numbers of his brave 24th men, fell among the guns. Brigadier Pennycuick was slain at the commencement. His son, Ensign Pennycuick, when he saw his father fall, rushed forward, and striding over his prostrate body, attempted to keep his assailants in check; but the fierce Sikhs rushed on, and hacked the gallant youth to pieces. Besides these brave chiefs, five captains, three lieutenants, and three ensigns of the 24th were killed, while many more were wounded; making in all 23 officers and 459 men. The Sikhs, seeing their advantage, cut down their opponents with savage fury, and at length compelled the shallow remnant of the regiment to fly in disorder."

The cavalry brigade was also brought forward in a way contrary to all the rules of warfare. Advancing in line through a dense forest, they came suddenly upon a strong body of Ghorchurras, intoxicated with the stimulating drug which the heroes of the East call to the aid of their valour. These fanatics, riding furiously towards them, killed some and wounded others, among whom was their brave colonel. At this moment a voice was heard to shout, "Threes about!" It was a fatal order. Wheeling round, the British dragoons fled, panic-struck, followed by the Ghorchurras, even among the ranks of the artillery. It was now that their chaplain, who was attending to some of the wounded in the rear, seeing them approach, grasped a sword, and leaped on a charger standing near him. "My lads," he exclaimed, "you have listened to my preaching, listen to me now. About, and drive the enemy before you!" Saying this, he placed himself at their head, and, encouraged by his gallant example, they once more wheeled about, and uniting with the rest of the regiment, who had been rallied by their colonel, charging furiously, drove back the enemy, and retrieved their honour. Among the officers slain on this occasion was Lieutenant A.J. Cureton, the son of Colonel Cureton, who was killed at Ramnuggur.

On the extreme left, however, the cavalry, under Sir Joseph Thackwell, were victorious wherever they encountered the enemy. The left brigade, under Brigadier Mountain, distinguished itself; while the right attack of infantry, under Sir Walter Gilbert, was perfectly successful: indeed, the disasters of that fatal evening were caused, in the first place, by engaging so late in the day; and in the case of the 24th Regiment, from the over-impetuosity of the officers; and in that of the 14th Light Dragoons, from being suddenly attacked on unfavourable ground, and from receiving wrong orders during the confusion into which they were consequently thrown. Completely did the regiment retrieve its honour in subsequent actions. The Sikhs retreated; the British remained masters of the field. Their loss was, however, very great. Twenty-six European officers and 731 men killed, and 66 officers and 1446 men wounded, was a heavy price to pay for so small an advantage. Never, indeed, had a British army in India, prepared for battle, suffered what was more like a defeat than on this disastrous occasion.

BATTLE OF GUJARAT, 21ST FEBRUARY 1849

After the battle of Chilianwala, the Sikhs were joined by a body of 1500 Afghan horse, under Akram Khan, a son of Dost Mahomed Khan. Compelled, however, by want of supplies, they quitted their entrenchments, and took up a fresh position with 60,000 men, and 59 pieces of artillery, between Gujerat and the Chenab. From this they probably intended marching on Lahore, but were prevented by a brigade under Major-General Whish, who was detached to guard the fords above and below Wuzeerabad, while Lord Gough advanced towards them—the whole army burning to avenge the loss of their comrades who had fallen on the 13th of January, many of whom, when lying wounded, had been cruelly slaughtered by the Sikhs. This time Lord Gough took good care to commence the action at an earlier hour in the day. At half-past seven in the morning on the 21st of February, the sky clear and cloudless, and the sun shining brightly on the extended line of bayonets and sabres, with the precision of a parade the British army advanced to meet the foe. The Sikh artillery opened at a long distance, thus exposing the position of their guns. With good judgment, Lord Gough therefore halted the infantry out of the range of fire, and pushed forward the whole of his guns, which were covered by skirmishers.

The Sikh guns were served well and rapidly; but the terrific fire of the British artillery at length compelled the enemy to fall back, when the infantry were deployed, and a general advance directed, covered by artillery.

A village in which a large body of the enemy's artillery was concealed lay directly in the line of Sir Walter Gilbert's advance. This was carried by the 3rd Brigade, under General Penny, in the most brilliant style, the enemy being driven from their cover with great slaughter. Here the 2nd European Regiment distinguished itself. At the same time a party of Brigadier Harvey's brigade, most gallantly led by Lieutenant-Colonel Franks, of the 10th Foot, drove a large body of the enemy from another village. The infantry continued to advance, while the heavy guns as well as field batteries kept pace with them, unlimbering in successive positions for effective action. The rapid advance and admirable fire of the horse artillery and light field batteries, strengthened by two reserved troops of horse artillery under Lieutenant-Colonel Brind, broke the enemy's ranks at all points. The other villages were stormed; the guns in position carried, 53 pieces falling into the hands of the victors; the camp with baggage and standard captured, and the whole army of Sher Singh routed in every direction. The cavalry had hitherto been restrained from taking too active a part in the action, though the brigades on either flank were occasionally threatened and attacked by large masses of the enemy's horsemen. Each time, however, by their steady movements and spirited manoeuvres, ably supported by the horse artillery attached to them, the British cavalry put the foe to flight. A large body of Ghorchurras, with some Afghan cavalry, appearing on the right, a brilliant and successful charge was made on them by some troops of the 9th Lancers with the Scinde Horse, when several standards were captured. The 14th Light Dragoons and other cavalry regiments, by their bold front and gallant conduct whenever the enemy approached, contributed much to the success of the day.

The enemy on all sides now took to flight. The right wing and General Campbell's division passed in pursuit to the eastward of Gujerat, and the Bombay division to the westward.

Then, from either flank the horse, unbroken and in perfect order, swept forward to do the work of final retribution. The two columns speedily got into communication. Onward they moved in union, cutting down, dispersing, riding over, and trampling the flying or scattered infantry, capturing guns and wagons, strewing the paths with dead and dying; forward they moved in their irresistible course, and converted a beaten army into a shapeless, hideous mass of helpless fugitives.

The Sikh army was soon dispersed over the country, the ground strewed with the dead and wounded, and their weapons and military equipments, which they cast from them in the hopes that they might be taken for peasants or camp followers instead of soldiers.

For twelve miles did the avenging horsemen pursue the foe; and it was not till half-past four that they drew rein, when they returned exultingly to camp. Such was the battle of Gujerat, one of the most important and decisive ever fought in India. By it the power of the Sikhs was completely broken, while it taught a lesson to the Afghans, who now for the first time had united to them, and made them feel that it was their best policy to obtain the friendship rather than the enmity of England. This great battle was won chiefly by artillery; though the infantry, by their gallant advance, drove back the enemy, and the cavalry, by their brilliant charges and their rapid pursuit, entirely broke and destroyed the force of the enemy. The flying army was followed up by Sir Walter Gilbert, Sir Colin Campbell, and Colonel Bradford, in three different directions, on the 3rd of March. Sir Walter Gilbert came up with a portion of the fugitives, which still held together under Sher Singh and Chuttur Singh, at Horrmuck, on the 11th of March, when they surrendered; and three days afterwards, the remainder of their forces, amounting to 16,000 men, laid down their arms at Rawalpindee, and 41 pieces of artillery were given up. Dost Mahomed was pursued as far as the Khyber Pass.

In consequence of these operations, the Punjab was annexed to the Government of India.

"Gujerat" is borne by the 3rd, 9th, and 14th Light Dragoons, and the 10th, 24th, 29th, 32nd, 53rd, 60th, and 61st Regiments—while the army received the thanks of Parliament. Sir Charles Napier had been hurried out to take command, out found on his arrival that the work to be done had been achieved, and that the brave Lord Gough's last battle was a crowning victory.

The Crimean War
1854-55

The Crimean War
1854-1855

The settled resolve of the Russian Government to crush the power of the Turks, and to take possession of Constantinople, was the cause of the declaration of war by England and France against Russia.

The war became at once popular among the British people when the news was spread that a Russian fleet, consisting of six men-of-war and several smaller vessels, had darted out of Sebastopol, and, taking advantage of a dense fog, had entered the harbour of Sinope, where they found a Turkish squadron of eight frigates, two schooners, and three transports, totally unprepared for battle. Admiral Nachimoff, the Russian commander, fiercely attacked them, and though the Turks fought bravely, so great was their disadvantage, that in a few hours 5000 men were massacred, and every ship, with the exception of two, was destroyed. To prevent the recurrence of such an event, the allied fleets of England and France entered the Black Sea on the 3rd of January 1854. War was not officially declared against Russia till the 28th of March. The Guards and other regiments had, however, embarked early in February; first to rendezvous at Malta, and subsequently at Varna, on the Turkish shore of the Black Sea. The British troops, under Lord Raglan, amounted to 26,800 men of all arms; that of the French, under Marshal Saint Arnaud, to nearly the same number, 26,526; and there were also 7000 Turks, under Selim Pasha; making in all 60,300 men, and 132 guns, 65 of which were British.

On the morning of the 14th September, the fleet conveying this magnificent army anchored off the coast, near Old Fort, distant about eighteen miles south of Eupatoria. The first British troops which landed in the Crimea were the men of Number 1 company of the 23rd Welsh Fusiliers, under Major Lystons and Lieutenant Drewe. The landing continued during the whole day, without any casualties. The first night on shore the rain fell in torrents, and the troops, who had landed without tents or shelter of any sort, were drenched to the skin. On the following morning the sun shone forth, and the disembarkation continued. No enemy was encountered till the 19th, when two or three Russian guns opened fire, and a body of Cossacks were seen hovering in the distance. The Earl of Cardigan instantly charged them, and they retreated till the British cavalry were led within range of the fire of their guns, when four dragoons were killed and six wounded,—the first of the many thousands who fell during the war.

The evening of the 19th closed with rain.

BATTLE OF THE ALMA
20TH SEPTEMBER

Wet and weary the allied troops rose on the morning of the 20th September of 1854, to march forward to the field of battle. On their right was the sea, on which floated the British fleet; before them was the river Alma, down to which the ground sloped, with villages, orchards, and gardens spread out along its banks. "On the other side of the river, the ground at once rose suddenly and precipitously to the height of three or four hundred feet, with tableland at the top. This range of heights, which, particularly near the sea, was so steep as to be almost inaccessible, continued for about two miles along the south bank, and then broke away from the river (making a deep curve round an amphitheatre, as it were, about a mile wide), and then returned to the stream again, but with gentler slopes, and features of a much less abrupt character." The road crossed the river by a wooden bridge, and ran through the centre of the valley or amphitheatre. Prince Menschikoff had posted the right of his army on the gentler slopes last described, and as it was the key of his position, great preparations had been made for its defence. About half-way down the slope a large earthen battery had been thrown up, with twelve heavy guns of position; and higher up, on its right rear, was another of four guns, sweeping the ground in that direction. Dense columns of infantry were massed on the slopes, with large reserves on the heights above. A lower ridge of hills ran across the amphitheatre, and at various points batteries of field-artillery were posted, commanding the passage of the river and its approaches. In front of this part of the position, and on the British side of the river, was the village of Borutiuk.

On their left, close to the sea, the acclivities were so abrupt that the Russians considered themselves safe from attack. The river, which ran along the whole front, was fordable in most places, but the banks were so steep, that only at certain points could artillery be got across. A numerous body of Russian riflemen were scattered among the villages, gardens, and vineyards spread along the banks. The Russian right was protected by large bodies of cavalry, which constantly threatened the British left, though held in check by the cavalry under Lord Lucan. The right of the allies rested on the sea, where, as close in shore as they could come, were a fleet of steamers throwing shot and shell on to the heights occupied by the Russian left.

At about eleven a.m. the allied armies advanced, the whole front covered by a chain of light infantry. On the extreme right, and about 1500 yards in advance of the line, was the division of General Bosquet; next, on his left, was that of General Canrobert; then the Prince Napoleon's, with General Forey's in his rear, in reserve. The English then took up the alignment, commencing with the 2nd division (Sir De Lacy Evans), then the light division (Sir G. Brown), and, in rear of them, the 3rd and 1st divisions respectively—the whole in column; Sir G. Cathcart, with the 4th division, being in reserve on the outward flank; the English cavalry, under the Earl of Lucan, considerably farther to the left, also protecting the exposed flank and rear.

The French advancing, gained the heights, took the enemy somewhat by surprise, and almost turned his left. He then, however, brought forward vast masses of troops against them, and it became necessary for the British more completely to occupy them in front.

The two leading English divisions (the light and 2nd), which had advanced across the plain in alignment with the French columns, on coming within long range of the enemy's guns deployed into line (two deep), and whilst waiting for the further development of the French attack, were ordered to lie down, so as to present as small a mark as possible. The Russian riflemen now opened fire, and the village burst into flames. Lord Raglan, with his staff, passing the river, perceived the position of the enemy on the heights he was about to storm. He instantly ordered up some guns, which, crossing the river, opened fire, and afterwards moving up the heights, harassed the Russian columns in their retreat.

Now, with skirmishers and rifles in advance, the two leading divisions advanced towards the enemy, General Codrington's brigade leading straight for the Russian entrenched battery. The two brigades of the 2nd division were separated by the burning village. The brigade of General Pennefather moved to the left of the village, close to the Sebastopol road, and found itself in the very focus towards which the Russians were directing their heaviest fire, both of artillery and musketry. Still undaunted, though suffering terrible loss, they pressed the Russians hard, and fully occupied their centre. While other operations were going on, the light division, under Sir

George Brown, having moved across the plain in a long thin line, became somewhat broken among the vineyards and inequalities of the ground. As they approached, however, they found some shelter; and at length the word was given to charge. They sprang from their cover, and with a rattling fire rushed at the foe; and General Codrington's brigade, 33rd and 23rd Regiments, and 7th Fusiliers, with the 19th on their left and the 95th on their right, were now in direct line, and in full view of the great Russian battery. The whole British line now opened a continuous fire—the Russian columns shook—men from the rear were seen to run; then whole columns would turn and fly, halting again and facing about at short intervals; but with artillery marching on their left flank, with Codrington's brigade streaming upwards, and every moment pouring in their fire nearer and nearer as they rushed up the slope, the enemy's troops could no longer maintain their ground, but fled disordered up the hill. The Russian batteries, however, still made a fearful havoc in the English ranks; and a wide street of dead and wounded, the whole way from the river upward, showed the terrific nature of the fight.

Breathless, decimated, and much broken, the men of the centre regiments dashed over the entrenchment and into the great battery in time to capture two guns. But the trials of the light division were not over. The reserves of the enemy now moved down. The English regiments, their ranks in disarray and sorely thinned, were forced gradually to relinquish the point they had gained, and doggedly fell back, followed by the Russian columns. It seemed for a moment as if victory was still doubtful; but succour was close at hand. The three regiments of Guards (having the Highland brigade on their left) were now steadily advancing up the hill, in magnificent order. There was a slight delay until the regiments of Codrington's brigade had passed through their ranks, during which time the struggle still wavered, and the casualties were very great; but when once their front was clear, the chance of the Russians was at an end, and their whole force retreated in confusion. The several batteries of the different divisions, after crossing at the bridge, moved rapidly to their front, and completed the victory by throwing in a very heavy fire, until the broken columns of the enemy were out of range. And now from rank to rank arose the shout of victory. Comrades shook hands, and warm congratulations passed from mouth to mouth that the day was won, and right nobly won. What cared then those gallant men of the toil, and thirst, and hunger, and wounds they had endured! Those heights on which at early morn the legions of Russia had proudly stood, confident of victory, had been gained, and the foe, broken and damaged, were in rapid retreat.

In this fight the Royal Welsh Fusiliers especially distinguished themselves by their heroic valour; and no less than 210 officers and men, upwards of a quarter of their number, were killed or wounded during the battle. The brave young Lieutenant Anstruther carried the colours; and when he fell dead under the terrific fire from the chief redoubt, they were picked up by Private Evans, and by him given to Corporal Luby. From him they were claimed by the gallant Sergeant Luke O'Connor, who bore them onwards amid the shower of bullets, when one struck him, and he fell; but quickly recovering himself, and refusing to relinquish them, onward once more he carried them till the day was won, and he received the reward of his bravery, by the praises of his General on the field, and the promise of a commission in his regiment; and a better soldier does not exist than Captain O'Connor of the 23rd.

Captain Bell, of the same regiment, seeing the Russians about to withdraw one of their guns, sprang forward, and putting a pistol to the head of the driver, made him jump off, and springing into the saddle in his stead, galloped away with it to the rear, but was soon again at his post, and, all the officers above him having been killed or wounded, had the honour of bringing the regiment out of action. Colonel Chester and Captain Evans were both killed near the redoubt. Captain Donovan, of the 33rd, captured another gun; but the horses not being harnessed to it, the driver took to flight, and it could not be removed. Nineteen sergeants of that regiment were killed or wounded, chiefly in defence of their colours. The colours of the Scots Fusilier Guards were carried by Lieutenants Lindsay and Thistlethwayte. The staff was broken and the colours riddled, and many sergeants fell dead by their side, yet unharmed they cut their way through the foe, and bore them triumphantly up that path of death to the summit of the heights. The action lasted little more than two hours. In that time 25 British officers were killed, and 81 wounded; and of non-commissioned officers and men, 337 were killed, and 1550 were wounded. But death was not satiated, and many brave officers and men died from cholera even on the field of victory. One name must not be forgotten—that of the good and brave Dr. Thompson, who, with his servant, remained on the field to attend to the wants of upwards of 200 Russians who had not been removed.

Lieutenant Lindsay, who carried the colours of the Scots Fusilier Guards, stood firmly by them, when, as they stormed the heights, their line was somewhat disordered, and by his energy greatly contributed to restore order. In this he was assisted by Sergeants Knox and McKechnie, and Private Reynolds. Sergeant Knox obtained a commission in the Rifle Brigade for his courage and coolness on this occasion.

SIEGE OF SEBASTOPOL

On the 17th of October commenced one of the most extraordinary sieges to be found recounted in the page of modern history. Five bombardments took place; three sanguinary battles were fought under these walls, and numerous sorties and skirmishes occurred. Sixty guns and mortars were landed and brought into position by the British; but the Russians were not idle, and not only was the Malakoff tower strengthened, but the Redan and other formidable batteries were thrown up. The French were on the left, and had fifty-three guns and mortars in position.

At half-past six a.m. on a beautiful morning on the 17th of October, the English and French batteries suddenly opened, completely taking the enemy by surprise; but though the guns from the top of the Malakoff tower were overthrown by the English guns, the Russians kept up a steady fire from the earthen batteries round, and from the Redan and Barrack batteries.

The French siege-guns were, however, of less use, and totally inadequate for the work; consequently at half-past ten a.m. they ceased firing, one of their magazines also having blown up, and killed or wounded 100 men. This undoubtedly was one of the main causes of the failure of the attempt. The fleets at the mouth of the harbour were warmly engaged, and suffered considerably.

The Russians lost Admiral Kermileff, killed, and Admiral Nachimoff, of Sinope celebrity, was wounded, with about 500 men killed and wounded.

The English lost 44 killed, and 266 wounded.

The French were greatly in want of guns, whereas the Russians had the means of increasing their garrison to any extent; and, by sinking their ships, they added 500 to the fortifications and obtained their crews to work them. Sickness and fighting had sadly reduced the English forces, who now numbered only 16,000 men, though the French had still 35,000 fit for service; yet they also soon suffered greatly from sickness and want of food and shelter.

To those who have not before them a plan of Sebastopol, a slight description of the place and the surrounding country will be necessary. It is situated on the south side of an inlet of the sea, with another smaller inlet running up on the east side called Dockyard Creek, and one on the west, some little distance from the entrenchments, called Quarantine Bay. Thus it has water on three sides. Ships of war were stationed in each of the smaller inlets, with their guns bearing on the ravines leading down to them. On the north side of the harbour, at the mouth, was Fort Constantine, with several batteries, and farther inland the Star Fort, while across the harbour's mouth was a line of powerful ships of war.

Only one side, therefore, remained open to attack. At the commencement of the siege, on the east was a round stone tower, built on commanding ground, and mounting four guns, called the Malakoff, and on the west a crenelated wall terminated by another tower overlooking the Quarantine Harbour; and between them, at one or two intermediate points, there were a few earthworks not completed, and apparently not armed.

Now these defences do not appear to be very formidable, and it is probable that, had the allies left their sick and wounded to the tender mercies of the Cossacks, and pushed on at once after the battle of the Alma, they might have entered the city; but they would have entered a trap in which they would have met certain destruction. The Russian fleet commanding the town would have thundered down on them, and they in their turn would have been subjected to an immediate attack from the powerful Russian forces hastening towards the place. It was therefore decided by the allied chiefs to wait till their siege-trains were landed, and then to lay regular siege to the place.

The river Chernaya ran into the head of the harbour from the east, passing under the heights of Inkerman. A range of hills and high ground extended from its mouth to the town and small harbour of Balaclava, with a broad valley intervening, in which the British cavalry was encamped, with a line of Turkish redoubts in their front, and the village of Kadikoi on their right. On the northern end of this range of heights above Inkerman, the Guards with the 2nd division were posted; while the French, under General Bosquet, were encamped extending along the whole line of heights, till they were terminated by the valley where the cavalry camp was pitched. The other three English divisions faced Sebastopol itself. Balaclava harbour is surrounded by heights, on which some powerful batteries were placed, and only one mountain road led up to them near the sea. Some way below them was the village of Kamara. The weakest points of the position were at the two ends of the long range of heights at Inkerman and Balaclava, and on both these the Russians made their fiercest attacks.

In the valley the only infantry regiment was the gallant 93rd Highlanders, posted in front of the village of Kadikoi.

Battle of Balaclava
25th October

The enemy had for some days before the 25th of October been observed hovering in the neighbourhood of Balaclava; and on the morning of that day, reinforcements of 20,000 infantry, 40 guns, and a strong force of cavalry arrived, under General Liprandi. The heights above Balaclava were now garrisoned by the marines landed from the fleet; and they, with the 93rd and a few detachments from other regiments, were under the immediate command of Sir Colin Campbell. Early in the morning the Russians, in great force, attacked the Turkish batteries, which they succeeded in capturing,—the English gunner in each, with noble self-devotion, spiking the guns before he attempted to escape. One large body of the enemy now attacked the 93rd, under Lieutenant-Colonel Ainslie, but were bravely repelled. Another, and the most powerful, turned towards the cavalry. As they did so, Lord Lucan ordered General Scarlett to charge, although the ground was far from favourable for the operation. It was the moment every trooper ardently longed for. Nothing could stop their impetuosity; but all descriptions would be tame after that of Mr. Russell, for never has there been sketched a more vivid picture.

As lightning flashes through the cloud, the Greys and Enniskilleners passed through the dark masses of the Russians. The shock was but for a moment. There was a clash of steel, and a light play of sword-blades in the air, and then the Greys and the redcoats disappeared in the midst of the shaken and quivering columns. In another moment we saw them emerging with diminished numbers, and in broken order, charging against the second line. It was a terrible moment. 'God help them, they are lost!' was the exclamation of more than one man, and the thought of many. With unabated fire the noble hearts dashed at their enemy. It was a fight of heroes. The first lines of Russians, which had been utterly smashed by our charge, and had fled at our flank, and towards the centre, were coming back to swallow up our handful of men. By sheer steel and sheer courage Enniskilleners and Scots were winning their desperate way right through the enemy's squadron, and already grey horses and redcoats had appeared right at the rear of the second mass, when, with irresistible force, like one bolt from a bow, the 4th Dragoon Guards, riding straight at the right flank of the Russians, and the 5th Dragoon Guards, following close upon the Enniskilleners, rushed at the remnant of the first line of the enemy, went through it as though it were made of pasteboard, and put them to utter rout. The Russian horse, in less than five minutes after it met our dragoons, was flying with all its speed before a force certainly not half its strength. A cheer burst from every lip. In their enthusiasm, officers and men took off their caps, and shouted with delight, and then, keeping up the scenic character of their position, they clapped their hands again and again. Lord Raglan at once despatched Lieutenant Curzon, his aide-de-camp, to convey his congratulations to Brigadier-General Scarlett, and to say, 'Well done!'

We may suppose the heights overlooking the plain or valley crowded with eager spectators—the enemy below—the Russian hosts beyond.

This was not that desperate charge known as the "Balaclava Charge," which took place soon afterwards.

The Charge of the Light Brigade.

That the reader may understand the circumstances which led to that terrible charge, a description of the ground must be given.

From the lofty plateau of the Chersonese, on which the British army was posted, a long ridge of elevated ground extends to the eastward, on the top of which runs the Woronzoff road. Along this ridge was a line of forts armed with carriage guns, which had just before been captured by the Russians from the Turks who had garrisoned them. To the south was the broad valley, with the heights of Balaclava on the farther side, in which the charge of the heavy cavalry, under General Scarlett, took place. On the north side of the ridge was a narrower valley, with the Fedhoukine hills to the north.

It was towards the latter part of that memorable day, the 25th of October, that the British cavalry were drawn up under Lord Lucan at the western end of this narrow valley directly under the steep heights of the Chersonese. On the summit, at the very edge of the heights, Lord Raglan with General Airey and other officers had taken their post, so as to overlook the Woronzoff ridge and the Fedhoukine hills with the whole of the intermediate valley. The eastern end of the valley was occupied by some powerful batteries of Russian guns, supported by large bodies of cavalry and several regiments of infantry, while the heights on both sides were crowned by Russian artillery and infantry. Lord Raglan, perceiving that it was the intention of the Russians to carry off the guns they had captured from the Turks, ordered up General Cathcart's brigade to prevent them from effecting their object. Some delay occurred before the brigade began its march; and the Commander-in-Chief, seeing that the Russians would succeed in carrying off the guns if not at once attacked, despatched Captain Nolan, an officer on General Airey's staff, with a written order to Lord Lucan to charge the Russians with the light brigade of cavalry commanded by Lord Cardigan, and to recapture the guns. Lord Lucan and Lord Cardigan saw only the heavy guns in their front—those to which Lord Raglan referred being concealed from their view by the high ground. They, therefore, supposing that they were to attack the guns which they did see, naturally demurred about performing an act which might prove the destruction of the whole brigade, while the aide-de-camp, who thought only of the guns on their right, insisted in strong language that the order must be obeyed. Supposing that the order was understood, Captain Nolan then placed himself on the left of the light brigade, intending to charge with it. Lord Cardigan, still under a wrong impression, obedient to the order which he conceived had been sent him, placed himself at the head of his gallant light cavalry, and gave the order to advance. Instead of wheeling with their left shoulders forward towards the slope on their right front, as the Commander-in-Chief expected them to do, the cavalry continued straight down the valley, Lord Cardigan, on his tall charger, at a distance of some five horses' lengths in front of the line, leading them.

Scarcely had they gone a hundred paces when Captain Nolan, dashing out from the left of the line, galloped diagonally across the front, waving his sword and pointing eagerly towards the Russians on the right. There might yet have been time to remedy the fatal error into which the cavalry guards had fallen, but at that moment a shell burst close to the brave aide-de-camp. His sword fell from his hand, while his arm still remained extended; his horse wheeling, dashed back towards the advancing ranks, passing between the 13th Light Dragoons, and he fell to the ground a lifeless corpse.

Steadily on went those 600 men, almost to certain death, a perfect marvel of discipline and heroic courage. From the Woronzoff heights on the right, from the Fedhoukine hills on the left, came showering down upon them shot and shell and rifle bullets, thinning their advancing ranks. Each gap made by the deadly missiles was immediately filled up. On went the devoted band. More and more dropped. Riderless horses galloped back, some falling in their course, others uttering cries of agony from the wounds they had received. Here and there human forms could be distinguished lying in the quiet of death, others writhing on the ground, or endeavouring to drag themselves back up the valley. As the brigade, still as steady as if on parade, dashed forward, the guns in their front opened their fire, filling the air with dense masses of smoke. Right up to them they charged, Lord Cardigan still leading. Amid the guns they forced their way, cutting down the gunners, who either fled or endeavoured to find shelter under the carriages.

Lord Lucan, in the meantime, followed with the heavy cavalry to support the light brigade, but having lost many men, he judiciously retired, at once seeing that his brigade would be destroyed before they could even reach the guns, and they were now compelled to remain inactive while the action continued, as their brethren in the light cavalry had been in the morning. At this juncture a portion of the French cavalry—the famous regiment of D'Allonville—moved forward, sweeping round the western base of the Fedhoukine hills, up which they charged, rushing forward as fast as the uneven nature of the ground would allow them, on the Russian artillery and infantry posted there, and which had caused such fearful loss to the light cavalry as they passed. As the French approached, the artillery limbered up and galloped off to the eastward, while the infantry quickly retreated, although not until many a gallant Frenchman's saddle had been emptied. Some minutes of awful suspense had passed since the last of the red line of cavalry had been seen rushing into the smoke. Those posted on the height of Chersonese could discern, as the smoke cleared away, a dark mass in the distance, and the glittering of sword-blades, while the sounds of musketry and the confused murmur of voices which came up the valley indicated that the fight was still raging. The guns which had dealt death into their ranks had ceased to roar. They had fought their way through, attacked, and put to flight the Russian cavalry. Then breaking into several bodies, after enduring a heavy fire from the rifles of the infantry, had wheeled round and were making their way back towards the point from which a few minutes before they had set forth in brilliant array. One body had to encounter a whole regiment of lancers drawn up on their flank. Although the Russians thrust at them with their long spears, every blow was parried, and they passed by unscathed. At length, here and there a single horseman was seen moving slowly back, he or his charger sorely wounded. Now more and more appeared, several dropping as they returned, the whole centre of the valley, as far as the eye could reach, being strewed with bodies of men and horses. The number of those coming up the valley now increased. Among them appeared the tall form of their leader, he and his horse uninjured; then came larger parties, followed by single horses and men on foot, still exposed to the fire from the Woronzoff ridge. Presently a number of Cossacks came galloping up after the retreating cavalry, spearing some, and taking others prisoners; but the Russian guns on the causeway again opening fire, the Cossacks, to avoid being struck by their friends, were compelled to abandon the pursuit, many of those they had surrounded making their escape. Among the last who came in was Lord George Paget, who with Colonel Douglas led out the remnant of the 4th Dragoon Guards and a portion of the 11th Hussars. Of the Gallant Brigade, which half an hour before had numbered 600 horseman, not 200 now remained fit for duty. 113 officers and men had been killed, and 134 wounded, while upwards of 400 horses were killed or rendered unfit for service. Although the Russian batteries still kept up their fire, many of the troopers who had themselves escaped dashed back to search for their wounded officers or comrades, and several were thus saved from perishing on the battle-field.

The Russian loss was far greater. Sir George Cathcart, with the 4th division, coming up, the enemy fell back, and abandoned the attempt to carry off the guns. On the next day, the 26th of October, the Russians made an attack on the 2nd division, that part of the British force which was posted above the ruins of Inkerman.

About 8000 men, supported by artillery and skirmishers, advanced against this division; but so admirably did they sustain the attack, that when General Bosquet led up some French troops, they retreated, and were chased down the ridge towards the head of the bay. This attack has been called the Little Inkerman.

Battle of Inkerman 5th November. The allied commanders had decided on a general assault for the 7th of November; but the enemy, who had received immense reinforcements, anticipated their plans, and prepared for another terrific attempt to raise the siege, and to drive the allies into the sea.

The camp of the 2nd division was on the extreme northern end of the heights, above the ruins of Inkerman, with Careening Bay on the left, and the river Chernaya in front. The extreme right of the British position, and the left of the French, was the weakest point. Sir De Lacy Evans had pointed it out, and Sir John Burgoyne had especially urged the French General Biot to strengthen it, but he paid no attention to the advice; and at length the English, their strength already overtaxed, had erected a small work there, but no guns had yet been mounted. Of this the Russian generals were fully aware when they formed their plan of attack.

Two corps of the Russian army were detailed for the grand attack. One, under General Pauloff, was to march from the north side, and crossing the marsh from the causeway, was then to wind up the heights in front of the 2nd division, and force the English right. Simultaneously with General Pauloff's movement, the other corps, under General Soimonoff, was to leave Sebastopol by a road near the Malakoff, which would have brought it up in front of the British light division. Instead of this, by mistaking the ground, he moved to his left, and found himself in front of the English 2nd division; so that, when General Pauloff's leading regiments arrived, the ground intended for their attack was already occupied, and the battle had begun. The Russians, confined therefore in a narrow space, encumbered each other during the day, and could not find sufficient room to deploy. It was dark and wet, and a thick fog lay on the ground as the day dawned on the 5th of November. It is said that Major Sir Thomas Troubridge, who commanded the outposts of the first brigade of the light division, after relieving the advanced sentries, went down before daybreak towards the Mamelon, and sweeping the ground with a field-glass, descried the enemy on the opposite side of the ravine.

While he hastened to get the 2nd division under arms to meet the threatened attack, the advanced pickets were surprised, but behaved with the greatest gallantry, disputing every inch of ground with the Russian riflemen. One detachment, in falling back, held the Sandbag battery for a short time, but were driven out by the enemy.

The 2nd division, under General Pennefather, was formed at once on the ridge in front of their own camp, the other English divisions getting under arms and hastening to the front. The three regiments of Guards proceeded to the right, and General Bullar's brigade to the left of the 2nd division. General Codrington's brigade took up the ground in front of its own camp, on the left side of Careening Bay ravine, on the spot where it had been intended Soimonoff's corps should have deployed. On the noble Guards fell a large share of the work of that sanguinary day. Pressing forward, they drove the enemy out of the Sandbag battery; and, though fiercely assailed on both flanks, they maintained that forward position during the day, except for a short time. Once they had to retire before overwhelming numbers and a terrific fire of artillery; reinforced by the 20th Regiment, they again rushed forward and retook the redoubt.

In vast masses the Russians pressed on, their artillery of heavy calibre supporting their advance, and often throughout the day the fortune of the fight seemed doubtful; but never did troops behave with more heroic courage. Shrouded by a thick fog, each man, and each company, and each regiment, felt that they must in a great part depend upon themselves. Meantime, Sir George Cathcart, with part of the 68th Regiment, and a few other men, hearing that the enemy were attempting to force the extreme right, and that it was the point most open to danger, pushed rapidly forward, hoping to act on the flank of the Russian troops storming the Sandbag battery. He had not gone far when he discovered the enemy on his front, on his right flank below him, and on his left above him.

At that moment he fell, shot through the head, while several of his staff were killed with him. General Torrens, who had come up, was also wounded; the men were withdrawn to the ground on the flank of the battery, which they, with other troops, continued to maintain. By this time several of the Russian generals, with the officers of their staffs, and colonels of regiments, were killed, and their troops thrown into confusion. While the battle thus furiously raged and numbers were falling, the Russians, 5000 strong, made a sortie against the left of the French batteries, and succeeded in spiking several guns; but the French troops, rallying, charged them so furiously that they were driven back; some of the French, carried on by their ardour, entering the batteries with them. The brave French General Lourmel was killed; but the Russians lost 1000 men. For several hours had the battle of Inkerman raged; the English, but 8000 strong, supporting the whole brunt of the fight.

The termination seemed doubtful; fresh troops were brought against them, but yet not a man who stood on those bloody heights ever dreamed of yielding. Yet, overwhelmed at length, the Guards were pressed back. Not only were they assailed by the fire of the Russian field batteries, but by the guns of Sebastopol, and by those of the ships in Careening Bay. Suddenly the shrill tones of the French horns were heard above the rolling and rattling of the firing. The regiments of the first brigade, which arrived with that dashing intrepidity for which the French are distinguished, immediately pressed forward into the thick of the fight, and almost reached the Sandbag battery, the contest for which had been so often renewed. But even these fresh troops found difficulty in maintaining themselves, and were almost surrounded. A second brigade, however, quickly reinforced them, and several French batteries coming up on the right of the English ones, the enemy were at length completely driven from the ground, and had now no alternative but a difficult retreat down precipitous slopes. Heavy masses were observed retiring over the bridge of the Chernaya, and ascending the opposite heights, abandoning on the field of battle 5000 or 6000 dead and wounded.

"There is probably," says Colonel Adye, "no record of any battle in which such great numbers fought on so small a space. There are few which have been so stoutly contested, or in which the valour and perseverance of all the troops engaged have been throughout so conspicuous."

The conduct of the English infantry is immortal. Although enfeebled by previous fatigue and constant night watches, still, on the day of trial, for hours did 8000 men resolutely maintain themselves against successive columns of attack of vastly superior numbers; and at last, when almost overpowered, they found an ever ready and gallant ally at hand to save them in their hour of need.

This battle, too, brought out conspicuously the sterling courage and unmatched steadiness of the English artillery. Repeatedly were the Russian columns close to the muzzles of the guns, and were driven back by volleys of case. In some instances the batteries were actually run into, and the gunners bayoneted at their posts. Their carriages were repeatedly struck, and their loss was 96 men and 80 horses killed.

The casualties of the British army amounted to 2,590. Of these, 43 officers and 416 men were killed, and 101 officers and 1,332 men were wounded, while nearly 200 were missing. The Russians lost fully 15,000 men.

That of the 25,000 British infantry landed in the Crimea, only 8000 should have been forthcoming to take part in the battle, may seem surprising; but so it was. Three thousand had been killed, 5,000 were sick, 3,000 were in the trenches, and 6,000 of the 3rd division were at Balaclava. Of those present, the Guards had 1,300; 2nd division, 2,500; light division, 2,000; and 4th division, 2,200.

And now let us do justice to the memory of as gallant a soldier as ever led the armies of Old England to victory, by looking at the difficulties by which Lord Raglan was surrounded.

Of his already diminished numbers, 2,500 men were lying on the field of battle—eight of his generals had fallen—the hospitals were full—cholera was in his camp—no recruits were coming—winter had arrived—the men had no shelter—no transport to bring them food—no clothing, for the *Prince*, with 40,000 greatcoats, and stores of all sorts, had gone down. Never did an army with more heroic courage and endurance persevere to finally conquer, though its brave General sank under the load of anxiety pressed on him, and the unjust accusations brought against his fame.

FINAL BOMBARDMENT

The allies had now been nearly a year before Sebastopol. The batteries opened on the 5th of September, and continued firing till noon of the 8th, when the French signal was given for the advance. Onward they rushed, and the Malakoff was taken by surprise without loss, its defenders being at dinner. The tri-colour flying from the parapet was the signal for the British to advance. A column of the light division led, and that of the second followed. The men stormed the parapet, and penetrated into the salient angle. Here Major Welsford, 97th, who led the storming party, was killed, and Colonel Handcock was mortally wounded. A most sanguinary contest ensued, but it was found impossible to maintain the position. Colonel Windham hurried back, and brought up the right wing of the 23rd, when a most brilliant charge was made, but it was of no avail: 29 officers killed and 125 wounded, with 356 non-commissioned officers and men killed, 1,762 wounded, showed the severe nature of the contest. Many gallant deeds were done, but the following men deserve especial notice, for bringing in wounded men from the advanced posts during daylight on the 8th:—Privates Thomas Johnson,

Bedford, Chapman, and William Freeman, of the 62nd. A considerable number performed the same merciful but dangerous work during the night. It was intended to renew the attack on the following morning with the Highland brigade under Sir Colin Campbell; but explosions were heard during the night, and when a small party advanced, the Redan was found deserted, and it was discovered that, by means of admirable arrangements, the whole Russian army were retiring by a bridge of boats to the north side, while they in the meantime had sunk all the ships of war in the harbour.

Thus was Sebastopol won undoubtedly by the gallantry of the French, for the possession of the Malakoff at that time ensured the capture of the town; but Britons may well feel proud of the heroism displayed by their countrymen from first to last of that memorable siege, and it is an example of the stuff with which English redcoats are filled: officers were killed and fully 5,000 men, while upwards of 15,000 died of disease.

In October, Kinburn was taken by General Spencer; and the supplies of the Russians being cut off, they were compelled to sue for peace.

While this most bloody war showed England's might, the undaunted bravery of her soldiers, and their admirable discipline and perseverance, it also showed wherein her weakness lay—that her commissariat was imperfect, and that much of her machinery had grown rusty from want of use. She has profited by the terrible lessons she has received; and though there is still room for improvement, the British soldier need no longer fear that sad state of things from which so many of his gallant comrades suffered in the Crimea.

GALLANT DEEDS OF THE CRIMEAN WAR

Here I must pause to tell of some few of the many gallant deeds done during that long and terrible year of warfare. First, how at; the bloody fight of Inkerman, Captain T. Miller, R.A., defended his guns with a handful of gunners, though surrounded by Russians, and with his own hand killed six of the foe who were attempting to capture them. How Sergeant—Major Andrew Henry, R.A., also nobly defended his guns against overwhelming numbers of the enemy, and continued to do so till he fell with twelve bayonet wounds in his body. How at the desperate charge of the Guards to retake the Sandbag battery, Lieutenant-colonel the Honourable H.M. Percy, Grenadier Guards, in face of a hot fire, charged singly into the battery, followed by his men; and how afterwards, when he found himself, with men of various regiments who had charged too far, nearly surrounded by Russians, and without ammunition, from his knowledge of the ground he was enabled, though he was wounded, to extricate them and to take them, under a heavy fire, to a spot where they obtained a supply of ammunition, and could return to the combat; and how he engaged in single combat, and wounded a Russian soldier. How Sergeant Norman and Privates Palmer and Baily were the first to volunteer to follow Sir Charles Russell to attempt retaking the Sandbag battery. Onward dashed those gallant men; the Russians could not withstand the desperate onslaught, and fled before them.

I have described those two cavalry charges at Balaclava. Several noble acts of heroism resulted from them. First, I must tell how, when Lieutenant-Colonel Morris, 17th Lancers, lay desperately wounded on the ground, in an exposed situation, after the retreat of the Light Cavalry, Surgeon Mouat, 6th Dragoons, voluntarily galloped to his rescue, and, under a heavy fire from the enemy, dressed his wounds; and how Sergeant-Major Wooden, 17th, also came to the rescue of his fallen colonel, and with Mr. Mouat bore him safely from the field. How, likewise, when Captain Webb, 17th Lancers, lay desperately and mortally wounded, Sergeant-major Berryman, 17th Lancers, found him, and refused to leave him, though urged to do so. How Quarter-master-sergeant Farrell and Sergeant Malone, 13th Light Dragoons, coming by, assisted to carry him out of the fire.

Worthy of note is the conduct of Private Parkes, 4th Light Dragoons. In that fearful charge Trumpet—Major Crawford's horse falling, he was dismounted, and lost his sword. Thus helpless, he was attacked by two Cossacks, when Parkes, whose horse was also killed, threw himself before his comrade, and drove off the enemy. Soon afterwards they were attacked by six Russians, whom Parkes kept at bay; and he retired slowly, fighting and defending Crawford, till his own sword was broken by a shot.

Sergeant Ramage, 2nd Dragoons, perceiving Private McPherson surrounded by seven Russians, galloped to his comrade's assistance, and saved his life by dispersing the enemy. On the same day, when the heavy brigade was rallying, and the enemy retiring, finding that his horse would not leave the ranks, he dismounted and brought in a Russian prisoner. He also on the same day saved the life of Private Gardner, whose leg was fractured by a round shot, by carrying him to the rear from under a heavy cross fire, and from a spot immediately afterwards occupied by Russians.

Officers and men vied with each other in the performance of gallant deeds. Major Howard Elphinstone, of the Royal Engineers, exhibited his fearless nature by volunteering, on the night of the 18th June, after the unsuccessful attack on the Redan, to command a party of volunteers, who proceeded to search for and bring back the scaling-ladders left behind after the repulse; a task he succeeded in performing. He also conducted a persevering search close to the enemy for wounded men, twenty of whom he rescued and brought back to the trenches.

Lieutenant Gerald Graham, on the same day, several times sallied out of the trenches, in spite of the enemy's fire, and brought in wounded men and officers.

On that day, also, when assaulting the Redan, Colour-sergeant Peter Leitch first approached it with ladders, and then tore down gabions from the parapet, and placed and filled them so as to enable those following to cross over. This dangerous occupation he continued till disabled by wounds.

Sapper John Perie was on that day conspicuous for his valour in leading the seamen with ladders to storm the Redan. He also rescued a wounded man from the open, though he had himself just been wounded by a bullet in his side.

Private John Connors, 3rd Foot, distinguished himself at the assault of the Redan, on the 8th September, in personal conflict with the enemy. Seeing an officer of the 30th Regiment surrounded by Russians, he rushed forward to his rescue, shot one and bayoneted another. He was himself surrounded, when he spiritedly cut his way out from among them.

Few surpassed Lieutenant William Hope, 7th Fusiliers, in gallantry. After the troops had retreated, on the 18th June, Lieutenant Hope, hearing from Sergeant Bacon that Lieutenant and Adjutant Hobson was lying outside the trenches, went out to look for him, accompanied by Private Hughes, and found him lying in an old agricultural ditch running towards the left flank of the Redan. He then returned, and got some more men to bring him in. Finding, however, that he could not be removed without a stretcher, he ran back across the open to Egerton's pit, where he procured one; and in spite of a very heavy fire from the Russian batteries, he carried it to where Lieutenant Hobson was lying, and brought in his brother officer in safety. He also, on the 8th of September, when his men were drawn out of the fifth parallel, endeavoured, with Assistant-Surgeon Hale, to rally them, and remained to aid Dr. Hale, who was dressing the wounds of Captain Jones, 7th Foot, who lay dangerously wounded. Dr. Hale's bravery was conspicuous; for after the regiment had retired into the trenches, he cleared the most advanced sap of the wounded, and aided by Sergeant Fisher, 7th Royal Fusiliers, under a very heavy fire, carried several wounded men from the open into the sap.

Private Sims, 34th Regiment, showed his bravery and humanity on the 18th June, when the troops had retired from the assault on the Redan, by going into the open ground outside the trenches, under a heavy fire, in broad daylight, and bringing in wounded soldiers.

Major Elton, 55th Regiment, exhibited the greatest courage on several occasions. On the night of the 4th August he commanded a working party in the advanced trenches in front of the Quarries; and when, in consequence of the dreadful fire to which they were exposed, some hesitation was shown, he went into the open with pick and shovel, and by thus setting an example to his men, encouraged them to persevere. In March, he volunteered with a small body of men to drive off a body of Russians who were destroying one of the British new detached works, and not only succeeded in so doing, but took one of the enemy prisoner.

Colour—Sergeant G. Gardiner, 57th Regiment, showed great coolness and gallantry on the occasion of the sortie of the enemy, 22nd March, when he was acting as orderly sergeant to the field officers of the trenches, in having rallied the covering parties which had been driven in by the Russians, and thus regaining and keeping possession of the trenches. Still more conspicuous was his conduct on the 18th June when attacking the Redan. He remained and encouraged others to stay in the holes made by the explosion of shells, from whence, by making parapets of the dead bodies of their comrades, they kept up a continuous fire until their ammunition was exhausted, thus clearing the enemy from the parapet of the Redan. This was done under a fire in which nearly half the officers and a third of the rank and file of the party of the regiment were placed *hors de combat*.

Major Lumley, 97th Regiment, especially distinguished himself at the assault on the Redan, 8th September. He was among the first inside the works, when he was immediately engaged with three Russian gunners, reloading a field-piece, who attacked him. He shot two of them with his revolver, when he was knocked down by a stone which for the moment stunned him. On his recovery he drew his sword, and was in the act of cheering on his men, when he received a ball in his mouth, which wounded him most severely.

Sergeant Coleman, also of the 97th Regiment, exhibited

coolness and bravery unsurpassed, when, on the night of 30th August, the enemy attacked a new sap and drove in the working party. He, however, remained in the open, completely exposed to the enemy's rifle-pits, until all around him had been killed or wounded; then, taking on his shoulder one of his officers, mortally wounded, he retreated with him to the rear.

Of the many anecdotes of heroism exhibited during the war, none is more worthy of note than one told of Ensign Dunham Massy, of the 19th Regiment, then one of the youngest officers in the army. At the storming of the Redan he led the grenadier company, and was about the first of the corps to jump into the ditch, waving his sword, and calling on his men to follow. They nobly stood by him, till, left for two hours without support, and seized by a fear of being blown up, they retired. He, borne along, endeavoured to disengage himself from the crowd, and there he stood, almost alone, facing round frequently to the batteries, with head erect, and with a calm, proud, disdainful eye. Hundreds of shots were aimed at him, and at last, having succeeded in rallying some men, and leading them on up the side of the ditch, he was struck by a shot and his thigh broken.

Being the last, he was left there with many other wounded. Hours passed by—who can tell the agony suffered by that mass of wounded men! Many were groaning, and some loudly crying out. A voice called faintly at first, and at length more loudly, "Are you Queen Victoria's soldiers?"

Some voices answered, "I am! I am!"

"Then," said the gallant youth, "let us not shame ourselves; let us show these Russians that we can bear pain as well as fight like men."

There was a silence as of death; and several times, when the poor fellows again gave way to their feelings, he appealed to them in a similar strain, and all was silent.

The unshakeable spirit of the young hero ruled all around him. As evening came on, the Russians crept out of the Redan, and plundered some of the wounded—though, in some cases, they exhibited kind feelings, and even gave water. Men with bayonets fixed strode over Massy's body. Sometimes he feigned death. A man took away his haversack. A Russian officer endeavoured to disengage his sword, which he still grasped; nor would he yield it. The Russian, smiling compassionately, at length left him. When the works were blown up in the night by the retreating Russians, his left leg was fearfully crushed by a falling stone. He was found in the morning by some Highlanders, and brought to the camp more dead than alive from loss of blood. Great was the joy of all at seeing him, as it was supposed that he was killed. In spite of his dangerous wounds, he ultimately recovered.

Privates and non-commissioned officers vied with each other in acts of gallantry and dash, as well as of coolness and calm heroism.

Privates Robert Humpston and Joseph Bradshaw, Rifle Brigade, 2nd battalion, especially exhibited their cool bravery. A Russian rifle-pit situated among the rocks overhanging the Woronzoff road, between the third parallel right attack and the Quarries, was occupied every night by the Russians, much impeding a new battery being erected by the British. These two men, seeing the importance of dislodging the enemy, at daybreak of the 22nd April started off of their own accord, made so furious an attack on the astonished Russians that they killed or put to flight all the occupants of the rifle-pit, and held it till, support coming, it was completely destroyed.

Private B. McGregor, also of the same corps, finding that there were two Russians in a rifle-pit who considerably annoyed the troops by their fire, he, being in the advanced trenches, crossed the open space under fire, and taking cover under a rock, dislodged them, and took possession of the pit, whence he fired on the enemy.

Several of the officers, too, of the Rifle Brigade exhibited conspicuous gallantry. At the battle of Inkerman, Brevet-Major the Honourable Henry H. Clifford led a dashing charge of his men against the enemy, of whom he killed one and wounded another; and one of his men having fallen near him, he defended him against the Russians, who were trying to kill him, and carried him off in safety.

Lieutenant Claude T. Bouchier and Lieutenant William J. Cuninghame highly distinguished themselves at the capture of the rifle-pits, on the 20th of November 1854.

There were numerous instances in which, at the risk of their own lives, both officers and men saved the lives of their comrades who lay wounded in exposed positions. Private John Alexander, 19th Regiment, after the attack on the Redan on the 18th of June, knowing that many wounded men lay helpless on the ground, in spite of the storm of round shot, bullets, and shells still raging, went out from the trenches, and, with calm intrepidity, brought in, one after the other, several wounded men. He also, being one of a working party, on the 6th of September 1855, in the most advanced trench, hearing that Captain Buckley, of the Scots Fusilier Guards, was lying dangerously wounded, went out under a very heavy fire, and brought him safely in. Sergeant Moynihan, of the same regiment, also rescued a wounded officer near the Redan, under a very heavy fire; and on the assault of the Redan, 8th of September 1855, actually encountered, and with his own hand was seen to have killed, five Russians in succession. Other acts of gallantry are recorded of this brave soldier, who, as a reward for them, and for a long-continued career of excellent conduct, has been since deservedly promoted to a lieutenancy, and subsequently obtained his company in the 8th Foot.

Sergeant William McWheeney, 44th Regiment, showed probably as much bravery in saving the lives of his comrades, and in other ways, as any man in the army. At the commencement of the siege he volunteered as a sharpshooter, and was placed in charge of a party of his regiment, who acted as sharpshooters. In the action on the Woronzoff road, the Russians came down in such overwhelming numbers that the sharpshooters were repulsed from the Quarries in which they had taken post. On that occasion Private John Kean, one of his party, was dangerously wounded, and would have been killed, had he not, running forward under a heavy fire, lifted the man on his back, and borne him off to a place of safety. On the 5th of December 1854 he performed a similar act. Corporal Courtenay, also a sharpshooter, was, when in the advance, severely wounded in the head. Sergeant McWheeney then lifted him up, and, under a heavy fire, carried him to some distance. Unable to bear him farther, he placed him on the ground; but, refusing to leave him, threw up with his bayonet a slight cover of earth, protected by which the two remained till dark, when he brought off his wounded companion. He also volunteered for the advanced guard of Major-General Eyre's brigade, in the Cemetery, on the 18th of June 1855. During the whole war he was never absent from duty.

Private McDermot, also, at the battle of Inkerman, seeing Colonel Haly lying wounded on the ground, surrounded by Russians about to despatch him, rushed to his rescue, killed the man who had cut down the colonel, and brought him off.

In like way, at the same time, Private Beach, seeing Lieutenant-Colonel Carpenter lying on the ground, several Russians being about to plunder and probably kill him, dashed forward, killed two of them, and protected the colonel against his assailants, till some men of the 41st Regiment coming up put them to flight.

Sergeant George Walters, 49th Regiment, also highly distinguished himself at Inkerman, by springing forward to save Brigadier-General Adams, who was surrounded by Russians, one of whom he bayoneted, and dispersed the rest.

Captain Thomas Esmonde especially exhibited his courage and humanity in preserving the lives of others. On the 18th of June he was engaged in the desperate and bloody assault on the Redan. Unwounded himself, he repeatedly returned, under a terrific fire of shell and grape, to assist in rescuing wounded men from the exposed positions where they lay. Two days after this, he was in command of a covering party to a working party in an advanced position. A fire-ball, thrown by the enemy, lodged close to them. With admirable presence of mind, he sprang forward and extinguished it before it had blazed up sufficiently to betray the position of the working party under his protection. Scarcely had the ball been extinguished, than a murderous fire of shell and grape was opened on the spot.

Lance-Sergeant Philip Smith, on the 18th June, after the column had retired from the assault, repeatedly returned under a heavy fire, and brought in his wounded comrades.

Several acts of coolness, similar to that recorded of Captain Esmonde, were performed.

On the 2nd September, Sergeant Alfred Ablet, of the Grenadier Guards, seeing a burning shell fall in the centre of a number of ammunition cases and powder, instantly seized it, and threw it outside the trench. It burst as it touched the ground. Had it exploded before, the loss of life would have been terrific.

Private George Strong, also, when on duty in the trenches, threw a live shell from the place where it had fallen to a distance.

Corporal John Ross, of the Royal Engineers, exhibited his calmness and judgment, as well as bravery, on several occasions. On the 23rd of August 1855 he was in charge of the advance from the fifth parallel right attack on the Redan, when he placed and filled twenty-five gabions under a very heavy fire, and in spite of light-balls thrown towards him. He was also one of those who, in the most intrepid and devoted way, on the night of the memorable 8th September, crept to the Redan and reported its evacuation, on which it was immediately occupied by the British.

Corporal William Lendrim, of the same corps, also, on the 11th April, in the most intrepid manner, got on the top of a magazine, on which some sandbags were burning, knowing that at any moment it might blow up. He succeeded in extinguishing the fire. On the 14th of February, when the whole of the gabions of Number 9 battery left attack were capsized, he superintended 150 French chasseurs in replacing them, under a heavy fire from the Russian guns. He likewise was one of four volunteers who destroyed the farthest rifle-pits on the 20th April.

Sergeant Daniel Cambridge, Royal Artillery, was among those who gallantly risked his own life to save those of his fellow-soldiers. He had volunteered for the spiking party at the assault on the Redan, on the 8th of September, and while thus engaged he was severely wounded; still he refused to go to the rear. Later in the day, while in the advanced trench, seeing a wounded man outside, in front, he sprang forward under a heavy fire to bring him in. He was in the open, shot and shell and bullets flying round him. He reached the wounded man, and bore him along. He was seen to stagger, but still he would not leave his helpless burden, but, persevering, brought him into the trench. It was then discovered that he had himself been severely wounded a second time.

The gallantry of Sergeant George Symons was always conspicuous, but especially on the 6th of June 1855, when he volunteered to unmask the embrasures of a five-gun battery, in the advanced right attack. No sooner was the first embrasure unmasked, than the enemy commenced a terrific fire on him; but, undaunted, he continued the work. As each fresh embrasure was unmasked, the enemy's fire was increased. At length only one remained, when, amid a perfect storm of missiles, he courageously mounted the parapet, and uncovered the last, by throwing down the sandbags. Scarcely was his task completed when a shell burst, and he fell, severely wounded.

Driver Thomas Arthur, of the same corps, had been placed in charge of a magazine, in one of the left advanced batteries of the right attack, on the 7th of June, when the Quarries were taken. Hearing that the 7th Fusiliers were in want of ammunition, he, of his own accord, carried several barrels of infantry ammunition to supply them, across the open, exposed to the enemy's fire. He also volunteered and formed one of the spiking party of artillery at the assault on the Redan.

Among the numberless acts of bravery performed at the battle of Inkerman, few are more worthy of record than one performed by Lieutenant-Colonel Sir Charles Russell, Bart., of the Grenadier Guards. The Sandbag battery, the scene of so many bloody encounters during that eventful day, had been at length entered by a strong party of Russians, its previous defenders having been killed or driven out by overwhelming numbers. Sir Charles Russell, seeing what had occurred, offered to dislodge the enemy, if any men would accompany him. The undertaking seemed desperate; but notwithstanding this, Sergeant Norman and Privates Anthony Palmer and Bailey immediately volunteered; others afterwards followed their example. On they went, following the gallant Sir Charles at furious speed, and into the battery they rushed. Bailey was killed, but Palmer escaped, and was the means of saving his brave leader's life. The Russians were driven out, and the battery was held by the British.

Sir Charles Russell received the Victoria Cross. We now give an extract from a letter he wrote to his mother after the battle:

After the brave band had been some time in the battery, our ammunition began to fail us, and the men, armed with stones, flung them into the masses of Russians, who caught the idea, and the air was thick with huge stones flying in all directions; but we were too much for them, and once more a *mêlée* of Grenadiers, Coldstreams, and Fusiliers held the battery their own, and from it, on the solid masses of the Russians, still poured as good a fire as our ammunition would permit. There were repeated cries of 'Charge!' and some man near me said, 'If any officer will lead us, we will charge'; and as I was the only one just there, I could not refuse such an appeal, so I jumped into the embrasure, and waving my revolver, said, 'Come on, my lads; who will follow me?' I then rushed on, fired my revolver at a fellow close to me, but it missed fire. I pulled again, and think I killed him. Just then a man touched me on the shoulder, and said, 'You was near done for.' I said, 'Oh no, he was some way from me.' He answered, 'His bayonet was all but into you when I clouted him over the head.' And sure enough, a fellow had got behind me and nearly settled me. I must add, that the grenadier who accompanied me was publicly made a corporal on parade next morning. His name is Palmer. I did not know it, but I said, 'What's your name? Well, if I live through this, you shall not be forgotten.'

Corporal Shields, 23rd Regiment Royal Welsh Fusiliers, among many brave men especially distinguished himself, and he was among the earliest recipients of the order of valour. He received also the Cross of the Legion of Honour from the Emperor of the French for the following brave action:—

On the 8th of September 1855 he was among the foremost at the desperate attack on the Redan, and one of the very few who reached the ditch at the re-entering angle. Finding that Lieutenant Dyneley, adjutant of the regiment, for whom he had a great regard, had not returned, he immediately set forward by himself to search for him, exposed to the hot fire of the enemy, who, although they must have known that he was on an errand of mercy, continually aimed at him. After searching for some time, he found his young officer on the ground, desperately wounded, behind a rock, which somewhat sheltered him from the enemy's fire. Stanching the flow of blood as well as he could, he endeavoured to lift him on his back to carry him to the trenches, but the pain of being lifted in that way was more than Mr. Dyneley could bear. Reluctantly he was compelled to relinquish the attempt; and hurrying back to the trenches, he entreated one of the medical officers to render the young officer assistance. His appeal was not made in vain. Without hesitation, the brave Assistant—Surgeon Sylvester, always ready at the call of humanity, volunteered to accompany him. Together they passed across the hailstorm of bullets the Russians were incessantly sending from their walls, when the surgeon knelt down and dressed the wounds of his brother officer, and did all that he could to alleviate his sufferings. Unwillingly they quitted him that they might obtain more succour; and in the evening Captain Drew and other volunteers accompanied Corporal Shields, who then for the third time braved the bullets of the enemy, and together they brought in the young lieutenant. Unhappily, his wound was mortal, and he died that night. While praising the brave corporal, we must not forget the heroism of the young surgeon. For this action Corporal Shields was rewarded with a commission.

Major Gerald Littlehales Goodlake, Coldstream Guards, gained the Victoria Cross for his gallantry on several occasions. A number of the best marksmen in each regiment had been selected to act as sharpshooters. With a party of these he set forth, on a night in November 1854, towards a fort at the bottom of the Windmill ravine, where a picket of the enemy were stationed. Approaching with all the caution of Indian warriors along a difficult and dangerous path, they suddenly sprang on the astonished Russians, who took to flight, leaving their rifles and knapsacks behind. A short time before this, on the 28th of October, he was posted in this ravine, which, with the party of his men, not exceeding thirty, he held against a powerful sortie of the Russians, made against the 2nd division of the British army.

In truth, young officers brought up in luxury and ease vied with soldiers long accustomed to warfare and the roughest work in deeds of daring and hardihood.

These are only some few of the many acts of heroism, coolness, and gallantry performed during the war, and for which the Victoria Cross has been awarded. Undoubtedly many more were performed, which have not been noted, in consequence of the death of the actors or witnesses, and some gallant men, though equally deserving, have not brought forward their claims; but even from the few examples here given, it is shown of what materials the British soldier is formed.

The Campaign in Persia
1856–57

The Campaign in Persia
1856-1857

In 1856 the Persians, thinking that they would be supported by Russia, took possession of Herat, in direct infraction of their treaty with England. To convince them of their mistake, war was declared; and an expedition, under Major-general Stalker, was despatched to the Persian Gulf, which, on the 3rd of December, took possession of the island of Karrack. On the 7th, the troops landed at Ras Halala, about fifteen miles below Bushire. Their first exploit was an attack on the old Dutch fort of Reshire, on the 9th of December. The enemy made a stout resistance. Captain Augustus Wood, of the 20th Bengal Native Infantry, led the grenadier company, which formed the head of the assaulting column. He was the first to mount the parapet of the fort, when a considerable number of the enemy, suddenly springing out on him from a trench cut in the parapet itself, attacked him furiously, firing a volley at his men when only a yard or two distant. Although seven bullets struck him, he at once rushed at his assailants, and passing his sword through the leader's body, being followed closely by his grenadiers with their bayonets at the charge, quickly drove all before him, and established himself in the place. Brigadier Stopford was unfortunately killed in the attack, and other officers were wounded. Captain Wood was so severely wounded that he was compelled to leave the force for a time; but he returned to it even before his wounds were healed. He gained the Victoria Cross for his gallantry on that occasion.

The next morning the British force marched on Bushire, a town of some strength, and walled round; but some of the garrison ran away, and were drowned as they were escaping, and the remainder, 2,000 strong, laid down their arms.

Meantime, a much larger force was organised at Bombay to unite with that of Brigadier—General Stalker, with Lieutenant-General Sir James Outram as Commander-in-chief. General Stalker's division was considerably increased, and was called the first division, while a second division embarked under the command of Brigadier—General Havelock. Brigadier Hamilton, 78th Highlanders, commanded one of his brigades, and Brigadier Hale the other.

These forces arrived at Bushire at the end of January. On the 3rd of February, the army broke ground from the camp of Bushire, and marched on the village of Brasjoon, outside of which the enemy were said to be entrenched, and to have eighteen guns. Such was the case. A wall, with tower bastions, enclosed the whole, and detached square towers within overlooked all; while a ditch, fifteen feet deep, ran outside, and beyond it were gardens, with high thorn and cactus fences: altogether it was a very formidable position. Shortly before one o'clock on the 5th, the Persian videttes and reconnoitring parties were made out; but they very rapidly retreated. A smart brush, however, took place between the rearguard and a few of the British cavalry, in which Cornet Speers, of the 3rd Light Cavalry, and two or three troopers were wounded. By two o'clock the British were in possession of the entrenched camp, in which were large quantities of grain, camp equipage, and ammunition. The governor of the place also fell into their hands.

All the stores, guns, and ammunition which could not be carried off having been destroyed, the army commenced its return march to Bushire on the 7th, not expecting to encounter an enemy.

After moving a few hundred yards clear of the entrenchment, the troops were halted to witness the explosion of a large quantity of gunpowder, stated to be 36,000 pounds. A very magnificent spectacle it occasioned. The evening was darker than usual, and the rush of one mighty column into the heavens, with cloud over cloud of bright silvery-looking smoke, mingled with shells bursting like sky-rockets in the midst, attended by a report that made the hills echo again, and a concussion which shook the ground even where the advanced guard stood, formed altogether an event not likely to be forgotten by any who beheld it. The pile of ammunition was fired by Lieutenant Gibbard, of the Horse Artillery, and Lieutenant Hassard, the adjutant of the 2nd European Light Infantry, with rifles and shell-bullets of Colonel Jacob's invention, from a distance of about 150 yards. Both were thrown down by the shock of the concussion. From *Outram and Havelock's Persian Campaign*, by Captain Hunt, from which the account of the battle of Khoosh-Aub is chiefly taken.

The march was then renewed, the general belief being that the enemy were never likely to approach them. At midnight, however, a sharp rattle of musketry was heard, and it was supposed that the rearguard were attacked. Colonel Honnor so ably handled the protecting troops, that he kept the enemy at bay for some time. In about half an hour, however, after the first shots had been fired, the Persian cavalry advanced in great numbers, and the entire force was enveloped in a skirmishing fire. Horsemen galloped round on all sides, yelling and screaming like fiends, and with trumpets and bugles making all the noise in their power. One of their buglers got close to the front of a skirmishing company of the Highlanders, and sounded first the "Cease fire," and afterwards "Incline to the left," escaping in the dark. Several English officers having but a few years before been employed in organising the Persian troops, accounted for their knowledge of the English bugle-calls, now artfully used to create confusion.

The silence and steadiness of the men were most admirable, and the manoeuvring of regiments that followed, in taking up position for the remaining hour of darkness, was as steady as on an ordinary parade; and this during a midnight attack, with an enemy's fire flashing in every direction, and cavalry surrounding, ready to take advantage of the slightest momentary confusion. At length, having been roughly handled by the 78th, the cavalry, and horse artillery, the Persian horsemen kept at a respectful distance.

The army was then thrown into an oblong form—a brigade protecting each flank, and a demi-brigade the front and rear; field-battery guns at intervals, and a thick line of skirmishers connecting and covering all; the horse artillery and cavalry on the flank of the face fronting the original line of march, the front and flanks of the oblong facing outwards; the baggage and followers being in the centre. When thus formed, the troops lay down, waiting for daylight in perfect silence, and showing no fire or light of any kind. Sir James Outram met with a severe accident while carrying out these admirable arrangements; but they were well concluded by Colonel Lugard, the chief of his staff.

Scarcely was the formation completed, than the enemy brought five heavy guns to bear; and iron shot plunging into the 64th Regiment, knocked down six men, and killed one of them. Another shot, first taking off a foot from Lieutenant Greentree, severely wounded Captain Mockler of that regiment. Several of the camp followers and baggage animals in the centre were killed but the orderly conduct of the troops saved them from many casualties, and as no musketry fire was allowed after the guns opened, the enemy had no opportunity of improving his original range.

As the morning approached, the enemy's fire slackened, and it was believed that he had retreated; but as the mist cleared off, the Persians were seen drawn up in line, their right resting on the walled village of Khoosh-Aub and a date-grove, their left on a hamlet with a round fortalice tower. Two rising mounds were in front of their centre, which served as redoubts, and where they had their guns; and they had some deep *nullahs* on their right front and flank thickly lined with skirmishers. Their cavalry, in considerable bodies, were on both flanks. Soojah-ul-Moolk, the best officer in the Persian army, was at their head. The British army was drawn up in two general lines. The front line consisted of the 78th Highlanders, and a party of sappers on the right; then the 26th Regiment of Native Infantry, the 2nd European Light Infantry, and the 4th Rifle Regiment on the left of all.

The second line had Her Majesty's 64th Regiment on its right, then the 20th Regiment Native Infantry, and the Beloochee battalion on its left. The light companies of battalions faced the enemy's skirmishers in the *nullahs*, and covered both flanks and rear of their own army. A detachment of the 3rd Cavalry assisted in this duty; and as the enemy showed some bodies of horse, threatening a dash on the baggage or wounded men, they were of considerable service.

The lines advanced directly the regiments had deployed, and so rapidly and steadily did the leading one move over the crest of the rising ground (for which the enemy's guns were laid), that it suffered but little; the Highlanders not having a single casualty, and the 26th Native Infantry, their companion regiment in brigade, losing only one man killed, and but four or five wounded. The brigades in the rear, in consequence of the shot which passed over the regiments in front striking them, suffered far more, especially the 2nd European Light Infantry.

During this time the cannonade had been continuous; but as the Persian fire in some degree slackened, the British artillery advanced to closer action, making most beautiful practice, and almost silencing the opposing batteries. Some bodies of horse soon presented an opportunity for a charge, and the squadrons of the 3rd Cavalry, and Tapp's irregulars, who had hitherto been on the right front, dashed at them, accompanied by Blake's horse artillery, and made a sweeping and most brilliant charge, sabring gunners, and fairly driving the enemy's horse off the field. The 3rd Bombay Light Cavalry was led by Lieutenant-Colonel Forbes. Lieutenant Moore, the adjutant of the regiment, was, however, perhaps the first of all, by a horse's length. As the regiment approached the enemy, thrown into a somewhat disorderly square, his horse sprang into their centre, but instantly fell dead, crushing his rider, whose sword was broken by the concussion. The enemy pressed round him, but speedily extricating himself, he attempted with his broken weapon to force his way through the throng: he would most certainly have lost his life, had not Lieutenant Malcolmson, observing his danger, fought his way through the crowd of Persians, and, giving him his stirrup, carried him safely out from among them. The thoughtfulness for others, cool determination, devoted courage, and ready activity shown in extreme danger by this young officer, Lieutenant Malcolmson, were most admirable. Both these officers most deservedly gained the Victoria Cross.

Meantime, the infantry lines were still advancing rapidly, and in beautifully steady order, to sustain the attack, and were just getting into close action when the enemy lost heart, and his entire line at once broke, and fled precipitately. The men cast away their arms and accoutrements, and, as the pursuit continued, even their clothing. Two or three of the *sirbar*, or regular battalions, on the extreme right, alone retired with any semblance of order. The 3rd Cavalry charged through, and back again, one of the battalions which attempted to receive them with steadiness, and Colonel Forbes was severely wounded, while Captain Moore, a brother of the adjutant, had his horse killed under him. The rout of the enemy was complete, and the troopers, as well as irregulars, were fairly exhausted cutting down the fugitives. More than 700 were left on the field, and many horses; while numbers more were slain in the pursuit. The British loss was only 1 officer and 18 men killed, and 4 officers and 60 men wounded. Lieutenant Frankland, of the 2nd European Regiment, who was killed, was highly mentioned, as was Lieutenant Greentree, of the 64th, who lost his leg.

Subsequently, on the 2nd of May, a treaty of peace was signed at Bagdad, in which the Shah agreed to evacuate Herat, and to refrain from all interference in future in the internal affairs of Afghanistan.

The Indian Mutiny
1857–58

The Indian Mutiny
1857-1858

The year 1857 saw the commencement of the Indian Mutiny, a terrible outbreak of cruelty and fanaticism which, while it inflicted unspeakable anguish upon hundreds of our defenceless countrywomen and their children, desolated many an English home, and evoked the horror and compassion of the civilised world, was also the occasion of numberless acts of heroism and devotion, not only on the part of British soldiers and their native allies, but of all classes of civilians.

Among other causes which led to the rising of so many of the natives, was no doubt the impression made by the Crimean war, under the influence of which certain ambitious Mohammedan chiefs, combining with some Hindoo rulers, misled by false accounts of the result of the war with Russia, formed the idea that the time had arrived for destroying the power of Great Britain in India.

For this purpose they made use of the prejudices and superstitions of the Hindoo soldiery, and the avarice and worst passions of the Mohammedans; and a story that the new cartridges issued to the troops were made with pig's or bullock's fat—the one being an abomination to the Mohammedans, the other to the Hindoos, who eating it would lose caste—was believed by the more ignorant and fanatical, who saw in it a design to destroy their religion.

The first serious outbreak took place at Meerut, when 85 out of 90 men of the 3rd Light Cavalry refused to use the cartridges. They were condemned to a long imprisonment, and their sentence was read out on parade. The next day, Sunday, 10th May, while the Europeans were at church, news was brought that the 11th and 20th Regiments of Native Infantry were assembling tumultuously on the parade-ground. Colonel Finnis, who immediately rode out to quell the disturbance, was shot by a sepoy while addressing the 20th Regiment, and cut to pieces; thirty other Europeans were speedily slaughtered, and the cantonments given to the flames. Mr. Greathead, the commissioner, and his wife, were saved by the fidelity of their servants. The British troops in the place were not called out till the mutineers had time to escape to Delhi; where, on their arrival, an outbreak took place, and the greater number of the British residing there were butchered with the most horrible barbarity.

The Siege of Delhi
30th May to 20th September 1857

It was not till many of the mutineers had fled to Delhi that the inhabitants of that city dared to rise in arms against the British. At Delhi resided a pensioner of the British Government, the last representative of the Mogul Emperors—an old man, feeble in mind and body, yet capable of atrocious mischief—who had assumed the title of the King of Delhi. He and his sons and some of his ministers were undoubtedly promoters of the revolt. By agreement with this potentate, no British troops were quartered in the city, notwithstanding that the Government had made the city the principal depot for military stores in India. The city was also inhabited by a large Mohammedan population, who clustered round the king, and clung to the traditions of their former greatness.

On the 11th of May there arrived at Delhi, early in the morning, several parties of mutineers from Meerut. They gave the signal of revolt. With scarcely a moment's warning, military officers, civil servants of the Government, merchants, and others were set upon by the rebel sepoys and by the inhabitants of the city, and cut down without mercy. Ladies and children were butchered with every conceivable cruelty and indignity. Mr. Simon Fraser, the commissioner, was murdered in the palace of the king; so was Captain Douglas, of the Palace Guards, and Mr. Jennings, the chaplain, and his daughter and another lady. The regiments outside the walls in cantonments revolted, and many of the British officers were killed, though some, with a few ladies, who got over the city walls, effected their escape.

The magazine, which was within the city walls, not far from the palace, was of course in danger from the very beginning. The officers in charge had seen the mutineers crossing the bridge in the morning, and Lieutenant Willoughby had gone in with Sir T. Metcalf to endeavour to get the gates closed. On his return, he found eight of the officers attached to the establishment—Lieutenants Forrest and Raynor, Conductors Buckley, Shaw, and Scully, Subconductor Crowe, and Sergeants Edward and Stewart—with the native Lascars and servants. Preparations were instantly begun for the defence of the magazine till the arrival of relief from Meerut, which none doubted was at hand. The magazine consisted of a number of buildings enclosed by a high wall. The gates were closed and barricaded. Inside the gate leading to the park were placed two 6-pounders, doubly charged with grape. The two sergeants stood by with lighted matches, ready, should that gate be attacked, to fire both at once, and fall back upon the body of the magazine. At the principal gate two guns were put in position, with a *chevaux-de-frise* on the inside; and a little behind, but bearing on the same point, were two others. Farther in were placed four more pieces, commanding two cross passages. A train was laid to the powder-magazine, ready to be fired at a given signal. Arms were put in the hands of the natives in the establishment, which they took sulkily. They were getting insolent and disobedient— the Mussulmans particularly so. Scarcely had these arrangements been made, when the Palace Guards appeared and demanded the magazine in the name of the Badsha of Delhi. No answer was given.

The king, they heard soon after, had sent word that ladders would be immediately brought from the palace to scale the walls. The natives in the magazine scarcely concealed their hostility. One man was seen to be communicating with the mutineers outside through the gate, and ordered to be shot if he was observed doing so again. The enemy, who had thus learned what was ready for them, did not attempt to force the gates; but in a short time the scaling-ladders arrived. On their being placed against the walls, the whole of the Lascars deserted, climbing over the sloped sheds on the inside, and down the ladders. It was found that they had hid the priming-pouches. The enemy now appeared in hundreds on the walls. The guns were immediately pointed at them, and worked with wonderful rapidity considering the small number of the party. Nine Britons, alone in that great Mohammedan city, betrayed and deserted as they were, bravely thought only of holding their post till the death. The enemy kept firing down upon them. In a few minutes several of the little band were wounded; it was clear that in a few more they would all be shot. Willoughby then gave the signal for firing the powder store. Scully, who had distinguished himself in this dreadful emergency by his perfect coolness, in the most careful and methodical manner lighted the trains. The explosion took place almost immediately. The wall adjoining was thrown to the ground; numbers of the enemy were buried among the ruins; and thousands of bullets from the cartridges in store were hurled far off, striking down people in the streets. Wonderful as it may seem, half the gallant defenders of the magazine crept out alive, partly stunned, blackened, scorched, and burned, yet able to make their way through the sally-port by the river for the Cashmere gate. Lieutenants Forrest and Raynor and Conductor Buckley succeeded in escaping to Meerut. Willoughby was seen at the Cashmere gate, and set out for Meerut with three more, who were all murdered in a village on the road. Scully, who was much hurt, was killed, when trying to escape, by a *sowar*. The explosion of the magazine was of course seen from the flagstaff tower, and was heard even at Meerut.

That afternoon, the sepoys who remained in the lines either deserted or revolted—a general flight took place; the Brigadier was one of the last to leave; and thus was Delhi lost.

No sooner had the Europeans gone, than the treacherous old king hoisted the green flag, and proclaimed himself Emperor of India. He had imprisoned within his palace walls forty-nine Europeans, chiefly women and children. Having for a week allowed them to be treated with the greatest cruelty, he gave them up to be further ill-treated, and finally murdered, by his soldiery. Their bodies were piled in a rotting heap at the Cashmere gate.

The day of vengeance was, however, not long delayed. On the 8th of June a small army, under Major-General Sir Henry Barnard, was collected at Alleepore, one march from Delhi. It consisted of four guns, 2nd troop 1st Brigade, 2nd and 3rd troops 3rd Brigade Horse Artillery; 3rd company 3rd Battalion Artillery, and Number 14 Horse Field-Battery; 4th company 6th Battalion Artillery: detachment Artillery recruits; Headquarters' detachment Sappers and Miners; Her Majesty's 9th Lancers; two squadrons Her Majesty's 6th Dragoon Guards; headquarters and six companies 60th Royal Rifles; headquarters and nine companies of Her Majesty's 75th Regiment; 1st

Bengal Fusiliers; headquarters and six companies 2nd Fusiliers; Simoor battalion Goorkhas. On the morning of the 8th this little army advanced from Alleepore towards Delhi. They encountered, strongly entrenched, a body of mutineers 3000 in number. The enemy's guns were well worked; the British artillery were unable to cope with them. There was only one thing to be done. The order was given to charge and capture the guns. With a ringing cheer, Her Majesty's 75th rushed on amidst a hailstorm of musketry, and the sepoys fled in terror to their next position; for they had constructed a line of defence from the signal-tower to the late Maharajah Hindoo Rao's house, and disputed every inch of the ground. However, by nine o'clock the army of retribution was in possession of the parade-ground and cantonments.

The latter, indeed, were now covered with masses of blackened walls, while the compounds were strewed with broken furniture, clothing, and books. Here, at about a mile and a half from the walls of Delhi, the army encamped, and waited for reinforcements.

The British advanced position was a strong brick-built house, on the top of a hill overlooking the city. Near it three batteries were constructed, which played night and day on the city. The mutineers had also three batteries, which kept up a continual fire on the British camp. They also generally sallied out each afternoon with a couple of guns and some cavalry—the greater portion of their force, however, consisting of infantry. The latter advanced skirmishing up, especially towards the large house, among rocky ground, covered with brushwood, which afforded them ample shelter. They always courted this system of desultory fighting, in which the strength of the native soldiers is best brought out. The British soldiers, on the contrary, too often lost their lives from want of caution. Disdaining the advantages of cover, fluttered with fury and impatience, and worn-out or stupefied by the heat, they were often shot down as they pressed incautiously forward to close with their wily foes.

However, after a time, the British soldiers made a very visible improvement in skirmishing; and as they were also well manoeuvred by their officers, they were perfectly able to cope with the enemy.

Hindoo Rao's hill was looked upon as the post of honour, and round it most of the affrays took place. It was held by Major Reid, with the Simoor battalion, and two companies of Rifles.

His losses were afterwards filled up by the infantry of the Guides. The Goorkhas were crowded into the large house from which the place took its name. Its walls were shattered with shells and round shot, which now and then struck through the chambers. Ten men were killed and wounded in the house by one shot, and seven by another the same day. Nobody was then secure of his life for an instant. Through the whole siege, Major Reid kept to his post. He never quitted the ridge save to attack the enemy below, and never once visited the camp until carried to it wounded on the day of the final assault.

The gallant Rifles here, as on every other occasion where they have had the opportunity afforded them, made good use of their weapons. On one occasion ten riflemen at the Sammy house made such execution among the gunners at the Moree bastion, that the battery was for a time abandoned. The Goorkhas, the inhabitants of the hill-country of Nepaul, and who happily had remained faithful to the British standard, were great adepts at skirmishing, and gallant little fellows in the main. A story was told of a Goorkha and a rifleman, who had in a skirmish followed a Brahmin soldier. The last took refuge in a house, and closed the door. The rifleman tried to push it open, but the Goorkha went to the window, and coiling his compact little person into its smallest compass, waited for his enemy. Soon the point of a musket, then a head and long neck appeared: the Goorkha sprang up, and seizing him by the locks, which clustered out of the back of his *pugarie*, he cut off his head with his *cookri*, ere the Brahmin could invoke Mahadeo. The little man was brought along with his trophy by the rifleman, to receive the applause of his comrades.

The annoyance which the batteries on Hindoo Rao's hill caused to the city was so great, that the mutineers commenced the construction of a battery on the right of it, to enfilade the whole British position. It was necessary to prevent this. About 400 men of the 1st Fusiliers and 60th Rifles, with Tombs' troop of horse artillery, 30 horsemen of the Guides, and a few sappers and miners, were got ready. The command was given to Major Tombs. Their destination was kept secret. Orders were given and countermanded, to confound the enemy's spies. Major Reid descended from Hindoo Rao's hill with the Rifles and Goorkhas, while Tombs advanced towards the enemy's left, and our batteries poured their fire on the Lahore gate, whose guns might have reached our squadrons. At first their cavalry, seeing the fewness of our *sowars*, prepared to charge them, but recoiled at sight of our troops coming up behind. Their infantry, taken by surprise, fled without offering the least resistance—many leaving their arms and clothes behind them. Some threw themselves into a mosque. The walls of its courtyard were loopholed, and they began to fire at our men. Tombs had two horses killed under him. His bold bearing and loud voice made him the aim of the enemy. He ordered the riflemen to go up and fire into the loopholes till the doors could be forced. A train of gunpowder was got ready, a bag was attached to the gates, they were blown open, and 39 sepoys were killed in the mosque. A 9-pounder gun was taken. Major Reid, on his side, was also successful. He destroyed a battery and magazine, and set a village and *serai* on fire. The whole British loss was 3 killed and 15 wounded—Captain Brown, of the Fusiliers, dangerously.

Sir Henry Barnard showed his admiration of the gallantry and conduct of Tombs in the most enthusiastic manner. Visiting the mess-tent of the Umballa artillery, he gave the highest and most enthusiastic praise to the young officer, declaring that he had never seen greater coolness and courage, and a more perfect knowledge of his profession, than had been shown by Major Tombs.

Tombs, on first entering the Company's army, had served with great distinction in the wars of the Punjaub, and his talents had been marked by the keen and wise eye of Sir Charles Napier. He had been made brevet-major when only a lieutenant of artillery. His gallantry at Ghazeoodeenugger had made him conspicuous from the beginning of the siege of Delhi.

In one of the first skirmishes—and it was a very severe one—which took place under Hindoo Rao's hill, Lieutenant Quintin Battye was mortally wounded through the stomach, the ball coming out at his back. He was a joyous, boyish, but noble fellow, whose every thought was honour. He was carried into camp, and was well aware that his last hour was approaching. A comrade went to see him. He smiled, and quoted the old tag, which, when so quoted, ceases to be trite: "Well, old fellow, '*Dulce et decorum est pro patria mori*'; you see it's my case. It is sweet and proper to die for one's country." Poor fellow! he did not survive his wound twenty-four hours. He was a good swordsman, and an excellent rider; and his impatience for an opportunity of distinguishing himself had been remarked at every station he had passed on the march.

Several accounts have been published describing the way in which Major Tombs saved the life of Lieutenant Hills. The following is among them:

On the morning of the 9th of July an outlying post of the British camp was unwisely confided to the care of a picket of the 9th Irregulars, who had hitherto remained true to their colours. A large body of rebel cavalry came down and talked them over, and were shown by them the way into the camp. A body of cavalry who were in their way—an inlying picket—proved for the moment unsteady, and thus the rebels reached the post at which two of Major Tombs' guns were placed. This post—a mound to the right of the camp—was under charge of Lieutenant Hills. At about eleven o'clock there was a rumour that the enemy's cavalry were coming down on his post. Instantly Lieutenant Hills hurried to the spot, to take up the position assigned to him in case of alarm; but before he reached the spot, and before there was time for his guns to form up, he saw the enemy close upon them. Issuing rapid orders to his sergeant, he charged single-handed the head of the enemy's column, cut the first man down, struck the second, and was then ridden down, horse and all. Rapidly recovering himself, however, he was attacked by three of the enemy. One he killed outright, another he wounded; but, in a combat with a third, he was brought to the ground. At that moment his commanding officer, Major Tombs, galloped up, having crossed the path of the enemy's cavalry, and escaped the certain death which would have been his fate had he met them. Seeing the critical position of his subaltern, he nobly charged his assailants, shot one and sabred the other, and then dragged the lieutenant out from under his horse, receiving, as he did so, a sword-cut on his head, but the thick turban he wore saved it from injury. The enemy passed on to the native troop of horse artillery, in the hopes of getting them to join; but, failing this, galloped out of the camp.

In the meantime, Captain Fagan, who had been writing in his tent, hearing the noise, started up, and without waiting for his sword, led a few foot artillerymen, who were ready armed, in pursuit. Fifteen of the enemy were shot down by the party, and the captain returned with a sword and a Minie carbine, of which he had relieved a ressaldar of the 8th Cavalry.

None but Europeans now remained in the camp. In consequence of their behaviour on this occasion, the 9th Irregulars were sent away, while the Golundazees who composed Renny's artillery were ordered to be disarmed. This latter measure was considered unnecessary. The brave fellows served in the batteries during the remainder of the siege; and, at the time of the assault, were sent in with the stormers to turn the guns captured in the bastions upon the enemy.

Notice having been received in the camp that the Nemuch brigade was advancing upon Agra, the only city in the Doab which remained faithful to the British, a force was sent out to oppose them. It consisted of 450 of the 3rd Europeans, Captain D'Oyley's battery, and about 50 mounted volunteers. It was determined to attack the enemy, who were several thousand strong. They came in front of the village, with 11 guns. The British force met them with half a battery on each wing, supported by the volunteer horse. A long artillery fight took place, and the enemy were driven back but not followed up. The foot were kept alternately advancing and lying down. Two *tumbrils* were blown up, and a gun dismounted. The enemy sent some cavalry to turn our flank, but they were met by our guns and some volunteer horse. It was now that Captain D'Oyley was mortally wounded, but still he continued giving his orders. At last, beginning to faint away, he said, "They have done for me now. Put a stone over my grave, and say that I died fighting for my guns." The enemy were ultimately driven out of the village, but the British ammunition falling short, advantage could not be taken of the success which had been obtained.

GALLANTRY OF BRIGADIER CHAMBERLAIN

Brigadier Chamberlain's gallantry was on all occasions very conspicuous. On the 14th of July a desperate attack was planned by the enemy on the British batteries.

They came out in great force to storm the pickets under Hindoo Rao's hill, and the Subzi Mundi. The British, however, under good cover, kept them back for several hours, making great havoc among them, and losing only 12 men. When Chamberlain appeared, he ordered the infantry and two troops of horse artillery into the Subzi Mundi. The Goorkhas descended from the fatal hill, a cheer running along the gardens, thickets, and rocks, to the length of the British line. The enemy were supported by the fire from their walls; grape thrown from their large guns fell up to 1,100 yards, but our men pushed on.

A native officer was seen sitting on his horse, waving his arm to cheer his men. Our troops recoiled from a wall lined with the enemy, when Chamberlain, leaping his horse over it among them, dared his men to follow. Influenced by his example, they charged, and drove the enemy through the gates with immense slaughter. The British force was, however, compelled to fall back in some confusion by the tremendous fire from the walls; and a large body of horse was advancing against them, when some infantry, consisting of the 1st Fusiliers and Guides, collected by Majors Jacob, Hodson, and Greville, and a few horsemen, came to their rescue, and again turned the enemy. There was great difficulty in getting off the wounded. Many soldiers were seen bearing their comrades in their arms; and Lieutenant Thompson, of the horse artillery, was shot through the leg while trying to save one of his men from falling into the hands of the enemy. Seventeen men were killed, and 16 officers and 177 men wounded. Among the latter was Brigadier Chamberlain, who had his arm shattered below the shoulder. He received his wound at the time he leaped the wall and charged the enemy who had sheltered themselves behind it. Captain Norman was appointed, in consequence, to carry on the duties of the Adjutant-General.

On the 31st July, another fierce attempt was made by the rebels to gain the rear of the British camp, followed by another attack the next day, but both were vigorously repulsed.

A welcome reinforcement a few days after this arrived, of 2000 Europeans and Sikhs, under Brigadier—General Nicholson.

On the 24th of August, General Nicholson obtained a brilliant victory over the enemy at Nujjuffghur, about twenty miles from Delhi, and thus prevented an attack which had been intended by the rebels on the rear of the British camp.

On the morning of the 4th of September, the long-expected siege-train arrived from Meerut, and now all felt sure that the moment for storming the central stronghold of the mutiny was not far off.

The most gallant action fought at this time was that of Nujjuffghur. Information had been received in camp that 7000 of the enemy had marched from Delhi, with the object in view of taking the British army in the rear. Immediately a force consisting of 1000 European and 2000 native troops, under the gallant Brigadier-General Nicholson, was despatched to meet the enemy, who were found posted at Nujjuffghur. The Brigadier formed the 1st and 61st Europeans in line, reminding them in a short speech of the renown gained by several regiments in the Crimea from reserving their fire till they were close on the foe. The word was given, "Line will advance." Steadily as on parade they stepped off with fixed bayonets, and not till close to the enemy did they utter their hearty British cheer, and rush fiercely forward towards the *serai* they were ordered to attack, on which four guns were mounted. The sepoys fled, and their guns were captured; a bridge was next taken; and in all thirteen guns fell into the hands of the victorious column, while ammunition and stores were destroyed, and numbers of the enemy were killed or wounded.

Towards the termination of a severe engagement in the Subzi Mundi, near Delhi, on the 10th of July, Lieutenant Wilberforce Greathead had, with part of the artillery and others, thrown himself into a *serai*, where they were surrounded by a host of rebels, who opened a hot fire on them. As they were not in a position to stand a siege, it was agreed that they should force their way out. All were prepared. The gate was thrown open. The officers led. Out rushed the gallant band. They killed the men immediately in front with their swords, and the British soldiers pressing on, the rebels gave way, and fled in disorder to Delhi. It was a trying moment. The odds against the British were ten to one. One officer was killed, another was wounded, and twenty-nine men were killed or wounded.

The capture of a rebel post before Delhi called Ludlow Castle, on the 12th August, was a very gallant affair. While still dark, the column destined to make the attack under Brigadier Showers marched down the Flagstaff road, and aroused the rebels by a rattling fire of musketry and a bayonet charge. So completely were the enemy taken by surprise, that all who could escape fled to the town, leaving four field-guns in the hands of the victors, which were brought back in triumph to camp. Brigadier Showers was severely wounded, and Colonel Greathead was sent down to take the command. With the coolness and forethought for which he is well-known, he brought the force out of action, taking good care that not a wounded man should be left behind. Colonel Greathead afterwards much distinguished himself. The qualifications for command which he possesses are such as all young officers should endeavour to obtain—coolness, decision, and forethought, with gallantry unsurpassed. Without these virtues, bravery, and even a perfect knowledge of his profession, will not make a man fit to command.

STORMING OF DELHI

On the night of the 13th of September, two Engineer officers were sent to examine the breaches made in the walls of Delhi. They stole through the enemy's skirmishers, descended into the ditch, and ascertained that the breaches were practicable, but that they might both be improved by a longer cannonade. As, however, the enemy had begun greatly to strengthen the fortifications, it was decided that the assault should take place at once. The infantry were accordingly divided into five columns of about 1000 men each, destined to carry the city in different places. The first was composed of detachments of the 75th, 1st Fusiliers, and 2nd Punjaub Infantry, to storm the breach near the Cashmere bastion.

The second was made up from Her Majesty's 8th and 2nd Fusiliers, and 4th Infantry, to carry the breach in the Water bastion. It was commanded by Brigadier Jones.

The third column was composed of Her Majesty's 52nd Foot, the Kumaon battalion, and the 1st Punjaub Infantry. This was to blow open and enter by the Cashmere gate.

The fourth, composed of Goorkhas and the Guides, with some companies of European troops, and the Cashmere contingent, was under Major Reid, and was to assault Kissengunge, and enter by the Lahore gate.

The fifth column, consisting chiefly of native troops, was destined for a reserve.

At one o'clock a.m. on the 14th, the men turned out in silence, not a bugle nor a trumpet sounding, and noiselessly moved down to the trenches. The batteries all the time kept up an incessant fire on the city, which was responded to as usual.

When the troops arrived at the trenches, they lay down, awaiting the signal which was to be given at daybreak. This was to be the blowing in of the Cashmere gate. The party selected for this hazardous operation consisted of Lieutenants Home and Salkeld, of the Engineers; Sergeants Carmichael, Burgess, and Smith; Bugler Hawthorne to sound the advance; and eight native sappers.

This work was to have been done before dawn; but, through some mistake, it was daylight before they reached the spot. Lieutenant Home walked through the outer barrier gate, which he found open, and crossed the broken drawbridge with four men, each carrying a bag of powder. The enemy in alarm shut the wicket, and Home had time to arrange his bags and jump into the ditch. The firing party followed, with four more bags of powder and a lighted port-fire. The enemy now understood what the party were about. The wicket was open, and through it, from above and from every side, came the bullets of the sepoys. Lieutenant Salkeld was wounded in two places, but passed the light to Sergeant Carmichael, who fell dead while attempting to fire the train. Havildar Madhoo was also wounded. The port-fire was next seized by Sergeant Burgess. Scarcely had he time to apply it successfully to the powder, than he too sank with a mortal wound. Sergeant Smith ran forward to see that all was right, while Bugler Hawthorne lifted up Lieutenant Salkeld; and barely had they time to leap for safety into the ditch than the explosion took place, and instantly afterwards the storming column burst through the shattered gates. For ever associated with the storming of Delhi will be the names of the two young Lieutenants Home and Salkeld, and the brave men who accompanied them.

Bugler Hawthorne, after sounding the advance, bore away Salkeld on his shoulders, and did not leave him till he had bound up his wounds and deposited him in a place of safety. The four heroes who survived were recommended for the Victoria Cross, but Salkeld died of his wounds, and the gallant Home lost his life by accident not two weeks afterwards; so that two only, Sergeant Smith and Bugler Hawthorne, received their honours.

Meantime the storming columns had marched on with deep and steady tramp. The Rifles ran forward in skirmishing order, and the heads of the first two columns issued from the Koodsia Bagh at a quick march. No sooner were their front ranks seen, than a storm of bullets showered upon them from every side. At the breach of the Cashmere gate, for some minutes it was impossible to put ladders down into the ditch. The ladders were thrown down, but they were quickly again raised against the escarp. Numbers are struck down, some to rise no more; others again scramble up,—the groans of the wounded, the feeble cries of the dying, the shouts and shrieks of the combatants, mingle together in wild confusion.

First to mount the breach was Lieutenant Fitzgerald, of the 75th: but the young hero fell dead on the spot. On came stout hearts and strong hands behind him. The enemy gave way. The British were in at last, and the glorious old colours over the broken wall. The second column had also burst through; and that line of ramparts which had so often turned back the brave soldiers of England was now their own.

The first and second columns swept along the circuit of the walls, taking the Moree bastion and the Cabul gate. On approaching the Lahore gate they found, however, that they should have to push through a narrow lane, barricaded and swept by some pieces of artillery, while the enemy fired on them from the houses. In vain was the attempt made; the hero Nicholson was shot through the chest, Lieutenant Speke killed, Major Jacob mortally wounded, and Captain Greville severely.

The third column, ably guided by Sir T. Metcalf, had also to retire before the massive walls of the Jumma Musjid. Part also of the 4th, under Major Reid, hastening to the support of the Cashmere contingent, was almost overpowered. Major Reid was wounded, and his troops retreated; but the guns mounted on Hindoo Rao's hill poured shrapnel into the enemy. The gallant Chamberlain came among the infantry a little recovered from his wound; while Brigadier Hope Grant brought up his old Lancers, with three regiments of Punjaub cavalry, and Hodson's Sikh and Paton sabres, to their aid. However, from the nature of the ground, the troopers could neither charge nor retire. They were compelled, therefore, to sit on their horses till some infantry could come to their relief. The horse artillery did what they could to keep the enemy back, but they became every moment bolder, and spread out, mending their sight and taking better aim.

Lieutenant Macdowell, second in command of Hodson's Horse—an eye-witness—says:

> The steadiness with which the cavalry confronted this most anxious position for two hours is as deserving of praise as the courage of the infantry who carried the breaches. At three a.m. we moved down in column of squadrons to the rear of our batteries, and waited there till about five a.m., when the enemy advanced from the Lahore gate with two troops of artillery, no end of cavalry, and a lot of infantry, apparently to our front. I think that they intended to try and take their old position now that we had got theirs. In an instant, horse artillery and cavalry were ordered to the front, and we then went at

a gallop through our own batteries, the men cheering us as we leaped over the sandbags, and halted under the Moree bastion under as heavy a fire of round shot, grape, and canister, as I have ever in my life been peppered with. Our artillery dashed to the front, unlimbered, and opened upon the enemy, and at it they went, hammer and tongs. We had no infantry with us; all the infantry were fighting in the city. The enemy came out against us with large bodies of infantry and cavalry, and then began the fire of musketry. It was tremendous. There we were (9th Lancers, 1st, 2nd, and 4th Sikh Guide Cavalry, and Hodson's Horse), protecting the artillery, who were threatened by their infantry and cavalry. All this time we never returned a shot. Our artillery blazed away, of course; but we had to sit in our saddles, and be knocked over. However, I am happy to say we saved the guns. The front we showed was so steady as to keep the enemy back, till some of the Guide infantry came down and went at them. Here we had had to sit for three hours in front of a lot of gardens, perfectly impracticable for cavalry, under a fire of musketry which I have seldom seen equalled, and the enemy quite concealed. Had we retired, they would at once have taken our guns. Had the guns retired with us, we should have lost the position.

Night put an end to the desperate struggle. A considerable portion of the city remained in the hands of the victors, but in other parts the rebels still held out. During this day's operations the casualties amounted to 1170 killed, wounded, and missing.

The victorious British continued making progress day by day, driving the enemy before them through the city. The magazine still remained in the power of the rebels. Lieutenant-Colonel Deacon, of the 61st Regiment, led the attack. In silence his men approached the city: not a trigger was pulled till the stormers and supports reached the walls; when, with a loud cheer, they rushed on at the enemy, who, taken by surprise, threw down the port-fires at their guns, and fled before them. Some were bayoneted close to the breach as they attempted to escape, and others, flying, were followed by the 61st and the 4th Punjaub Infantry.

Captain Norman accompanied a party under Lieutenant-Colonel Rainey, and spiked a gun which was in position, pointing at the College garden battery, in spite of the desperate defence of the enemy. Assistant-Surgeon Reade and Colour-Sergeant Mitchell, of the 61st, also spiked a gun. Frequent attacks were made by the rebels on the troops within the walls under Colonel Farquhar, but they were vigorously repulsed on each occasion.

On the morning of the 20th, the enemy were driven from the Lahore gate, and possession was secured. The troops now pushed triumphantly on, capturing the other gates and bastions, till all the defences of the rebel city were in the power of the British. The gate of the palace was blown in early on the 20th, and here Major-General Wilson established his headquarters. Major Brind, of the Artillery, with a detachment of fifty men of the 8th Foot, and twenty of the 1st Bengal European Fusiliers, under the command of Major Bannatyne, forced an entrance in the most brilliant way into the Jumma Musjid, and contributed much to the success of the operations.

The guns from the bloodstained battlements of Delhi thundering forth a royal salute, as the rising sun gilded the summit of its domes and minarets, on the 21st of September 1857, proclaimed that Delhi was once more under the rule of Great Britain.

PURSUIT OF THE FOE

In terror, the hordes of the rebel foe took to flight, abandoning most of their artillery, stores, and sick and wounded. The princes, the chief instigators of the atrocities committed, were captured by Major Hodson, and shot; and the old king was likewise taken, and sent as a prisoner for life to Rangoon.

A flying column, consisting of the 9th Lancers, 8th and 75th Regiments, the 2nd and 4th Punjaub Infantry, 200 of Hodson's Horse, with the 1st, 2nd, and 5th Punjaub Cavalry, and horse artillery, was immediately formed, and placed under the command of Lieutenant-Colonel E.H. Greathead, who proceeded in a south-easterly direction, in order to cut off the mutineers on the right bank of the Jumna. After defeating a body of the enemy at Boolundshuhur on the 28th of September, the column took and destroyed the fort of Malaghur. Here, while blowing up the fortifications, the gallant and young Lieutenant Home lost his life.

On the evening of the 10th October, as the troops, wearied with a long march in the heat of the sun, were preparing to encamp, they were attacked by a numerous body of the enemy, whom they routed with great slaughter, the 9th Lancers especially distinguishing themselves. The column defeated the enemy in various engagements. On the 14th of October it was joined by Brigadier Hope Grant, who, as superior officer, took the command; and finally, on the 8th of November, reached the Alumbagh, before Lucknow.

The following officers and men obtained the Victoria Cross for gallant deeds performed during these operations:—

Lieutenant John Charles Campbell Daunt, 11th (late 70th) Bengal Native Infantry, and Number 2165, Sergeant Denis Dynon, 53rd Regiment, gained that honour, for conspicuous gallantry in action, on the 2nd of October 1857, with the mutineers of the Ramgurh battalion at Chotah Behar, in capturing two guns, particularly the last, when they rushed forward and secured it by pistolling the gunners, who were mowing the detachment down with grape, one-third of which was *hors de combat* at the time. Lieutenant Daunt highly distinguished himself by chasing, on the 2nd of November following, the mutineers of the 32nd Bengal Native Infantry across a plain into a rich cultivation, into which he followed them with a few of Rattray's Sikhs. He was dangerously wounded in the attempt to drive out a large body of these mutineers from an enclosure, the preservation of many of his party, on this occasion, being attributed to his gallantry.

Conductor James Miller, Ordnance Department, Bengal, gained the Cross on 28th October 1857, at great personal risk, by going to the assistance of a wounded officer, Lieutenant Glubb, of the late 38th Regiment of Bengal Native Infantry, whom he carried out of action. He was himself subsequently wounded, and sent to Agra. Conductor Miller was at the time employed with heavy howitzers and ordnance stores attached to a body of troops commanded by the late Colonel Cotton, C.B., in the attack on the rebels who had taken up their position in the *serai* at Futtehpore Sikra, near Agra.

On the 17th of October the fort of Jhujjur was captured by Brigadier Showers, and this achievement is looked upon as the close of the operations against Delhi.

LIEUTENANT KERR AT KOLAPORE

Among the many dashing exploits performed at this time, was one for which Lieutenant William Alexander Kerr, adjutant of the South Mahratta Horse, gained high renown. He was with his regiment at Sattara, the inhabitants of which had already exhibited a mutinous disposition, when information was received that the 27th Regiment of Bombay Native Infantry, stationed at Kolapore, a town about 75 miles off, had mutinied and murdered their officers. For the safety perhaps of the whole Presidency, the mutiny must be immediately crushed. Kerr instantly volunteered to lead a body of his men against the rebels. He knew that he could trust his fellows. Not a moment was to be lost. The bugle sounded to horse. He addressed them, and told them what was to be done. They promised to follow him to the death. Across rivers and *nullahs*, swollen by heavy rains, they went, and in twenty-six hours pulled rein before the gates of Kolapore. The mutineers had barricaded all the entrances to the place, and were already flushed with a momentary success over a body of infantry sent against them. Without guns the barricades were difficult to remove, but Kerr was not to be disheartened. He and a faithful *sowar*, Gumpunt Row, dismounting from their horses, with crowbars in their hands advanced to the attack, leading on the rest of the troop also on foot. The first defences, in spite of showers of bullets, were forced; the rebels gave way, but took refuge in a loopholed house with other barricades in front. These were to be removed before an entrance could be effected. Again the gallant lieutenant vigorously plied his crowbar; the barricade was forced; a shot carried away the chain of his helmet. Gumpunt Row was wounded, but still he fought on by the side of his leader, and twice saved his life from the bayonet-thrusts of the foe. Kerr, passing his sword through the body of a sepoy who had fired his musket in his face and almost blinded him with the powder, rushed on, and, wounded though he was, killed another enemy, entered the house, and the defenders, to the number of 34, armed with muskets and bayonets, were all either killed, wounded, or captured. Of his own brave followers, not one escaped unhurt; 8 were killed on the spot, and 4 afterwards died of their wounds. It was not only a brave deed, but well-executed, and so well timed that it contributed greatly to crush the spread of the mutiny throughout the Presidency. Lieutenant Kerr most deservedly obtained the Victoria Cross.

DEFENCE OF CAWNPORE
7TH AND 25TH JUNE 1858

The saddest episode in the bloodstained history of the sepoy mutiny is the storming of Cawnpore. Cawnpore was one of the most pleasant stations of the Indian army. The cantonments were entirely separated from the native town, and spread in a semicircular form over an extent of six miles along the banks of the river. On the highest ground in the cantonments stood the church and the assembly rooms, and on another part a theatre and a café, supported by public subscriptions. Round them were scattered, amid gardens and groves, numberless bungalows, the residence of officers, with barracks for troops, and a separate bazaar for each regiment; while numerous tents for the troops kept under canvas increased the picturesque effect and animation of the scene. The native town at the time of the mutiny contained 60,000 inhabitants. In cantonments there were 3000 sepoy troops, and, including officers, 300 European combatants, and upwards of 700 European civilians, merchants, railway officials, shopkeepers, and women and children. General Sir Hugh Wheeler was the commandant of the division. It was not till the middle of May that full credit was given to the fact that the great sepoy army of India was in revolt.

A spot was then selected, in which the Europeans entrenched themselves. In the centre was the old dragoon hospital, and round it a mud wall was thrown up four feet high. Ten guns were placed round the entrenchments, three commanding the lines on the north-east, and three on the south to range the plain which separates the cantonments from the city. Of the other four, one was a 3-pound rifled gun, and three were brought by Lieutenant Ashe, of the Bengal Artillery. Supplies of food were also laid in, but very inadequate to the wants of so large a number of people. The outbreak of the troops commenced on 6th June, when the 2nd Native Cavalry deserted their post, taking with them their horses, arms, colours, and regimental treasure-chest. Some few, but very few, of the natives proved true to their oaths. Among them was the old *subadar*-major of the regiment, who defended as long as he had the power the colours and treasure, which were in the quarter guard. The old man was found in the morning severely wounded, and lying in his blood at his post. He remained with the British, and was killed by a shell in the entrenchment.

The native commissioned and non-commissioned officers and a few privates of the 53rd Regiment of Native Infantry also remained faithful. The British troops who defended the entrenchments of Cawnpore for so long a period, and against such fearful odds and so treacherous an enemy, consisted of 60 men of the 84th Regiment, 74 men of the 32nd, 15 men of the Madras Fusiliers, and 59 men of the Company's artillery, besides the officers attached to the sepoy regiments. The siege was noted, perhaps, more for the patient suffering and endurance of those within the lines, especially of the women and children, and for its most dreadful and terrible termination, than for many especial acts of bravery performed by its defenders. The fact is, that the whole defence was one continual act of heroism; and had more forethought been exhibited in providing a sufficient store of food, and had no confidence been placed in the promises of that abominable wretch the Nana, it might have proved as successful as that of Lucknow, which in many respects it resembled.

On the morning of Sunday the 7th June, the bugle-call summoned the whole garrison to the lines; and soon after Lieutenant Ashe with his guns went out to meet the enemy, but he was speedily compelled to return. In a short time the mutineers opened their fire from a 9-pounder, the shot striking the crest of the mud wall, and gliding over into the *puckah*-roofed barrack. This was about ten o'clock; a number of ladies and children were outside the barrack. The consternation among them was indescribable. As the day advanced, the firing became hotter. Shrieks and cries most heartrending burst from them as the shot struck the walls of the barrack. This was the commencement of the horrible sufferings they had to endure, and which only terminated with their yet more terrible destruction. They soon learned the uselessness of giving vent to their fears in cries, and from henceforth never uttered a sound except when groaning from the dreadful mutilation they were compelled to endure. The following were the arrangements made for the defence:

On the north, Major Vibart, of the 2nd Cavalry, assisted by Captain Jenkins, held the redan, which was an earthwork defending the whole of the northern side. At the north-east battery, Lieutenant Ashe, of the Oude Irregular Artillery, commanded one 24-pounder howitzer and two 9-pounders, assisted by Lieutenant Sotheby. Captain Kempland, 56th Native Infantry, was posted on the south side. Lieutenant Eckford, of the Artillery, had charge of the south-east battery with three 9-pounders, assisted by Lieutenant Burney, also of the Artillery, and Lieutenant Delafosse, of the 53rd Native Infantry. The main guard, from south to west, was held by Lieutenant Turnbull, 13th Native Infantry. On the west, Lieutenant C. Dempster commanded three 9-pounders, assisted by Lieutenant Martin. Flanking the west battery, the little rifled 3-pounder was stationed, with a detachment under the command of Major Prout, 56th Native Infantry; and on the north-west, Captain Whiting held the command. At each of the batteries infantry were posted, fifteen paces apart, under the cover of the mud wall, four feet in height. This service was shared by combatants and civilians alike, without any relief: each man had at least three loaded muskets by his side, with bayonet fixed in case of assault; but in most instances our trained men had as many as seven and even eight muskets each.

The batteries were none of them masked or fortified in any way, and the gunners were in consequence exposed to a most murderous fire. The entrenchments were commanded by eight or more barracks in the course of erection, from 300 to 400 yards distant, on the Allahabad road. A detachment, consisting chiefly of civil engineers, was accordingly placed in two or more of them, and they became the scene of several desperate encounters. Even to obtain ammunition it was necessary to send across to the entrenchments under fire of the mutineers, who had obtained possession of the outer barracks. Food also had to be obtained in the same way; but volunteers were never found wanting for this hazardous service. Every day the pickets swept through these barracks to dislodge the enemy, who scarcely ever remained for a hand-to-hand fight. Scarcity of food, the shot of the enemy, and the excessive heat of the weather, carried off day after day numbers of the gallant defenders. Want of food was greatly felt—the defenders were glad to shoot the horses of the enemy for the purpose of making soup; and on one occasion a Brahmin bull coming near the lines was killed. To get it was now the difficulty. An officer, with ten followers, rushed out, and dragged it within the entrenchments under a hot fire from the enemy.

The well in the entrenchment was one of the points of greatest danger, as it was completely exposed to the enemy's fire; and even at night the creaking of the tackle was the signal for the mutineers to point their guns in that direction. Still, brave men were found, chiefly privates, who incurred the risk of drawing water for the women and children, when all money reward had become valueless. A gentleman of the Civil Service, Mr. John McKillop, constituted himself captain of the well, drawing for the supply of the women and children as often as he could. After numerous escapes, he received his death-wound in the groin from a grape-shot, with his last breath entreating that someone would draw water for a lady to whom he had promised it. Dreadful were the sufferings of all from thirst; and children were seen sucking pieces of old water-bags to try and get a drop of moisture on their parched lips. One of the barracks was thatched; part of it was used as an hospital. That at length caught fire; and while the heroic garrison were dragging forth their wounded countrymen from the flames, the mutineers poured in on them incessant volleys of musketry, and a continued shower of round shot.

The enemy, imagining that all the attention of the garrison was devoted to extinguishing the flames, advanced to the assault, with the intention of storming Ashe's battery. Not a sound did they utter, and, fancying that they were undiscovered, were allowed to come within 60 or 80 yards of the guns before one was fired, or a movement made to indicate that they were perceived. Just as they must have supposed their success certain, the 9-pounders opened on them with a most destructive discharge of grape. The men shouldered in succession the muskets which they had by their sides ready loaded, and discharged them into their midst. In half an hour the enemy took to flight, leaving a hundred corpses on the plain. No sooner had the ashes of the barrack cooled, than the soldiers of the 32nd Regiment, though the enemy were firing on them, raking with their swords and bayonets, made diligent search for their medals. Several of them were found, though much injured by fire. This fact shows the high appreciation in which the British soldier holds his decorations.

Numbers of the officers and men had already fallen.

Soon after the destruction of the hospital, Captain Moore determined to make a dash upon the enemy's guns, in the hope of silencing some of them. Accordingly a party of fifty, headed by the captain, sallied out at midnight towards the church compound, where they spiked two or three guns. Proceeding thence to the mess-house, they killed several of the native gunners asleep at their posts, blew up one of the 24-pounders and spiked another, and returned with the loss of one private killed and four wounded. Gallant and successful as was the exploit, it availed the garrison nothing, as the next day the enemy brought fresh guns into position. In vain did they look for relief. So completely were the roads closed by the rebel sepoys, that news of their condition did not reach Lucknow, only fifty miles distant, till near the termination of the affair.

The 23rd of June 1857 was the centenary of the battle of Plassy, and the sepoys believed on that day they should finally throw off the British yoke. On the night of the 22nd, the barrack held by the British under the command of Captain Mowbray Thomson was threatened with a grand attack. Numbers of rebels were seen gathering from all directions at this barrack, and Captain Thomson, believing that he should be overpowered, sent to the entrenchments for reinforcements. The answer was that none could be spared. Captain Moore, however, shortly after came across to see how affairs stood. He proposed that they should themselves sally out as if they were about to make an attack. He himself had but a sword, Lieutenant Delafosse an empty musket. Captain Moore vociferated to the winds, "Number one to the front"; and hundreds of ammunition pouches rattled on the sheaths as the astonished foe vaulted out from the cover afforded by heaps of rubbish, and rushed for shelter to the barrack walls. The gallant little party, which consisted but of 13 privates and 3 officers, fired a volley, and with bayonets at the charge followed the enemy, who dared not face them. The party returned to their barrack, laughing heartily at the success of their feint.

All night long a series of false charges and surprises were made on the barrack, and not a man for an instant left his post. Towards dawn, the enemy being more quiet, Mr. Mainwaring, a cavalry cadet, one of Captain Thomson's picket, begged him to lie down, while he kept a look-out. Scarcely had the captain closed his eyes when Mainwaring shouted, "Here they come!" The enemy, with more pluck than they had hitherto shown, advanced close up to the doorway of the barrack. Mainwaring's revolver despatched two of the enemy. Stirling, with an Enfield rifle, shot one and bayoneted another. Captain Thomson fired both charges of his double-barrelled gun, killing two more.

The defenders of the barrack consisted of but seventeen men, while the enemy left eighteen corpses lying outside the doorway. At the same time the mutineers surrounded the entrenchments on all sides with cavalry and infantry, and horse and bullock batteries of field-artillery. Their cavalry, however, started on the charge at a hand gallop, so that when they neared the entrenchments their horses were winded, and a round from the British guns threw their ranks into hopeless confusion; all who were not biting the dust wheeling round, and galloping off in dismay. One of the expedients adopted by the enemy was to roll before them large bales of cotton, under which they managed to approach very near the walls. A well-directed fire from the batteries soon, however, set fire to these novel defences, and the skirmishers, panic-struck, took to flight before the main body had begun to advance.

For seventeen days and nights had the gallant little band resisted all the efforts made by the overwhelming numbers of the foe to storm the position. At last it only remained for the enemy to starve them out; and this operation they forthwith commenced, abandoning all attempts to take the place by assault. Of the fifty-nine artillerymen, all, with the exception of four, had perished at the batteries, while the guns themselves were so knocked about that two only could be made to carry grape. Even in these, in consequence of the irregularity of the bore, the canisters could not be driven home. A new style of cartridge was therefore invented, formed by stockings supplied by the women; and into these the contents of the canisters were emptied. Among the most gallant defenders of the fort, and one of the few survivors of the siege, was Lieutenant Delafosse. Being much annoyed by a small gun in Barrack Number 1, he resolved to silence it if possible. Giving his own worn-out gun a monster charge of three 6-pound shots, and a stockingful of grape, he rammed them all well down. He fired; his faithful piece of artillery did not burst, and his troublesome little antagonist was never again heard.

Another gallant exploit on the part of Lieutenant Delafosse occurred at the north-east battery on the 21st June. A shot had entered the *tumbril* of a gun, blew it up, and ignited the woodwork of the carriage, thus exposing the ammunition all around to destruction. The rebels, observing what was taking place, directed their fire to the spot with redoubled fury. Delafosse, with perfect self-possession, went to the burning gun, and, lying down under the firing mass, pulled away portions of the wood, and scattered earth with both hands on the flames. Two soldiers followed this courageous example, each with a bucket of water, which the lieutenant applied till the fire was extinguished.

In time, the sepoys discovering that they were not likely to capture the fort while any of the heroic garrison remained alive, resolved to starve them to death. Their sufferings from want of food at last became so great, that on the 25th of June General Wheeler entered into arrangements for the evacuation of the place with Nana Sahib. The next day the survivors proceeded to the river to embark on board boats prepared for them, when, with a treachery almost unparalleled in history, by the order of that demon in human shape, they were fired on and mostly killed. The rest, with few exceptions, were brought back to Cawnpore, when the men were shot, and the women and children, after being kept prisoners for some time and treated with the utmost indignity and barbarity, were indiscriminately slaughtered, and their bodies thrown into a well. One boat only escaped down the river, by which the life of Lieutenant Delafosse, who has given a narrative of what he witnessed, was preserved. Of all the gallant men and heroic women who endured the sufferings which have been described, he, with two or three others, alone escaped.

Terribly, however, ere long were they to be avenged.

LUCKNOW
1857–1858

The drama of Lucknow may properly be divided into four acts. 1st, The defence by Sir Henry Lawrence and Brigadier Inglis; 2nd, The succour of Lucknow by Sir Henry Havelock and Sir James Outram, 25th September; 3rd, The relief of Lucknow on the 22nd November 1857 by Sir Colin Campbell, when the hard-pressed garrison were carried out from overwhelming numbers of the enemy; and 4th, The siege of Lucknow by the British force under Sir Colin Campbell and Sir James Outram. Sir James Outram had previously been established in the strong position of the Alumbagh, from which the rebels had in vain endeavoured to dislodge him.

DEFENCE OF LUCKNOW
29TH JUNE TO 25TH SEPTEMBER 1857

Sir Henry Lawrence, with a small body of troops, was stationed at Lucknow, when, on the 29th of June, hearing that a large body of rebels was approaching, he marched out to make a reconnaissance.

The force fell into an ambuscade, and some of the native artillerymen proving traitors, it was compelled to retire with a very heavy loss of officers and men, and three pieces of artillery.

Immediately on his return, Sir Henry prepared for the defence. The whole garrison amounted only to 1616 officers and men fit for duty, and with 80 officers and men sick and wounded. Sir Henry's first care was to withdraw the garrison from the old fort of Muchee Bowen; and in the course of the night of the 1st July, such provision as could be removed having been carried off, it was blown up with vast quantities of gunpowder and ball cartridges. An entrenched position had been commenced round the British Residency, and to complete this all the energies of the garrison were first devoted. Long, however, before all the proposed batteries were thrown up, the rebels, assembling in vast numbers, began the blockade of the place. Unhappily, Sir Henry Lawrence was mortally wounded by a shell on the 2nd of July, and closed a distinguished career on the 4th. Brigadier Inglis then succeeded to the command. At this time only two batteries were finished. No spot was safe: the sick and wounded were killed in the hospital, and women and children in private houses suffered the same fate. On the 20th of July, the enemy, after exploding a mine, attempted to storm the defences, but were driven back, after a desperate struggle which lasted four hours. Day and night a murderous fire was kept up on the garrison, who were already suffering dreadfully from sickness, while famine stared them in the face. On the 10th of August, the enemy attempted another assault, after, as before, springing a mine. On the 18th, a similar attempt was made. On this occasion three officers were blown up, though without injury, and the enemy established themselves in one of the houses of the British position; they were, however, driven out in the evening by a gallant charge of the 32nd and 48th Regiments. No men could have behaved more splendidly than did those of these two regiments. The 32nd was reduced to less than 300 men. The artillery behaved admirably, and suffered so much, that at length there were only 24 European gunners to work guns, including mortars in position; so that, although ably assisted by the men of the 32nd and by civilian volunteers, they had to run from gun to gun to defend the points most threatened by the enemy.

Five sorties were made during the siege by the British, for the purpose of destroying buildings which commanded the entrenchments, and of spiking guns. On all these occasions, both officers and men of the 32nd Regiment particularly distinguished themselves. In a sortie made on the 7th July, for the purpose of examining a house strongly held by the enemy, to ascertain whether or not a mine was being driven from it, Lieutenant Lawrence, 32nd Regiment, was the first to mount the ladder and to enter the window of the house, in effecting which he had his pistol knocked out of his hand by one of the enemy. On the 26th of September, he charged with two of his men in advance of his company, and captured a 9-pounder gun. A veranda having fallen on the 30th June, Mr. Capper, of the Bengal Civil Service, being entangled among the ruins, Corporal Oxenham rushed forward amid a shower of bullets, to which he was exposed for ten minutes while extricating him from his dangerous situation. Private Dowling on three several occasions rushed out and spiked the enemy's guns; on one, killing a *subadar*, who attempted to defend his gun. Captain Henry George Browne, 32nd Regiment, later of the 100th Regiment, performed a similar conspicuous act of bravery, having, on the 21st August 1857, gallantly led a sortie at great personal risk, for the purpose of spiking two heavy guns, which were doing considerable damage to the defences. Captain Browne was the first person who entered the battery, which consisted of the two guns in question, protected by high palisades, the embrasures being closed with sliding shutters. On reaching the battery, Captain Browne removed the shutters, and jumped into the battery. The result was, that the guns were spiked, and it is supposed that about 100 of the enemy were killed.

The Succour of Lucknow
25th September

At length, on the 25th September, early in the morning, a messenger arrived with a letter from General Outram, announcing his approach to Lucknow. Hours passed by; many of the enemy were seen retreating across the river, and every gun which could be brought to bear was fired at them, though all the time the rebels engaged in besieging the entrenchments never ceased firing, both with artillery and rifles. At four p.m. there was a report that some officers and a European regiment had been seen advancing in the distance. At five p.m. volleys of musketry were heard, growing louder and louder, and soon afterwards the British troops were seen fighting their way through one of the principal streets; and though men fell at every step, onward they gallantly pushed, till the rearguard heavy guns were inside the position. The relieving force was under the command of Sir James Outram. It had suffered severely in the gallant exploit. Of 2600 who had left Cawnpore, nearly one-third had been either killed or wounded in forcing their way through the city, so that nothing could be done for the relief of the place. The united body was therefore as closely besieged as before.

We must now describe more particularly how this gallant exploit had been accomplished.

On the return of General Havelock from Persia, he was appointed to the command of a movable column, consisting of 1964 men. He immediately commenced his march on Cawnpore, hoping to relieve the prisoners there confined by the miscreant Nana Sahib. Having been joined by Major Renard with 800 men, a victory was obtained, on the 12th July, over a large body of the rebels near Futtehpore.

Twice on the 15th he engaged the rebels, at Aeng, and the bridge of Pandoo Nudder. On the 16th he drove Nana Sahib from a strong position at Ahirwa.

The next day, the fatal 17th, the wretch butchered the women and children left in his power, blew up the magazine at Cawnpore, and retreated to Bithpor. Here he was unable to make a stand, and once more made a hasty retreat. General Havelock, on this, leaving General Neill at Cawnpore, pushed on for Lucknow. He again encountered the mutineers near Uano on the 29th July, when the 78th Highlanders, the 1st Fusiliers, and the 64th Regiment were chiefly engaged. The same corps next captured Busherut Gunge, a walled town with wet ditches. Three times the same place was attacked and taken while General Havelock was waiting at Cawnpore for reinforcements.

On the 16th September, Sir James Outram arrived. Though superior officer, he refused to supersede Major-General Havelock, but accompanied the force as Chief-Commissioner of Oude. The relieving force, now amounting to about 2500 men and 17 guns, crossed the Ganges, and, on the 21st September, attacked the rebels at Munghowar, who fled, four guns being captured, two of which were taken in a cavalry charge led by Sir James Outram.

On the 23rd, they arrived before the Alumbagh, an isolated building, a country palace situated in a large walled park to the south-east of the city of Lucknow, and about three miles from the Residency. From this place the enemy were driven, four guns were taken, and it was occupied by the relieving army. As the British troops were wearied with their long march in pelting rain, the assault was deferred till the 25th. All the 24th they were bombarded by the enemy, and an attack was made by 1000 cavalry on the baggage, which was defeated by the soldiers of the gallant 90th, though not without the loss of several officers and men.

The morning of the 25th arrived. The generals breakfasted at a small table placed in the open field; and while they and their staff were afterwards examining a map of the city spread out on it, a 9-pound shot from the enemy's battery struck the ground five yards from it, and bounded over their heads. Soon after eight the welcome order to advance was given. Sir James Outram commanded the first and leading brigade, with all the artillery, heavy and light.

The second brigade, under General Havelock, followed in support. Scarcely had Sir James's brigade passed the advanced pickets, than it was assailed by a heavy fire in front, on either flank, and from two guns planted near a house called from its colour the Yellow House. The enemy had flanked his road under cover of long, high grass, and a murderous fire was poured on the columns from a double-storied house, full of musketeers, from the loopholed walls of the surrounding gardens, from two guns that raked the road from his right flank, and from another that commanded his front. In the face of this desperate opposition, Captain Maude, with his brave artillerymen, pushed on, though not without the loss of one-third of their number.

A canal passes between the Alumbagh and Lucknow. At the bridge over it the enemy had determined to make their stand, and dispute the entrance to the city. It was defended by six guns on the Lucknow side, one of them a 24-pound-er, which completely swept the bridge and the approach to it, while all the houses near it were loopholed and filled with musketeers. Here nearly every man of Captain Maude's two guns was killed or wounded, though he and Lieutenant Maitland remained unhurt, and they frequently had to call for volunteers from the infantry to replace the artillerymen falling around. A charge was now made by the Madras Fusiliers, when Lieutenant Arnold, at the first word of command, dashed on to the bridge with nineteen of his men. The enemy, believing this little band to be the main body, sent a discharge of grape, which they had reserved for the occasion, among them. Lieutenant Arnold fell, shot through both legs, and most of his men were swept down. Lieutenant Havelock alone remained on the bridge. Waving his sword, he called to the Fusiliers to advance. Then, bravely led by their regimental officers, they dashed forward with a cheer, and, not giving the enemy time to reload, rushed on the guns, amid a storm, of bullets, wrested them from the enemy, and bayoneted the gunners.

The British army now entered the city, and the 78th Highlanders were pushed forward on the Cawnpore road to the Residency, to cover the passage of the troops and baggage, etcetera; while the remainder turned short to the right, and began to thread the narrow lane leading towards the king's stables.

The 78th Highlanders held their position at the head of the street, as the baggage, the wounded, and the followers defiled over the bridge. As soon as the enemy perceived that it was an unsupported rearguard, it was assailed by overwhelming numbers, but continued firmly to hold its own. In this unequal struggle, which lasted nearly three hours, its ammunition was more than once exhausted and renewed.

On one occasion, the enemy becoming more bold, brought two brass 9-pounders to bear on the Highlanders; but they immediately left the shelter of the houses, captured the guns, hurled them into the canal, and then calmly resumed their defensive position. Repeatedly tried through this campaign, and always found worthy of its high reputation, never did the valour of this gallant regiment shine brighter than in this bloody conflict.

Among others, Lieutenant-Adjutant Herbert McPherson was conspicuous in the splendid charge on the two guns, while Assistant-Surgeon Valentine McMaster exhibited the most devoted gallantry in the way in which he risked his life for the purpose of binding up the wounds, and securing the retreat of the men under his charge disabled by the bullets of the enemy.

The main body, turning to the right, advanced to a point between the Motee Mahal and the old mess-house of the 32nd. It was between this spot and the Residency, a distance of three-quarters of a mile, that the strength of the enemy was concentrated; and here the fiercest conflict, after that of forcing the bridge, occurred. At length, however, the enemy were driven back by the heavy guns, and, after passing through a hot fire from the roofs of neighbouring houses, the force was halted under shelter of a wall of one of the palaces, to allow the long column, the progress of which had been impeded by the narrowness of the streets, to come up. The main body was now within 500 yards of the Residency, but surrounded with enemies. The generals, however, determined to push on. The Highlanders and a regiment of Sikhs were called to the front; Sir James Outram, though wounded, and General Havelock placed themselves at their head, and through an incessant storm of shot pushed on to the Residency.

> The loopholed houses on either side poured forth a stream of fire as they advanced: every roof sent down a shower of missiles on them. Deep trenches had been cut across the road to detain them under the fire of the adjacent buildings. At every angle they encountered a fearful volley; but, animated by the generals, officers and men pushed on, till at length the gate of the Residency was reached, and the hard-pressed garrison welcomed them with their hearty cheers. The remainder of the troops quickly followed, and entered the Residency. Numbers had fallen, and among them General Neill, who was with the 1st Madras Fusiliers, and soon after the shelter was quitted was shot dead, falling instantly

183

from his horse, and never speaking more. The united forces were, however, too weak to attempt to retreat. They were consequently again besieged in the Residency, though able to keep the foe at bay.

RELIEF OF LUCKNOW

At length, on the 10th of November, Sir Colin Campbell, with a thoroughly equipped force of 5000 men, arrived in the neighbourhood of the Alumbagh. It was important that the generals in the Residency should communicate with him, and Mr. Cavanagh, an officer of the Civil Service, volunteered to proceed to his camp with plans of the city, and suggestions as to the route he should take. Perilous as was the adventure, Mr. Cavanagh accomplished the undertaking. A semaphoric communication was soon afterwards established between the Alumbagh and the Residency. By its means Sir Colin was enabled, on the 12th, to announce his intention of advancing by the Dilkoosha at seven a.m. on the 14th. The garrison therefore prepared to co-operate with him.

At the time appointed, the advance began; but several large buildings, strongly fortified, had to be stormed,—the Dilkoosha, Martiniere, and finally the Secunderbagh, in which place upwards of 2,000 rebels were killed. These operations occupied till the afternoon of the 17th, when the mess-house was gallantly stormed by a company of the 90th, a picket of the 53rd, with some Punjaub infantry. Beyond this the enemy again made a desperate stand; but the advance was sounded—the troops pushed on—house after house was taken—nowhere could the rebels withstand them, and complete communication was established with the Residency.

It was now resolved to remove the non-combatants, the women, children, and sick and wounded, as well as the troops, from Lucknow. By masterly arrangements, the enemy were completely deceived. The women and children, the sick and wounded, were first withdrawn on the night of the 18th, many ladies walking a distance of six miles to the Dilkoosha encampment over rough ground, and at one spot exposed to the fire of the enemy,—Lady Inglis, the heroic wife of Brigadier Inglis, setting the example. When they were in safety, arrangements were made to withdraw the garrison.

On the 20th and 21st, Captain Peel, with the guns of his Naval Brigade, aided by Havelock's guns in the palaces, breached the Kaiserbagh. The enemy, believing that an assault would immediately follow, stood on the defensive. Orders were then given for the garrison to withdraw through the line of pickets at midnight on the 22nd. Brigadier Hope's brigade covered all their movements, and Brigadier Greathead's brigade closed in the rear, and formed the rearguard as the troops retired through a long narrow lane, the only road open for them towards the Dilkoosha. That position was reached by four o'clock in the afternoon of the 23rd of November, without the loss of a man. On the previous day, one of the gallant defenders of Lucknow, the good and brave Sir Henry Havelock, had breathed his last in the Dilkoosha, from dysentery, brought on by exposure and the unwholesome food on which he had been compelled to exist.

Of course all the property in the Residency, which had been so long bravely defended, had to be left at the mercy of the rebels; but that was a slight gain compared to the rage and vexation they must have experienced at finding themselves so completely out-manoeuvred, and that the foes they hoped to crush had escaped them.

SIEGE AND CAPTURE OF LUCKNOW
2ND AND 21ST MARCH

When Sir Colin Campbell retired with his rescued countrymen from Lucknow, on the 27th of November 1857, he left a force under Sir James Outram in the strong position of the Alumbagh, to keep the enemy in check in the city, thus locking up a large number, and preventing them from committing mischief throughout the country.

On the 12th and 16th of January, and at other subsequent times, the rebels endeavoured to dislodge Sir James Outram from his position, but were each time driven back with loss. Meanwhile, Sir Colin Campbell defeated the enemy on the 6th of December,—estimated at 25,000 men and 36 guns.

He remained at Cawnpore till the 4th of February, when the first portion of his army crossed the Ganges, on their road to Lucknow. While marching on Lucknow, Brigadier Franks, on the 19th, successively defeated two bodies of the enemy at Chanda and Amerapore; and, on the 23rd, gained a still more important victory over their united forces near Sultanpore. Sir Colin, with reinforcements and siege-train, arrived at the Alumbagh on the 1st of March, and no time was lost in carrying out the contemplated operations against Lucknow.

The Dilkoosha palace was first seized, when a gun was captured. This palace then formed the advanced post on the right, and the Mahomed Bagh on the left, heavy guns being placed in them, to keep down the fire of the enemy. Sir James Outram being withdrawn from the Alumbagh, crossed to the left bank of the Goomtee, and, on the 9th, drove the enemy before him at all points, till he was enabled to occupy the Tyzabad road, and to plant his batteries so as to enfilade the works on the canal. A two gun battery of the enemy had in the most gallant way been attacked by an officer with half his company, and the guns spiked, thus securing the most advanced position of the troops from artillery fire. It thus became very important that the skirmishers on the opposite side of the river should be made acquainted with this success. To carry the information, Lieutenant Thomas Adair Butter, 1st Bengal Fusiliers, plunging into the Goomtee, swam across it under a heavy fire, and, climbing the parapet, remained for some time still exposed to the shots of the enemy. He, however, happily escaped without a wound, and, leaping down, delivered his message. For this act of cool bravery, he was prominently mentioned by General Outram in general orders, and deservedly received the Victoria Cross.

On the afternoon of the same day, Brigadiers Sir Edward Lugard and Adrian Hope, with the 42nd, 53rd, and 90th Regiments, stormed and captured the Martiniere College. And now the operations against the Kaiserbagh could be carried out more effectually, and science and engineering skill were brought into play. Building after building was captured, and well secured, before the infantry were allowed to advance. A large block of palaces, known as the Begum Kotee, having been breached under the direction of Brigadier Napier, it was stormed on the morning of the 12th, with the greatest gallantry, by the 93rd Highlanders, supported by the 4th Punjaub Rifles and 1,000 Goorkhas, led by Brigadier Adrian Hope. This was looked upon as one of the severest struggles and most gallant actions during the siege.

Brigadier Napier now, by aid of sappers and heavy guns, pushed forward the approaches through the enclosures, the infantry immediately occupying the ground as he advanced, the guns and mortars being moved on as the positions were gained where they could be placed. Brigadier Franks, early on the morning of the 14th, carried the Imambarrah; and Major Brasyer, with a regiment of Sikhs, pressing forward in pursuit, entered the Kaiserbagh, and then the third line of the enemy's defences was won, and the spot where so many desperate encounters had taken place was once more occupied by the British. Moosabagh, the last position of the rebels on the Goomtee, was cannonaded and captured by Sir James Outram and Sir Hope Grant on the 19th; and, on the 21st, Sir Edward Lugard, after a fierce struggle, took the last stronghold in the possession of the rebels in the heart of the city.

Brigadier W. Campbell, at the head of the 2nd Dragoon Guards, followed the fugitives for the distance of six miles, killing vast numbers, and completely routing them. The inhabitants were now invited to return, and Lucknow was once more placed under British rule.

Gallant Deeds of the Mutiny

At no time in the history of the world has more calm courage, devotion, perseverance, and gallantry been shown than was exhibited by the soldiers of England during the Indian Mutiny. Many of their gallant deeds have already been recounted, but it is impossible to recount them all.

Not only soldiers, but non-combatants were conspicuous on many occasions for their gallantry. The surgeons especially exhibited the most heroic courage. The name of Surgeon Herbert Taylor Reade deserves to be mentioned. During the siege of Delhi, while he was attending to the wounded at the end of one of the streets, on the 14th of September, a party of rebels advanced from the direction of the Bank, and, having established themselves in the houses in the street, commenced firing from the roofs. The wounded were thus in very great danger, and would have fallen into the hands of the enemy, had not Surgeon Reade, drawing his sword, and calling upon about ten soldiers who were near him to follow, dashed bravely forward under a heavy fire, and, attacking the rebels, dislodged them from their position, and put them to flight. Two of his followers were killed, and five or six wounded, in this gallant act, for which he was deservedly decorated with the Victoria Cross. He also accompanied his regiment on the assault of Delhi, and, on the morning of the 16th September, was one of the first up at the breach of the magazine. On this occasion, he, with a sergeant of his regiment, spiked one of the enemy's guns.

Surgeon Joseph Jee, C.B., was another medical officer whose bravery was conspicuous. After that gallant charge made by the 78th Highlanders, when two guns were captured near the Char Bagh, as they, forming part of Sir

Henry Havelock's force, were entering Lucknow on the 25th September 1857, numbers were left wounded on the ground. He hastened among them, exposed to a severe fire and the risk of being cut off, and succeeded, by great exertions, in getting them removed in cots, or on the backs of their comrades, until he had collected the *dooly*-bearers, who had fled. He remained by the wounded till later in the day, when he endeavoured to convey them into the Residency, but was compelled to take refuge with his charge and their escort in the Motee Mahal, where they were besieged by an overwhelming force. Here, however, he remained during the whole night, voluntarily and repeatedly exposing himself to a heavy fire while he was engaged in dressing the wounds of the men who fell serving a 24-pounder in a most exposed situation. At length he set forward to accompany a number of the wounded into the Residency by the river bank, although warned of the danger of the undertaking. Seeing the importance, however, of placing them in safety, he persevered, and succeeded in accomplishing his object.

Surgeon Anthony D. Home, of the 90th, aided by Assistant-surgeon W. Bradshaw, on the same occasion, and under very similar circumstances, behaved in the same manner. When the relieving columns pushed their way forward towards the Residency, he was left behind in charge of the wounded. The escort had by casualties been greatly diminished, and, being entirely separated from the column, they were compelled to take refuge in a house on the approach of a large body of the enemy. Here they defended themselves till it was set on fire. Of four officers who were with the party, all were badly wounded—three of them mortally. The conduct of the defence therefore devolved on Mr. Home; and as it was by his active exertions, before being forced into the house, that the wounded were then saved, so now to his coolness and intrepidity the continued defence of the building was mainly due. Hour after hour passed by, one after the other dropping, till only he and six companions remained to fire. Still they persevered, though they had almost abandoned hope, and had resigned themselves to their fate. At length, a little after daybreak, they were aroused by distant firing. They did not, however, believe that it announced any help to them, but rather the return of more foes. Still it approached nearer and nearer, when a brave soldier of the 1st Madras Fusiliers, John Ryan, suddenly jumping up, shouted, "Oh, boys! them's our chaps!" The little band, leaping to their feet, united in a hearty cheer, crying out to their friends to keep on the right, while they fired into the loopholes from which the enemy were annoying them. In about three minutes, Captain Moorsom, who had led the party to their relief, appeared at the entrance-hole of the shed, and they beckoning to him, he entered.

It was by the admirable arrangements of this officer that the little band were brought safely off, and soon after reached the palace, with the rearguard of the 90th. On this occasion, Private McManus, 5th Regiment, kept outside the house, and continued behind a pillar, firing on the sepoys, to prevent their rushing into it, till he was himself wounded. He also, in conjunction with Private John Ryan, rushed into the street under a heavy fire, and took Captain Arnold, 1st Madras Fusiliers, out of a *dooly*, and brought him into the house, that officer being again hit while they were so doing.

Among the many gallant men we may mention Captain George Alexander Renny, and Gunner William Conolly, of the Bengal Horse Artillery. After the capture of the Delhi magazine, 16th September 1857, a vigorous attack was made on it by the enemy. Under cover of a heavy cross fire from the high houses on the right flank of the magazine, and from Selinghur and the palace, the enemy advanced to the high wall of the magazine, and endeavoured to set fire to a thatched roof. This was partially accomplished, but the fire was extinguished by a sepoy of the Beloochee battalion. However, the roof having been again set on fire, and the enemy pressing round, Captain

Renny, with great gallantry, mounted to the top of the wall of the magazine, and flung several shells with lighted fusees into the midst of the enemy. This had so considerable an effect, that the enemy almost immediately retreated.

The half troop to which Gunner Conolly belonged, under command of Lieutenant Cooks, having advanced at daybreak at a gallop, and engaged the enemy within easy musket range, the sponge-men of one of the guns having been shot, Conolly assumed the duties of second sponge-man; and he had barely assisted at two discharges of his gun, when a musket-ball through the left thigh felled him to the ground. Nothing daunted by pain and loss of blood, he was endeavouring to resume his post, when a movement in retirement was ordered. Mounting his horse, he rode to the next position the guns took up, and manfully declined going to the rear when the necessity of his doing so was represented to him. At about eleven a.m. he was again knocked down by a musket-ball striking him on the hip, causing him great pain and faintness. On hearing his commanding officer direct that he should be taken out of action, he staggered to his feet, exclaiming, "No, no; I'll not go there while I can work here."

Shortly afterwards he once more resumed his post. Later in the day the guns were engaged at 100 yards from the walls of a village, whence a storm of bullets was directed at them. Here, though suffering severely from his two previous wounds, he was wielding his guns with an energy and courage which attracted the admiration of his comrades; and while cheerfully encouraging a wounded man to hasten in bringing up the ammunition, he was a third time hit by a musket-ball, which tore through the muscles of his right leg. Even then, with the most undaunted bravery he struggled on, and not until he had loaded six times did he give way, and then only from loss of blood, when he fell fainting at his post into his commander's arms, and, being placed in a wagon, was borne in a state of unconsciousness from the fight.

Such are the materials of which are made the true British soldiers, the redcoats of Old England, who have nobly upheld her honour and glory in all parts of the world.

We do not pretend to give a catalogue of all the gallant deeds done during that sanguinary struggle worthy of being chronicled. Were we to attempt to give all, we should fail in so doing; and some, whose names were omitted, would complain that we treated their comrades with partiality. The numerous brave acts we have recorded are rather to show of what British soldiers of the present day are capable, and what is more, what sort of deeds are most highly appreciated, for on all, or nearly all, the men whose names we have mentioned, the Victoria Cross has been bestowed; and yet, probably, we have omitted half the recipients of that honour, not less deserving than those whose deeds we have recorded.

The Chinese War
1856–60

The Chinese War
1856-1860

The Chinese, in breach of the treaties into which they had entered in 1842, committed a series of aggressive acts against British subjects, the most memorable of which was the seizure of the crew of the *Arrow*, in 1856. War was consequently declared, and hostilities were commenced by our naval forces, which, under Sir Michael Seymour, after bombarding Canton in October, and destroying several war-junks on the 5th, captured the Bogue Forts, mounting more than 400 guns, on the 12th and 13th of November, and again attacked the suburbs of Canton on the 12th of January 1857. The fleet also destroyed a large number of Chinese war-junks in the Canton waters; but further operations on land were suspended till the Indian Mutiny had been quelled, and Lord Elgin had returned to China.

The British and French troops having united towards the end of December 1857, the city of Canton was summoned to surrender. On the refusal of the Chinese authorities to do so, a bombardment was commenced by the fleet on the 28th, and the British and French troops landed at Kupar Creek, to the south-east of the town. The English troops were divided into two brigades: the first, consisting of the first and second battalions of Royal Marine Light Infantry, was commanded by Colonel Holloway, of that corps; while the second, which was composed of the Royal Engineers and a volunteer company of Sappers, Royal Artillery, and Royal Marine Artillery, Provisional Battalion Royal Marines, the 59th Regiment, and

38th Madras Native Infantry, was under Colonel Hope Graham, of the 59th. Colonel Dunlop commanded the artillery. The troops amounted to 2900 men. Then there was the British Naval Brigade, consisting of 1829 men, and the French Naval Brigade, of 950.

The first attack was made on East or Linn Fort. The Chinese received their assailants with a hot fire, but were soon driven out, retreating to Cough's Fort. The ships kept up a continued cannonade during the day and the following night, and on the 29th it was determined to make a grand attack by escalade on the east wall of the city. The advance was led by the brave Major Luard, the 59th, under Major Burmister, covering the French Naval Brigade and Royal Marines. At an appointed time the ships were to cease firing, and the assault was to be made. The Chinese, meantime, were keeping up a hot fire on their approaching assailants from their walls. It was necessary to ascertain the best spot for placing the scaling-ladders. Captain Bate volunteered to go, and Captain Naun, of the Engineers, accompanied him. Captain Bate had run across an open space, and was looking down into the ditch, when a shot struck him. He fell. Dr. Anderson rushed out through a hot fire, accompanied by Captain Bate's coxswain, to his assistance, but he never spoke again. They escaped uninjured.

> Some minutes before the time, the French advanced, and the English could not be kept back. They had crossed the ditch, and were clustered under the walls before the scaling-ladders could be brought up. A young Frenchman had taken off his shoes and gaiters, and was trying to work himself up to the southern angle of the bastion, aided by Major Luard, who was propping him up with the muzzle of the Frenchman's own firelock, when a ladder was placed, and Luard, leaping on it, stood first upon the wall. He was followed by a Frenchman, the bandmaster of the 59th, and Colonel Hope Graham. At

the same time, Stuart, of the Engineers, was balancing in air on a breaking ladder at the north side of the bastion; but though he sprang to another, two or three Frenchmen got up before him. Here, also, Corporal Perkins and Daniel Donovan, volunteer sappers, pushing on with the French, were among the first over the wall. Meantime the Chinese had been tumbling down all sorts of missiles; but when the Allies were once upon the walls, the great body of them retired. They poured down into the city, and fired from the streets; they dodged behind the buildings on the ramparts, and thence took aim with their cumbrous matchlocks. A few single encounters occurred, and Major Luard's revolver disposed of one lingerer; but the Allies generally fired right and left, and pushed on to the right, so as to sweep the wall upwards towards the hill. Helter-skelter they went, driving the Tartars close into the town and before them along the wall, until, some hundred yards in front, they came upon Captain Fellowes and his bluejackets, who were just accomplishing another escalade. Commodore Elliot was well in front, and the admiral and general were not far behind.

The enemy were now driven entirely along the wall, and complete possession was taken of the eastern gate. Some casualties had occurred. Lieutenants Shinkwin and Ensign Bower, of the 59th, were both wounded, the latter mortally. The chiefs of the expedition, however, anxious to prevent the destruction of life, would not allow the troops to descend into the streets, though they had in reality entire command over the city. A whole week was allowed the Chinese authorities to consider the matter, and to sue for peace; but, as they continued obstinate, on the 5th of January the allied forces were poured down into the streets, when Commissioner Yeh, the Tartar General, and the Governor of Canton were speedily captured, very much to their own astonishment, and very little to the regret of the people over whom they ruled.

On the 20th of May, the forts at the mouth of the Peiho were taken, and then at length the Chinese commissioners, discovering that the Allies were in earnest, sued for peace. A treaty was signed at Tientsin on the 20th of June, when all the terms demanded by the Allies were agreed to, though the Chinese authorities had no intention, probably, of adhering to any of them.

Capture of the Taku Forts
21st August 1860

The Chinese Government having refused to ratify the treaty of Tientsin, the British and French forces once more prepared for active operations. Major-General Sir Hope Grant had been appointed to the command of the British troops, with the local rank of lieutenant-general,—Major-General Sir Robert Napier holding command of the second division under him. The expedition started from Hong Kong harbour early in June, and assembled at Talien Bay, ready for a descent on the Peiho.

On the 1st of August, the expedition, organised with great forethought, and in the most admirable manner, commenced disembarking at the mouth of the Peiho River. The village of Pehtang was immediately taken possession of.

The first engagement took place at Sinho, when the Tartar cavalry showed some courage, but were soon put to the rout—the Armstrong guns being here for the first time employed; the second division, under Sir Robert Napier, taking the principal part in the action. Soon after daybreak on the 13th, the first division received notice that they were to storm the fortified village of Tangkoo. A causeway ran from Sinoo to Tangkoo, with a marsh on one side, and a moist plain, intersected by ditches, on the other, which ditches had now been bridged over.

The fortifications of Tangkoo consisted of a long semi-circular crenelated wall, three miles in length, terminating at both ends on the banks of the river. The attack was made from the right of the causeway,—the English on the right near the river, the French along the road. Two hundred Rifles, commanded by Major Rigaud, advanced in skirmishing order, to support the batteries of Armstrong guns and some 9-pounders. The Royals and 31st followed, and then the Queen's 60th Rifles and 15th Punjaubees. Some Chinese batteries and junks were silenced; and then Sir John Michel ordered up the infantry, who rushed into the fortress, and bowled over the Tartars, as they scampered with precipitancy from the wall across the open into the village, while rockets, whizzing through the air over their heads in graceful curve, spread dismay among their masses, and hastened their speed.

The Taku forts were next to be taken. On the 20th, they were summoned to surrender; and the officer in command having refused to do so, preparations were made to storm them on the morning of the 21st. The French force consisted of about 1000 infantry, and six 12-pounder rifled cannon. The English mustered 2500 men, consisting of a wing of the 44th, under Lieutenant-Colonel McMahon; a wing of the 67th, under Lieutenant-Colonel Thomas, supported by the other wings of those two regiments; the Royal Marines, under Lieutenant-Colonel Gascoigne; a detachment of the same corps under Lieutenant-Colonel Travers, carrying a pontoon-bridge for crossing the wet ditches; and Ensign Graham, with his company of Royal Engineers, to conduct the assault. The whole were commanded by Brigadier Reeves.

Several gunboats had also come up the river to bombard the forts. At daylight the Chinese opened fire on their assailants, which was replied to by the gunboats and Armstrong guns; and soon a large magazine blew up with a terrific roar, the explosion shaking the ground for miles round. Soon after, another magazine in the lower north fort blew up. Still the Tartar troops defended themselves with the greatest bravery. The field-guns were advanced to within 500 yards of the forts, and redoubled their efforts. The fire of the forts having ceased, a breach was commenced near the gate, and a portion of the storming party were advanced to within thirty yards, to open a musketry fire. No sooner had the artillery fire slackened, than the enemy emerged from their cover, and opened a heavy fire of musketry on the Allies.

No less than fifteen men of the sappers carrying the pontoon-bridge were struck down, and the French who had pushed on were unable to escalade the walls.

While the fire was hottest, an hospital apprentice, Arthur Fitzgibbon,* who had accompanied a wing of the 67th, quitted cover, and proceeded, in spite of the shot rattling round him, to attend to a *dooly*-bearer whose wounds he had been directed to bind up; and while the regiment was advancing under the enemy's fire, he ran across the open to attend to another wounded man, when he was himself severely wounded.

At this juncture Sir R. Napier caused the two howitzers of Captain Govan's battery to be brought up to within fifty yards of the gate, in order more speedily to create a breach, when the storming party was joined by the headquarters wing of the 67th, under Colonel Knox, who had partly crossed by the French bridge, and partly swam over. A space having been made sufficient to admit one man, the brave band forced their way in by single file in the most gallant manner, Lieutenant Rogers, 44th Regiment, and (All marked thus were awarded the Victoria Cross) Lieutenant Burslem, 67th Regiment, being the first to enter, when they assisted Ensign Chaplain, who carried the regimental colours, to enter; and he, supported by Private Lane, 67th Regiment, was the first to plant them on the breach, and subsequently on the cavalier, which he was the first to mount. Accompanying Lieutenant Rogers was Private John McDougall, 67th Regiment, and Lieutenant E.H. Lewis, who gallantly swam the ditches, and were the first established on the walls, each assisting the others to mount the embrasures. Lieutenant Burslem and Private Lane more especially distinguished themselves in enlarging the opening in the wall, through which they eventually entered, and were severely wounded in so doing. At the same moment the French effected their entrance, and the garrison was driven back step by step, and hurled pell-mell through the embrasures on the opposite side, when a destructive fire was opened on them by Captain Govan's guns, which strewed the ground outside with dead and wounded. Preparations were then made to attack the lower fort, but the garrison of 2000 men and upwards yielded without firing a gun. Of the British, 17 men were killed, and 22 officers and 161 men wounded. The French had 130 casualties; several of their officers were killed. Fully 2000 Tartars must have been killed and wounded.

The Allies entered Tientsin on the 6th September, when every effort was made by the Chinese authorities to gain time by negotiations.

On the arrival of the Allies on the ground intended for the camp, it was found occupied by a large Chinese army, who had hastily thrown up batteries for their defence. Colonel Walker, with Commissary Thompson and a few orderlies, had ridden on at an early hour, to arrange about the camping-ground for the army. Mr. Parkes, Lieutenant Anderson, Mr. De Norman, and Mr. Bowlby went forward to ascertain the reason of the threatening attitude of the Chinese, not in any way apprehending danger. Captain Brabazon and Mr. Lock followed with a flag of truce, to order them to return.

On their return, the whole party, with several French officers and men, were surrounded by the Chinese. Some were cut down, and others were made prisoners; but Colonel Walker, suspecting what was about to occur, called out to those of his companions near him to charge for their lives through the midst of the enemy. At the word of command, they bent down to their horses' necks, and spurred their chargers through the Tartar ranks, which gave way before them; and though a fire was opened on them, one dragoon only was wounded. The action instantly commenced; but after lasting two hours, the enemy, unable to withstand the fierce charges of the cavalry and the hot fire of the Armstrong guns, gave way in all directions, being dreadfully cut up by the Dragoon Guards and Fane's and Probyn's Horse.

On the 21st, the Allies, being strengthened by the arrival of 1000 French troops, again advanced to meet the enemy. General Michel's division was on the left, and the cavalry brigade and the marines, and the 2nd Queen's taking the extreme left. While Sir Hope Grant was riding towards the French, to confer with General Montauban, a furious charge was made towards him and his staff by a large body of Tartar cavalry. The General and his followers, at once galloping to the right and left, disclosed the Armstrong guns, which had just before been ordered to move their position. They were, however, under the command of Lieutenant Rochfort, who, as he was about to obey the order, saw the threatening movement of the enemy. He therefore held his ground, and when the General and his staff rode aside, he was ready for action. At first the range was incorrect.

With perfect coolness he altered the elevation, and, as the Tartars came on, yelling furiously, opened a fire which, aided by the rifles of the 2nd Queen's, emptied many a saddle, and sent the enemy speedily to the right-about, with yells of terror and despair. Another body of Tartar cavalry were posted on an eminence which had a sudden fall at the foot of it, with a deep ditch in front. It was evident that they thought the cavalry could not pass this ditch, and that they might easily pick them off with their matchlocks.

The 1st Dragoon Guards, however, rode at it, and cleared the ditch, one or two men only getting out of the ranks. The dragoons then made a furious charge, and soon put the Tartars to flight. Finally, the Chinese entrenched camp was taken, and their army was driven back towards Pekin, completely broken and disorganised. During these operations, nearly 600 guns were captured by the Allies. The army now advanced towards Pekin; and on the 7th of October the Emperor was informed that unless the prisoners were restored, and one of the gates of the Imperial city was placed in the hands of the Allies, Pekin would be stormed.

These terms were agreed to. On the 13th of October, at noon, possession was taken of the gate by a small body of English and French; the money demanded was paid, and the surviving prisoners were delivered up; others had died under the barbarous treatment received by them.

The New Zealand War
1863–65

The New Zealand War
1863–1865

ENSIGN MCKENNA
AN EXAMPLE OF COOL COURAGE
AND DEVOTION

We do not like to hear of war in New Zealand. Long ago the native inhabitants of these magnificent islands desired to become subjects of Queen Victoria. Their offers were accepted, and New Zealand became a British colony.

Differences, however, arose between the settlers and the natives, chiefly about land; and from time to time the latter have attempted to assert their rights in a thoroughly barbarous fashion, by murdering all the white settlers they could fall on unprepared. It is difficult to say by whom they were instigated to revolt. The possession of certain lands claimed by settlers was the ostensible cause of each outbreak; and the natives invariably commenced hostilities, by murdering some settlers whom they attacked unawares. Such was the commencement of the last New Zealand War. One of their chiefs had been proclaimed king by the rebel tribes, who had declared their intention of driving the British from the northern island. Although the natives may be pitied for their ignorance, it was necessary immediately to put down such pretensions by force. Preparations were therefore made for attacking the enemy in their strongholds—a nature of warfare arduous and hazardous in the extreme, and requiring great judgment and discretion not only in the leaders, but in the non-commissioned officers and privates. Where British soldiers have an opportunity of exhibiting these qualities, they are generally found in their possession.

The 65th Regiment of Foot was stationed at Auckland at the commencement of the war in July 1863, and were about to return to England, when they were ordered to the front in search of the enemy. For two months a detachment under the command of Captain Swift was posted at Fort Alexandra, in the neighbourhood of Cameron Town, where Mr. Armitage, a magistrate, had his residence.

On the 7th of September, news was brought to the fort that Mr. Armitage, a few white men, and a large number of friendly natives residing near him, had been massacred by the enemy.

Captain Swift, on hearing this, immediately set out, with Lieutenant Butler, Sergeant McKenna, two other sergeants, a bugler, and a party of fifty men, into the bush in pursuit of the foe. Swamps were crossed, rivers forded, hills climbed, and dense woods penetrated, and other difficulties over-come, till towards the evening the gallant little band found themselves in an open space near the place where they expected to fall in with the enemy. A party of ten were sent in advance to feel the way.

The advance guard, however, lost the path, thus greatly reducing the main body. Again they advanced, when, having reached another opening in which the savages had been encamped, they once more halted. Hearing the sounds of the enemy's voices, they were advancing to chase them, when they found themselves exposed to a terrific fire from out of the bush on either side. Captain Swift was the first to fall; and directly afterwards Lieutenant Butler, while bravely animating his men, and having shot three of the enemy, received his death-wound. The command now devolved on Sergeant McKenna, who, leaving Corporal Ryan and two men with the wounded officers, with the rest of the force charged the enemy in the most spirited manner, and put them to flight. A fresh position was again taken up in an opening, on the left and front of which the Maories had collected. The sergeant, ordering his men to extend in skirmishing order across the opening, kept up a hot fire for a considerable time with the savages, bringing down some who had climbed up into trees for the purpose of taking more certain aim.

Any wavering or disorder on the part of the soldiers would have caused their immediate destruction. Their steady coolness alone seemed to overawe the natives, who, after losing several of their number, retired to a greater distance. They still, however, kept up a fire at the little body of British, by which another man was killed. Night was drawing on. McKenna saw that the time for retreating had arrived. He took his measures with admirable coolness and presence of mind. He ordered the front rank of skirmishers to fire a volley, and, giving a loud cheer as if about to charge, to retire down the hill by a sheltered path through the bush. The movement was executed with the utmost steadiness. When they were established below, the rear rank performed the same manoeuvre, and, finding a stream of clear water, were able to refresh themselves. They were not to retire unmolested. They were again attacked by the Maories, numbering, it was ascertained, nearly 300 men, who were, however, successfully driven back; and at eight o'clock the party commenced their arduous retreat through the bush, many of them severely wounded. It would be impossible to describe fully the difficulties of that midnight march through the tangled bush, with bloodthirsty foes swarming on every side. The judgment and coolness of the non-commissioned officers in charge of the party cannot be praised too highly. It was not till eight o'clock in the morning that they came in sight of the redoubt, and met a body of 100 men marching to their relief.

They then learned that Corporal Ryan and Privates Bulford and Talbot had, in the most devoted manner, remained with Captain Swift, after carrying him for some distance, till he died, and that the savages had at one time actually surrounded them, while they lay hid among the brushwood. Not till he had breathed his last, and they had covered up his body with branches, did they think of seeking their own safety by making their way towards the redoubt.

In the same truly devoted manner Privates Thomas and Cole had remained all the night with Lieutenant Butler. The dying officer complained bitterly of the cold, and not only did the two brave fellows cover him up with their own greatcoats, but one of them, Thomas, took off his own serge shirt and put it on him. They knew full well that their suffering superior would not live to report their conduct, or to reward them, and that very probably they would themselves be slaughtered by the savages. In the above narrative, we find an exhibition of courage, judgment, discipline, coolness, devotion, and affection rarely surpassed. Sergeant McKenna obtained the Victoria Cross and his commission.

Incidents of a skirmish in New Zealand, in the war of 1865, Lieutenant-colonel Havelock commanding.

GALLANTRY OF CAPTAIN HEAPHY, A.R.V

That British militia and volunteers, when opportunity offers, possess no lack of gallantry, they have often given proof, especially in the Cape Colony and New Zealand.

In the last war in New Zealand, Colonel Waddy, C.B., was in command of the advance force of the British, composed of regulars, militia, and volunteers, at Paterangi near a native *pah* or fort.

Under him was serving Lieutenant-Colonel Havelock.

To the right, facing the *pah*, at some distance from the camp, the river Mangapiko forms a complete bow or loop. At the narrow end or knot there is an old native *pah*, with the river flowing on either side of it. Inside the loop at the broad end is a thick scrub, and here 100 Maories from the Paterangi *pah* had formed an ambush.

A number of soldiers from the camp, unsuspicious of danger, had gone to the river to bathe directly opposite this scrub, there being a ford at the spot across the river.

Immediately the natives began to fire on the bathers, the inlying pickets of the 40th and 50th Regiments turned out, a party under Major Bowdler going to the right to attack the natives retreating up that part of the river, while Lieutenant-Colonel Havelock, with the men he could collect, accompanied by Captain Fisher, Captain Heaphy, and Captain Jackson, marched rapidly on the left a considerable distance towards the old *pah*, to cut off the retreat of the natives who had formed the ambush, or to intercept any others who might come from Paterangi to their relief. At the narrow end of the loop there was a deep gully, with an old canoe thrown over it as a bridge.

While Major Bowdler's party were attacking the natives who had taken post in the old *pah* on one side, Captain Fisher led a few men across the bridge on the opposite side, followed by Captain Heaphy, who had collected some men of the 40th and 50th Regiments. Large numbers of natives now came rushing up from Paterangi *pah*, and the fight became general over a wide extent of woody ground, the English soldiers often dashing forward incautiously at the enemy, and suffering considerably; Captain Fisher re-crossing the bridge to repel the Maori reinforcements. Colonel Havelock, who had no arms, and Captain Heaphy were left with a few men in the midst of the enemy. Captain Heaphy now shot a Maori, and, having secured his gun and pouch, gave Colonel Havelock his own breechloader and a few cartridges, continuing the fight himself with the Maori gun and ammunition. Captain Jackson, when wading the river, shot a Maori who had snapped both barrels at him, and then, hauling the man to the bank, secured his gun and pouch.

Meantime, Captain Fisher being hotly engaged and somewhat pressed by a large body of natives coming from Paterangi, Captain Heaphy collected a party of stragglers under fire, told them off into front and rear ranks, and, placing them under cover, directed their fire on the above-mentioned natives, who, receiving thus a cross fire, made no further headway.

A series of hand-to-hand encounters took place during the fight about the old tree-covered *pah*, between the Maories, crouching in the thick bush, and the British, who showed a keen eagerness to dart at and close with their lurking enemies. A private, Cassan of the 50th, having been desperately wounded, fell into one of the deep overgrown ditches near the *pah*, within reach of many Maories concealed there. Captain Heaphy, on hearing of this, called for volunteers and hastened down for the purpose of bringing off the wounded soldier, though exposed to a hot fire from the enemy directly above him. Two of his followers were shot dead, while five balls pierced his cap and clothes, and he was wounded in three places, providentially but slightly. He remained by the man, to defend him from the enemy, till Assistant-Surgeon Stiles of the 40th Regiment joined him, when the poor fellow was brought off, though he died directly after. Dr. Stiles greatly exposed himself, and took great pains to get the wounded removed to the camp.

When wounded, Captain Heaphy was urged by Colonel Havelock to go back to camp, but he remained in the skirmish to the end, after aiding Dr. Stiles in attending to other wounded. When the troops withdrew to camp after dark, while ten files of Major Von Tempsky's Rangers were covering the rear of the stretcher parties, he remained with them, only crossing the river with the last men. At the very moment of fording the stream, a ball, passing between him and Colonel Havelock, struck a man of the 40th farther in advance through the wrist, thus proving that the gallant Heaphy was under fire to the very end of the fight. Few will dispute that this brave officer of the Auckland Volunteer Rifles, in addition to the majority he forthwith obtained, deserved as much as any man the honour of the Victoria Cross.

The Abyssinian
Expedition
1867-68

The Abyssinian Expedition
1867-1868

A glance at the map of Africa shows us Abyssinia situated at the south of Egypt, beyond Nubia, with the Red Sea on the east, and a wild and little-known country of arid and sandy desert on the west, and a still more mountainous and barbarous country to the south. It has therefore long been considered a region inaccessible to an invading army. On the north, the unhealthy plains and valleys of Nubia render its approach dangerous and difficult, while a range of lofty mountains, rugged and precipitous, and deep valleys run almost parallel with the sea, having at their base a dry and sandy region, destitute of water, and productive of fever and agues. The centre of the country consists of lofty plateaus and rugged mountains, with deep valleys, lakes, and streams. The higher regions are healthy and fertile, but in the valleys, at certain seasons, pestilence destroys numbers who are subjected to its influence.

Dark-skinned people, though of different tribes, inhabit this region. A portion of the population who formerly dwelt in the eastern part of the country are Jews. The ruling race are the Amharas, who are a warlike and intelligent people, but of cruel and bloodthirsty disposition. They are Christians, having been converted about the fourth century, but their Christianity has been greatly corrupted. The country has for centuries remained in a state of chronic disorder, the chiefs rebelling against the sovereign, and being in a constant state of warfare amongst themselves. Notwithstanding, therefore, its many natural advantages, it has made no progress in civilisation or prosperity, and the great mass of the people are ignorant and barbarous in the extreme. The chiefs, too, are often cruel, bloodthirsty, turbulent, and grasping. Though their complexion is dark, their features are regular and handsome. They wear their hair plaited and wound round their head, covered thickly with butter. Their costume consists of drawers, a cotton shirt, with a white cotton-cloth cloak, called a *shama*, having a broad scarlet border, and, in addition, a lion-skin tippet with long tails. On their right side hangs a curved sword in a red leather scabbard, and a richly ornamented hilt, while a hide shield, ornamented with gold filigree bosses, and with silver plates, is worn on the left arm, and a long spear is grasped in the right hand. The most invincible enemies of the Amharas have been the heathen tribes of the Gallas, inhabiting the regions to the south of Abyssinia. At the end of last century, however, one of their chiefs, Rass Guka, obtained possession of the person of the then puppet emperor, and assumed supreme power. He outwardly conformed to the Christian religion, many of his people following his example.

When in 1838 the Egyptian troops of Mahomed Ali attempted to invade Abyssinia, they were defeated by Dejatch Confu, chief of Kuara, who had a nephew, Kasa by name. Kasa was deprived of his father at an early age, and his mother was reduced to a state of poverty, and compelled, it was said, to follow the humble calling of a *kosso* seller. He was sent to a convent to be brought up as a priest or scribe, but the convent being attacked by a robber chief, who put most of the inmates to the sword, Kasa escaped to the castle of his powerful uncle. Here, listening to the conversation of various chiefs, he imbibed an enthusiastic love of war and daring exploits.

On the death of his uncle, his cousins quarrelled. He sided with the eldest, was defeated, and became a robber chief. At length he unfurled the standard of rebellion, under the pretence of checking oppression and restraining violence. The queen of the usurping semi-Christian Galla race, of whom we have just spoken, long hated in the land, sent an army against him. Her troops were, however, speedily defeated. Finding that force would not prevail against him, the wily sovereign hoped to entrap him by guile, and offered him her granddaughter in marriage, having instructed the young lady how to betray him. The princess, however, admiring his character, became a most faithful wife, warning him of all the plots contrived for his destruction. At length the treacherous queen and her son, Kasa's father-in-law, were defeated in a pitched battle, and fled from the country. Kasa had still several chiefs and provinces to conquer.

The most important province was that of Tigre, governed by a warrior, Dejatch Oulie, whose army awaited him drawn up on the heights of Gemien. On the 3rd of February 1856 was fought one of the most desperate battles in the annals of Abyssinian warfare. It resulted in favour of Kasa, who was crowned under the name of King Theodorus. Many a battle had still to be fought; and King Theodore, as we will call him, lost not a moment in endeavouring to quell rebellion. He now became sovereign of Tigre and Amhara, the principal provinces of Abyssinia. Not content, however, with the power he had gained, his great ambition was to conquer the Galla tribes, whom he treated with the greatest cruelty.

Having reduced many of them to a temporary submission, he marched towards Tigre, where a rebellion had broken out. Here also he was victorious, but he treated those he had conquered in so barbarous a way, that he made enemies of the chiefs in all directions. It was about this time that a number of missionaries were sent into the country, for the purpose of preaching the gospel to the Jewish Falashas, at the instigation of Bishop Gobat, of Jerusalem. The principal one was the Reverend Mr. Stern, an English clergyman, who was accompanied by several German missionaries and their wives. In the camp of the king there were also a number of artisans of various nations, some of whom were engaged by the king to manufacture cannon and muskets. Mr. Stern, on returning to England, wrote an interesting volume, in which he made

217

some disparaging remarks on King Theodore. The book unfortunately found its way into the country, and these remarks were translated to the king. He had previously written a letter to the Queen of England, which for a long time remained unanswered. This and other circumstances greatly excited his anger; at the same time, he suspected that the English were disposed to assist the Egyptians, who he thought purposed invading his country.

The English Government, desirous of cultivating friendly relations with Abyssinia, had appointed Captain Cameron as consul to that country. He was stationed at Massowa, on the shores of the Red Sea. During an expedition into the interior, he was seized by Theodore, in revenge for the insult he considered he had received, the king having also thrown Mr. Stern and some of the other missionaries into prison.

At length Mr. Rassam was sent as ambassador to King Theodore, in hopes of obtaining the release of the prisoners. He was accompanied by Lieutenant Prideaux and Dr. Blanc. At the very moment that it appeared the king was about to release the prisoners, Mr. Rassam and his companions were themselves seized and treated with the greatest indignity. In vain every attempt was made by the English Government to obtain their release. Theodore would listen to no expostulations, and at length it was resolved to send an English army to compel him to deliver them up, although the difficulties of the undertaking were well-known.

Never was an expedition undertaken for a more generous object or with purer motives. It was simply for the release of the captives. The thought of conquest or the acquisition of territory did not for a moment enter into the views of the British Cabinet. The work to be done was to march an army of some thousand men a distance of 400 miles across a mountainous and little-known region, inhabited by tribes who might prove hostile, to the fortress in which the king had confined certain British subjects, and to compel him to release them. The persons, both military and civil, who were believed to be the best able to carry it out, were selected without favouritism or party consideration of any sort. Colonel Merewether, an officer of known talent, was appointed to make the preliminary preparations, and to select the spot best suited for the base of operations.

The reconnoitring party selected a place called Mulkutto, in Annesley Bay, on the shores of the Red Sea, for that object. In the previous month, Sir Robert Napier, then Commander-in-Chief of the Bombay Army, was appointed to command the Abyssinian expedition, and Major-General Sir Charles Staveley was nominated as second in command, with a force under them of 4000 British and 8000 native troops. The reconnoitring party consisted of the 10th Regiment of Bombay Native Infantry, the 3rd Regiment of Bombay Cavalry, a mountain train of four guns, with native gunners, and two companies of Bombay Sappers. Associated with Colonel Merewether were Colonel Phayre, Quartermaster-General of the Bombay Army, and Colonel Wilkins, of the Royal Engineers.

The first work of importance was the construction of a landing-pier, the beach being too gradually shelving to allow of landing without it. In a short time a pier was run out for 300 yards, where there was a depth of five feet at low-water spring tides, and a tramway was laid down from its head to some way up the beach, for bringing up stores. Wells were also dug, and the surrounding country carefully examined for water. Exploring expeditions were also made for a considerable distance, under a blazing tropical sun overhead, through a wild and unknown region.

On the 21st of October, the advance brigade arrived, under command of Colonel Field. H.M.S. *Satellite* also reached the bay, with apparatus for condensing sea-water, and she and other, steamers were able in a short time to produce 32,000 gallons a day, which was conveyed on shore by pipes raised on trestles above the sea. Officers also were sent in all directions to purchase mules and other beasts of burden for the transport service. A friendly understanding was soon established with the Shoho tribes, who gladly undertook to furnish guides and to convey stores into the interior. Friendly relations were also established with several powerful chiefs then in rebellion against Theodore, and who gladly offered all the assistance in their power.

Sir Charles Staveley now arrived with a brigade which had been embarked at Scinde, under Brigadier-General Collins, consisting of the 33rd Regiment, the G 14 Armstrong battery of six 12-pounder guns, under Captain Murray, the Beloochee regiments, and 3rd Scinde Horse. On the 3rd of January 1868, Lieutenant-General Sir Robert Napier, Commander-in-Chief of the expedition, arrived on board H.M.S. *Octavia*. He expressed his satisfaction at the progress made by the expedition, which had now obtained a firm footing on the highlands of Abyssinia.

A convenient port had been established on the desert shore; a road for cart traffic had been formed through a difficult mountain pass; the most determined robbers, the Shohos, had been turned into useful assistants; and an advance force had already gained the Abyssinian plateau, and friendly relations had been secured with the principal chiefs ruling over the territories up to Magdala itself. It must be understood that some time before this the British and other prisoners had been sent by Theodore to the fortress of Magdala, to reach which was therefore the main object of the expedition. Two plans were now open to Sir Robert Napier for the conduct of the campaign: one was, relying on the friendliness of the people for keeping communications open with his base, to push forward and attack Theodore on his flank march before he could reach Magdala, and thus prevent the prisoners again falling into his power.

Sir Robert, however, considered that in order to make any real and permanent advance, he must be entirely independent of the resources of the country, and that he should not have a force of much less than 10,000 men, with six months' supplies stored at Senafe; that Theodore might at any time abandon his guns should he hear of his approach, and push forward to

Magdala, which he could quickly reach without them. It was believed, however, that this he would never attempt doing, as it was the prestige of those guns which served as his only protection from being attacked and overwhelmed by the numerous rebel forces surrounding him. This latter plan, however, was not adhered to. Great efforts were made to improve the transport train. Owing to the want of care and barbarity of the natives who had been brought from India, a large number of the mules and camels died, but fresh supplies continued to arrive, and the whole organisation of the transport train was entrusted to Major Warden, who served in the same department in the Crimea. By the time the campaign was over, there was a corps of 12,000 muleteers, 400 native and 160 European inspectors, and 80 commissioned officers.

The most difficult piece of work to be accomplished was the conveyance of the artillery, next to the transport organisation. The guns and equipments were brought from England by Lieutenants Nolan and Chapman, who had prepared everything at Mulkutto for two batteries, A and B 21, the officers and men of which came from India. The guns were conveyed athwart-ships on mules, and they, with the ammunition and equipments for the two batteries, required go mules for their carriage. This may give some idea of the number of animals required for the work. A Naval Brigade, consisting of 80 men, with two rocket tubes, commanded by Captain Fellowes of the *Dryad*, was also organised.

The advance force halted in a beautiful district near Adigerat, upwards of 8500 feet above the sea. From this they pushed on to Antalo, where they halted for nearly a month, in consequence of having to wait for a supply of dollars, without which no purchases could be made. At length, on the 12th of March, the march to Magdala really commenced.

Colonel Phayre led the advance force, accompanied by a pioneer force consisting of two companies of the 33rd, two of native sappers, one of Punjaub Pioneers, and 80 sabres of native cavalry; the whole commanded by Captain Field, of the 10th Native Infantry. The rest of the force was divided into two brigades, under Sir Charles Staveley. With the first brigade marched the Commander-in-Chief and headquarters. It consisted of the 33rd Regiment, two companies of Beloochees, the head-quarter wing of the 10th Bombay Native Infantry, the 10th company of Royal Engineers, a battery of mountain guns, and the Scinde Horse.

The second brigade was composed of the 4th Regiment, a wing of the Beloochees, a company of sappers, Punjaub Pioneers, Naval Brigade, and Armstrong guns, and two mortars with elephants, the B battery of mountain guns, and the 3rd Bombay Cavalry. Sir Charles Staveley and his staff marched with this brigade. The road before them was rough and mountainous in the extreme, with difficult passes, mountain torrents to be crossed, and often lofty overhanging rocks above their heads.

Frequently, before the first brigade could advance, the roads had to be made practicable for mules and carts. The 33rd Regiment distinguished itself by the persevering way in which the men laboured, often going out as grass-cutters, laying out the camp, and working hard at road-making, along the whole line. All superfluous baggage had been sent to the rear.

The camp equipage now consisted of small bell-tents only, without tables, chairs, bedsteads, luggage, or any of the usual comforts of camp life. The rations were of the roughest and most unvarying description; seldom anything but tough beef and *chowpatties* were eaten, the Commander-in-Chief enjoying no greater luxuries than the private soldier.

During the halts the men were employed on the roads, and often even on marching days. For 17 days the force pushed on from the Buya camp, near Antalo, to the Wadela plateau, a distance of 118 miles, during which they crossed no less than six formidable ranges of mountains. Perhaps the severest march of the campaign was one performed on the 24th of March, from Marawa to Dildi, on the banks of the Tellare, a distance of 16 miles, up and down the steep spurs of the Lasta mountains. Starting soon after eight in the morning, with a long train of mules, they had to scramble up and down the rugged, tree-covered mountain-sides, the 33rd Regiment carrying, in addition to their arms, a heavy weight of blankets and water-proofs. Towards the end of it rain came on, and during some hours of the night the men came straggling in, footsore, hungry, and wet, and complaining not a little of their hardships.

The cold, too, was severe on that high ground after sunset. All luxuries about this time also began to fall short. No spirits remained, and but a small quantity of tea and compressed vegetables. Magdala was almost reached. The country now appeared open and covered with grass; long stages of grassy hill and dale, with occasional rocky ridges, and here and there among the hills a lovely lake, with streams and narrow valleys, formed the general aspect of the country. Round Magdala, situated itself on a high rock, rose numerous peaks and saddles above the large plateau on which it stands. They form a curve, Magdala being at the east end, and a peak called Sallasye at its base, and a smaller plateau called Fala at the south-west end. Sallasye and Magdala are connected by a saddle about a mile long called Islamgye, bounded on either flank by scarped precipices with sides below sloping rapidly down to the ravines, and covered with trees and bushes, some of the ravines nearly 3000 feet below the fortress.

Meantime, Theodore was advancing towards Magdala, having burnt his capital of Debra Tabor, likewise forming roads up the steep sides of mountains and across deep ravines for the transport of his heavy guns, on which he mainly depended for the success of his arms, with a force under him of about 6000 soldiers, a host of camp followers, and several European workmen. By the 18th of March his army had reached Arogye. At this time there were in Magdala the whole of the British prisoners, as well as 570 natives, many of them chiefs. Some days afterwards, the king sent for Mr. Rassam, Lieutenant Prideaux, and Dr. Blanc to visit him, and treated them with courtesy, but the very next day in a drunken fit he ordered nearly 200 of his native prisoners to be murdered. Some he killed with his own hands, others were thrown over the precipice of Islamgye. A letter was next addressed by Sir Robert Napier to the king, demanding the liberation of the captives. To this no answer was sent.

On the 8th of April, two brigades of the British army encamped on the Delanta plateau, in full view of the heights of Magdala. By the night of the 9th all preparations were completed for storming the fortress. Theodore had posted his army, consisting of 3000 soldiers armed with percussion guns, a host of spearmen, and several pieces of ordnance, on the flat-topped hill of Fala. Here he had come to conquer, as he thought it possible, with his cherished guns, or to die should he meet with defeat. Between the armies was the plain of Arogye. In front rose, more than 1000 feet above it, the lofty stronghold of the tyrant. To the left of Fala appeared the lofty peak of Sallasye, the two being connected by a lower saddle.

The British army consisted of 3733 men, of whom 460 were cavalry. They had two batteries of steel mountain guns, a battery of four Armstrong 12-pounder guns, and two mortars, besides which many of the troops were armed with the deadly Snider rifle, against which the weapons of the Abyssinians were almost useless. The Naval Brigade of 80 men were armed also with deadly rockets, especially calculated to create a panic among such troops as the Abyssinians.

The greater part of the day had passed, and Sir Robert had no intention of commencing an action, when, at forty-two minutes past four in the afternoon of the 10th of April, a gun was fired from the crest of Fala, 1200 feet above the Arogye plain. A few rounds followed, plunging into the ground close to the British, when several thousand men, the flower of Theodore's army, rushed impetuously over the crest of the hill down the precipitous slopes, yelling defiance, led by their chiefs on sure-footed Galla ponies. While the main body advanced across the plain, a large detachment hastened to attack the baggage train of the British on one side.

Immediately the Naval Brigade opened upon them with their rockets, while Sir Charles Staveley moved the infantry of his brigade down to the plain, the Snider rifles keeping up a fire against which the Abyssinians could not for a moment stand. Unable to get within range themselves, they were mown down in lines. Their old general, Fitaurari Gabriye, led them on again and again, but he soon fell, shot through the head; and night coming on, the shattered remnant retired towards the Fala saddle, still shouting defiance. Colonel Milward, who accompanied Penn's battery, had opened fire on the left, while Chamberlain with his pioneers drove back the enemy who were attacking the baggage train.

They still, however, persevered, but were finally checked by the baggage guard, consisting of two companies of the 4th under Captain Roberts. As the Abyssinian army retreated, Captain Fellowes and his bluejackets took up a fresh position farther in advance, sending their rockets into the flying crowd as they ascended the hillside. Of the Abyssinian force, nearly 800 were killed and 1500 wounded, most of the survivors flying in all directions, few returning to Magdala; while of the British force, Captain Roberts and six men of the 4th, twelve Punjaub Pioneers, and one Bombay sapper alone were wounded, two of them mortally.

The first brigade encamped on the Aficho plateau, without food, water, fires, or tents, while the second formed their camp on the plain of Arogye. Meantime Theodore, who had hitherto always headed his own troops, remained on the heights watching the combat. As night came on, and claps of thunder resounded over his head, he paced the ground at the foot of the Sallasye peak, waiting the return of his chiefs and soldiers. He called for his faithful old general Gabriye, but no answer came; for other trusted leaders,—there was no reply. He now saw that all hope of victory was gone. He must yield to the demands of an irresistible enemy or die. Fearful must have been the anxiety of the prisoners. Any moment he might have sent to order their destruction. Providentially, however, he resolved to try and obtain the friendship of the English by delivering up the captives. Lieutenant Prideaux and Mr. Flad were sent into the English camp to propose terms. The English general, however, would offer none short of an unconditional surrender, guaranteeing, however, honourable treatment for the king and his family.

On their return across the field of battle, the body of the old General Gabriye was found. He was lying flat on his back, with his arms stretched out, habited in a rich shirt of scarlet and gold. A Snider rifle bullet had passed through his temples. The dead and dying thickly strewn about had frightful wounds, many with half their skulls taken off.

On the arrival of two envoys, the king was found sitting on the brow of Sallasye. He immediately sent them back to the English camp with a document he had been dictating, refusing to deliver himself up. Soon after their departure, he put a pistol to his head, but the bullet was turned aside by his attendants. The king after this appears to have resolved to live, and to have conceived the hope of obtaining peace by releasing his captives. Many of his chiefs, however, had advised him to kill them, and fight to the last.

One alone—Basha Abito—urged that they should be preserved, lest a terrible vengeance should be exacted by their countrymen. Immediately the king had arrived at this decision, he ordered one of his officers to escort Mr. Rassam and all the prisoners at once to the English camp, believing, no doubt, that by so doing acceptable terms would be secured for him. Meantime Sir Robert Napier had sent Lieutenant Prideaux back with a message to the king, reiterating the contents of his former letter. The gallant young officer knew perfectly well the fearful risk he was running.

Happily he encountered a German workman, who informed him of the release of the captives, when he and Mr. Flad returned to the camp. The released prisoners were Mr. Rassam, Dr. Blanc, Lieutenant Prideaux, Consul Cameron, Mr. Stern the missionary, Mr. Flad, Mr. and Mrs. Rosenthal, young Kerans, secretary to Captain Cameron, and Pietro, an Italian servant. As may be supposed, they received the warmest welcome in the camp, and every attention was paid to them. The king now made another attempt at reconciliation, by sending a present of cattle. On finding that this was refused, he seems to have given way to despair.

Having spent the night on Islamgye, he summoned his soldiers, and ordered those not prepared to share his fortunes to the last to provide for their own safety. The whole army immediately disbanded, a few chiefs and personal followers only answering his call. After this he seems to have wished to make his escape, but he was cut off by the British on one side, while the Gallas were eagerly watching on the other to capture him.

On seeing the English advancing up Islamgye, he mounted his favourite horse Hamra, and, followed by some of his chiefs, furiously galloped up and down in circles, firing off his rifle as a challenge, perhaps wishing that some kind bullet might at the moment end his career. Probably he experienced a peculiar pleasure at that desperate moment in displaying his horsemanship and other soldierlike qualities. As the British advanced and opened fire, he was compelled to abandon his guns and retreat into Magdala, followed by the few chiefs who had remained faithful. Part of the British army now took possession of the heights of Islamgye, while a party of the 33rd Regiment, the 10th company of Royal Engineers, and a company of Madras sappers were ordered to assault the Koketbir gate of the fortress. The guns from Islamgye and the Fala saddle opened fire, and continued it during the afternoon.

The ascent to the fortress, or *amba*, as it is called, was by an excessively steep and narrow path, amidst large boulders, with perpendicular black cliffs on the right. The Koketbir gate consisted of a rough stone gateway 15 feet deep, with folding wooden doors. On either side the approach was defended by a thick hedge with stakes. Seventy feet higher up there was a second hedge, and another gate opening on the flat summit of the *amba*. As the British soldiers climbed up the rocky path, firing rapidly with their Sniders, they received a dropping fire in return, by which seven men were wounded and a few others slightly injured. The 33rd then made a dash at the hedge, climbed over it, and opened the door from the inside, when the rest of the storming party rushed in. The dead bodies of a few chiefs, richly dressed, were found lying in a heap inside the gate, but no enemy appeared.

Deserted by most of his followers, the king, after attempting to pile up large stones against the inside of the gate, took his seat on the rocks between the two gates, surrounded by his friends, watching the English guns with his glass. When the assault commenced, he and nine who had remained with him commenced firing at the English. By a volley fired into the little band, most of those who had hitherto survived were wounded. Theodore on this retired to some huts on the *amba*, about 50 yards from the second gate. Here, dismissing his remaining followers, he turned to his body-servant, Walda Gabir, saying that, sooner than fall into the hands of his enemies, he would kill himself. Then, putting a pistol to his mouth, he fired it, and fell dead. The bullet had passed through the roof of his mouth and through the back of his head. This was at about 4:10 p.m.

Some prisoners who had escaped pointed out the body of the king to the English. It was now put into a litter, and brought to Sir Charles Staveley. It appears that Theodore had eaten nothing for four days, supported only by *tej* and drams of *araki*. He was of medium stature, well-built, broad chest, small waist, and muscular limbs, his complexion being dark even for an Abyssinian, though with a finely cut aquiline nose, with a low bridge, his thin lips telling of his cruel disposition. He was in his 50th year and the 15th of his reign. The level area of the now well-known fortress was almost entirely covered with well-built circular thatched huts, most of them surrounded by a hedge or wall.

The king's own house, in which the Queen Terunish and her little boy resided, was an oblong building of two storeys. Other buildings were attached to it, with a sort of summer-house commanding a magnificent view of the country. Amidst the houses was a church in miserable condition; indeed, Magdala was not considered Christian ground, being in the territory of the heathen Gallas. The whole town contained about 3,000 persons.

The body of the king, having been embalmed, was buried by the Abyssinian priests, within the precincts of this wretched church, a small guard of the 33rd attending to keep order. The grave was shallow, and soon covered in with stones, and the surface strewn with straw. The queen came for protection to the British camp, and expressed her wish that the English would take charge of her son. She, however, died on the march, and her young son remained under charge of the English, by whom he has been brought up and educated. The huts in Magdala were burned, the gates of the fortress were blown up, and all the guns, to the number of 37, collected by Theodore, were burst.

The return march was performed as successfully as the advance, and before the end of the month of June the last man of the expedition had departed from Annesley Bay. The larger body returned to India, while the Commander-in-chief sailed in the *Feroze* for England. A peerage, a Grand Cross of the Bath, and a pension were conferred upon Sir Robert Napier; and two Knight Commanderships and 27 Companionships of the same order were bestowed on other officers; while 15 colonelcies, 18 Lieutenant-Colonelcies, and 13 majorities were distributed among the other officers of the expedition. The Abyssinian Expedition will ever be remembered for the judgment and forethought exercised in its preparation, the perseverance and energy of the officers employed, and the admirable conduct of the men.

The Ashantee War
1873-74

The Ashantee War
1873-1874

On that part of the West coast of Africa which runs east
and west, extending from the Bight of Benin to Cape Pal-
mas, a portion being known as the Gold Coast, are situated a
number of forts, some of which belonged to the Dutch and
Danes, who lately ceded them to the British Government.

The principal fort is Cape Coast Castle, and to the west of
it is the late Dutch fort of Elmina.

The largest river in this part of Africa is the Prah, which,
running for some distance from the north-east to the south-
west, takes an almost due southerly course, and falls into the sea
about 20 miles west of Cape Coast Castle. The whole region
is almost entirely covered by dense scrub or lofty trees, with a
thick undergrowth of shrubs and creepers, through which it
is impossible to pass, unless where native paths exist or a way
has been cut by the axe of the pioneer; while in all directions
marshes exist, emitting exhalations destructive to the health
and lives of Europeans exposed to their noxious influences.

The Ashantees, a large and warlike tribe who had fought
their way from the interior, established themselves early in the
last century to the north and west of the Prah, and founded
Coomassie as their capital, about 140 miles to the north of Cape
Coast Castle. Having devastated the country by fire and sword,
they soon after annexed the greater part of Denkera to their
kingdom, driving the surviving inhabitants to the south-east,
where they are at present settled near the Swat River, which
falls into the sea between Cape Coast Castle and Elmina.

The country between Cape Coast Castle and the Prah is inhabited by the Fantis, a tribe which, although at one time warlike, have greatly degenerated. Neither the Dutch nor the English have attempted to subdue any of the neighbouring tribes; and though the people residing in the immediate vicinity of the forts have been friendly, the Europeans have throughout their occupancy been subject to serious attacks from the savages in the neighbourhood.

The most formidable of these foes have been the Ashantees, who have on several occasions threatened Cape Coast Castle, and numbers of the garrison marching out to drive them back have been cut off.

The Fantis have been, since the commencement of this century, constantly attacked by the Ashantees, and in 1820 they placed themselves under the protection of England. A fatal expedition for their defence was undertaken in 1824 by Sir Charles Macarthy, who, crossing the Prah with a small force without waiting for the main body of his troops, being deserted by the Fantis and surrounded by the Ashantees, was with all his forces cut to pieces, three white men only escaping.

This and other successes over our native allies induced the reigning king of Ashantee, Coffee Calcalli, to hold the British power in contempt. The barbarous customs of the Ashantees almost surpass conception. Their religion is the grossest fetishism. Human life is utterly disregarded; and thousands of slaves are yearly slaughtered as sacrifices by the king, their bodies being thrown into a vast pit in the neighbourhood of his palace.

In 1873, this black potentate having made alliances with the chiefs of other tribes, sent a large Ashantee force across the Prah, with the avowed intention of capturing Elmina, which he asserted the Dutch had no right to dispose of to the English. Destroying the Fanti villages in their course, they advanced to within a few days' march of Cape Coast Castle. Every effort was made by Colonel Harley, who was then in command there, to induce the Fantis to withstand the enemy, while he collected such forces as were available for their support. One of the bravest and most disciplined races in that part of Africa are the Houssas, a body of whom were at once obtained from Lagos, and who, with some companies of the 2nd West India Regiment and a body of Fanti police, were marched to the front, under the command of Lieutenant Hopkins.

The Fantis, however, though far more numerous than their invaders, took to flight, and the force which had been sent to their assistance had to return.

The Ashantees now took possession of Dunquah, from whence they moved to the east towards Denkera. As serious apprehensions were entertained that both Elmina and Cape Coast Castle would be attacked, the English Government sent out H.M.S. *Barracouta*, Captain Fremantle, with a detachment of no marines, under the command of Lieutenant-Colonel Festing, of the Royal Marine Artillery.

They landed at Cape Coast Castle on the 9th of June, when Colonel Festing assumed command of the troops on the coast, and Captain Fremantle became senior naval officer on the station. Martial law was proclaimed; and as the inhabitants of the native town of Elmina showed a disposition to revolt, on the refusal of the chiefs to give up their arms the place was bombarded and set on fire, the rebels making their escape. A large body of Ashantees, two or three thousand strong, now approached Elmina, when they were gallantly attacked by Colonel Festing with the marines, and a party of bluejackets under Captain Fremantle, some men of the 2nd West India Regiment, and a body of Houssas.

The enemy advanced boldly along the plain, and were about to outflank the British force on the right, when Lieutenant Wells, R.N., of the *Barracouta*, attacked them with a heavy fire of Sniders, and drove them back, on which Colonel Festing, ordering the advance of the whole line, repulsed the enemy, who left 200 men dead on the field.

This was the first of several actions which ensued; but it was very evident that no adequate punishment could be inflicted on King Coffee and his subjects unless by a strong body of disciplined troops. This was the opinion of all the principal officers acquainted with the country. The British Government, however, not being at first thoroughly satisfied of the necessity of sending out troops from England, appointed Sir Garnet Wolseley, who had displayed his abilities as a general in the Red River Expedition, to proceed to Cape Coast Castle, with a well-selected staff of officers, and to make his report.

One of the most active officers at this time was Lieutenant Gordon, who had raised and drilled a body of Houssas, with whom he rendered good service during the war. He now formed a redoubt at the village of Napoleon, about five miles from Cape Coast, and several others being thrown up, the intermediate country to the south was well protected. A further body of marines arrived by the *Simoom*.

In the meantime Commodore Commerell, who had arrived in the *Rattlesnake* from the Cape of Good Hope, made an excursion with several other officers up the Prah, to communicate with the chiefs residing on its banks.

Having had an interview with the chiefs he found near the mouth of the river, he led his fleet of boats about a mile and a half up, when, without any warning, an enemy concealed in the bush opened a heavy fire on them. The commodore was badly wounded, and Captains Luxmoore and Helden were also severely hurt, as were several of the men. On this the commodore ordered the return of the boats to the *Rattlesnake*, when the town of Chamah was at once bombarded, and quickly destroyed.

In this unfortunate affair four men were killed and sixteen wounded, while so severe was Commodore Commerell's wound, that he was ordered immediately to return to the Cape.

Space will not allow a description of the numerous engagements with the enemy, in which all the officers employed exhibited the greatest courage and endurance, although none surpassed Lieutenant Gordon and his Houssas in the services they rendered.

On the 2nd October, Sir Garnet Wolseley arrived at Cape Coast Castle in the *Ambris*, having previously touched at Sierra Leone, and made arrangements with the governor for raising men from the various tribes along the coast; steps were also immediately taken to form an army of Fantis. The major-general, however, was soon convinced that the attempt was hopeless; and, after a month's experience of the native forces he was able to collect, supported as they were by marines, bluejackets, and West India regiments, he wrote home requesting that the regiments which had been selected might be immediately sent out.

In the meantime, Captain Glover, formerly of the navy, who had served as administrator of the Government at Lagos, proposed a plan to raise a force of 10,000 natives, and to march from the east on Coomassie, the base of operations being on the river Volta, on which some steam-launches and canoes were to be placed. Captain Glover's plan being sanctioned, he at once proceeded out with the officers he had selected to act under him.

He was now busily employed in raising the proposed troops, which, from a thorough knowledge of the people, he succeeded in doing in the most complete manner.

One of Sir Garnet Wolseley's first exploits was a well-conducted attack on several of the villages in the neighbourhood of Elmina held by the Ashantees. Keeping his plan secret until the moment the march was commenced, he was able to surprise the enemy, who, however, stood their ground until put to flight by the rockets and the Snider rifle. Several officers and men were, however, wounded—Colonel McNeill badly in the wrist, as was also Captain Fremantle.

The seamen and marines had been up all night, and marched 21 miles under a burning sun, yet there were only two cases of sunstroke, and only four men were admitted to hospital the following day.

Captain Rait and Lieutenant Eardley Wilmot, of the Royal Artillery, had drilled a number of Houssas as gunners for Gatling guns and rockets, who afterwards rendered admirable service.

Besides Captain Rait's artillery, two efficient regiments had been formed of between 400 and 500 men each, from the bravest tribes, the one under the command of Lieutenant-Colonel Wood, the other under that of Major Russell. Both these corps were well drilled by experienced English officers, and on all occasions exhibited the greatest bravery.

So well-conducted were the attacks made on the Ashantee forces which had invaded the Fanti territory, that at length, towards the end of October, they broke up their camp and began to retreat over the Prah. They were closely pursued; but many of the native allies, as on other occasions, refusing to proceed, the difficulty of carrying on reconnaissances fell mostly on the English officers.

In this work Lord Gifford especially distinguished himself. Colonel Festing commanded the force employed in the pursuit. He had with him Lieutenant Eardley Wilmot, in charge of eight Houssas of Rait's artillery. While pushing on gallantly in front, Lieutenant Wilmot was wounded in the arm, yet in spite of this he continued under fire, until an hour later he was shot through the heart; and Colonel Festing, when bringing in his body from where it was lying, was wounded by a slug in the hip.

Abrakrampa, one of the British advance posts, was garrisoned by the black regiment commanded by Major Russell, who had with him also a party of marines and bluejackets. He had received orders to send the latter back to Cape Coast, but just as they were about to march he received information that his camp would certainly be attacked. The report proved to be true. The enemy came on in great force; but each time that they attempted to break out of the bush, they were driven back by the hot fire kept up by the little garrison.

Major Russell immediately despatched a requisition for assistance, when a body of marines and bluejackets from the ships in the roads were landed and sent off. The Ashantees again and again renewed the attack, but were each time driven back.

The British force marching to the relief of the place suffered greatly from fatigue. They arrived, however, in time to assist in driving back the enemy, who now retreated towards the Prah at a more rapid rate than heretofore. While in pursuit of the enemy, large numbers of the native allies again took to flight, proving how utterly unreliable they were.

Sir Garnet Wolseley's chief object now was, having driven the enemy before him, to construct a road in the direction of Coomassie, and prepare halting-places for the European troops which were soon expected out.

Sickness, however, rendered a considerable number of the English officers incapable of duty.

The pursuit of the enemy by the force under Colonel Wood was especially harassing work. He and many of his officers were suffering from fever. The Ashantees frequently halted and fired on their pursuers, though on each occasion driven back.

As many bluejackets as could be spared from the ships were now landed, and several officers arrived out from England. The major-general was able to report on the 15th December 1873—"That the first phase of this war had been brought to a satisfactory conclusion by a few companies of the 2nd West India Regiment, Rait's artillery, Gordon's Houssas, and Wood's and Russell's regiments, admirably conducted by the British officers belonging to them, without the assistance of any English troops except the marines and bluejackets, who were on the station on his arrival." The Fanti country being cleared, a road towards the Prah was now energetically pushed forward. It was 12 feet wide, cleared of stumps or roots, swamps were either drained or avoided, or causeways made over them, and all the streams were bridged. This task was confided to Major Home, of the Royal Engineers.

The rough clearing of the first 25 miles had, however, already been performed by Lieutenant Gordon.

Stations were selected, and huts erected for the accommodation of the troops, and for stores and provisions. Means were taken to secure an ample supply of water, either by digging wells or from streams in the neighbourhood. At Prahsu the river Prah makes a sharp bend, within which a large camp was formed, with shelter for 2000 European troops, an hospital, and storehouses. Complete arrangements were made for the accommodation of the sick. The great difficulty was to obtain native carriers, who frequently deserted as soon as they were collected; and it was not until some time had passed that the transport service could be arranged in a satisfactory manner.

The plan which the major-general had arranged for the campaign was as follows:—The main body, consisting of three battalions of European troops, the Naval Brigade, Wood's and Russell's regiments and Rait's artillery, was to advance from Prahsu by the Coomassie road. On the extreme right, a native force under Captain Glover was to cross the Prah near Assum, and, as a connecting link between him and the main body, a column composed of natives, under the command of Captain Butler, 69th Regiment, was to cross the same river lower down; while, on the extreme left, another column of natives, commanded by Captain Dalrymple of the 88th Regiment, was to advance by the Wassaw road on Coomassie.

MARCH TO COOMASSIE

On the 26th December, the major-general with his staff left Cape Coast Castle for Prahsu, which he reached on the 2nd January. Here the Naval Brigade arrived the following day.

The disembarkation of the regular troops commenced the 1st of January at 1:45, and by 6:35 that evening the whole of the troops had landed, and the brigade had reached Inquabun, six miles from Cape Coast Castle.

They consisted of the 42nd Highlanders, the Rifle Brigade, a detachment of the Royal Engineers, the 23rd Fusiliers, a detachment of the Royal Artillery, numbering in all 2504 men. As, however, there was great difficulty in obtaining transport, the Fusiliers and Royal Artillery were re-embarked, to remain on board the ships until required. Two hundred of the Fusiliers were afterwards re-landed, and marched to the front. Besides these, there were the 2nd West India Regiment, of 350 men, Rait's artillery, 50 men, and Wood's and Russell's regiments, numbering together 800, afterwards increased by a detachment of the 1st West India Regiment, lately landed.

During the early part of January, the whole of the British troops reached Prahsu, and on the 20th, the bridge across the Prah being finished, the force intended for the attack on Coomassie marched out of the camp.

Lord Gifford, in command of a well-trained body of native scouts, had previously gone forward, followed by Russell's and Wood's regiments, which obtained possession of the crest of the Adansi Hills. Lord Gifford pushing ahead, the enemy's scouts retreated before him, and the inhabitants deserted the villages. The king, it was evident, by this time was seriously alarmed, and, hoping for peace, released the European prisoners in his hands. He first sent in Mr. Kuhne, a German missionary, who was followed by Mr. Ramseyer, another missionary, and his wife and their two children, and Monsieur Bannat, a French merchant, from whom much important information was obtained. As the army advanced, the villages taken possession of were fortified and garrisoned, so that communication with the rear should be kept up and the sick carried back to hospital. Already a considerable number of officers and men were suffering from sickness. Captain Huyshe died the day before the major-general left Prahsu. Thus, out of the whole European force of 1800 men forming the main body, 215 men and 3 officers were unfitted for duty.

Fommanah, a large village 30 miles from Coomassie, having been deserted by the enemy, was entered on the 24th. The king sent letter after letter to Sir Garnet Wolseley petitioning for peace, but as he did not forward the hostages which were demanded, the army continued its advance, while the answer sent to him was "that the governor meant to go to Coomassie."

In an attack on the village of Borborassie, in which the Naval Brigade, a company of Fusiliers, and another of Russell's regiment, with Rait's artillery, were engaged, Captain

Nicol, who led the advance, was unhappily shot dead, the first officer to fall north of the Prah. Information being received that the enemy was posted near the villages of Amoaful and Becquah, it was resolved immediately to attack them. The nature of the ground over which the operations were carried on must be described.

Excepting where the clearings for the villages existed, or native paths, the whole country was covered thickly with lofty trees, from which hung creepers innumerable, while below was thick brushwood, through which the pioneers had to cut a way before the troops could advance. Such a region afforded the enemy ample means of forming ambushes as well as for fighting under cover, of which they did not fail to take full advantage. The only other openings to be found were where swamps had prevented the growth of trees. Such was the difficult country in which Sir Garnet Wolseley had to manoeuvre his troops. The army advanced, with Lord Gifford's scouts skirmishing in front, Rait's guns and rockets leading, followed by the 42nd Highlanders, the 23rd Fusiliers, and the Rifle Brigade in succession, and on either flank the Naval Brigade and Russell's and Wood's regiments,—that on the right under command of Colonel Wood, and on the left of Colonel McLeod.

Lord Gifford, with 40 scouts, pushing ahead early in the morning, occupied the village of Egginassie by a rush. On the other side the enemy was found in considerable force. On this, Brigadier Sir Archibald Alison sent two companies of the 42nd Highlanders, forming the advance guard, up the main road to the front, and a section up a path which branched off to the left. Being soon hotly engaged, they were quickly supported by other companies under Major Macpherson, and the remainder of the regiment was immediately afterwards pushed forward. As company after company descended, their pipes playing, they were rapidly lost to sight in the thick smoke beneath, and their position could only be judged of by the sharp crack of their rifles, in contradistinction to the dull roar of the Ashantee musketry.

It was with the greatest difficulty, when fresh companies were sent to the support of those in action, that the latter could find their friends in the midst of the enemy's fire. The engineer labourers under Captain Buckle were cutting paths in the required directions, but so heavy a fire was brought to bear by the enemy, that their progress was much delayed. While at this time engaged in urging on his men, Captain Buckle fell mortally wounded. By one of the paths thus formed, Lieutenant Palmer brought his rockets into action, and, covered by their fire, two of the companies of Russell's regiment, led by Captain Gordon, made a splendid dash at the enemy. The Naval Brigade, under Captain Luxmoore, were engaged at the same period in exchanging a heavy fire with the Ashantees, who were making desperate attempts to retake the village. Before long, Major Macpherson and several other officers were wounded. Captain Rait's guns were now sent across the swamp, to attack a spot on which a dense mass of the enemy were collected together. After 14 or 15 rounds, which caused tremendous slaughter, they showed signs of giving way, and a rush being made, their position was carried. On the summit was found a large camp, in which their main body had been posted. This being quickly traversed by the British troops, the Ashantees again made a bold stand from a ridge behind it.

Once more Rait's guns were brought into action, followed by a heavy rifle fire, when, another charge being made, the fresh position taken up by the enemy was also carried. In the meantime, the right column, under Colonel Wood, which had been supported by the Fusiliers, was hotly engaged, and a considerable number of men were wounded, Colonel Wood and his aide-de-camp among them. So fierce was the opposition, that a second support of two companies of the Rifle Brigade was next ordered up. Pushing forward, they gallantly drove the enemy from their cover, and about half-past twelve the Ashantees took to flight.

As the cheers in front announced that the battle was gained, a rapid fire was heard in the direction of Quarman, showing that the Ashantees were attempting to cut off the communication with the rear. Four companies of the Rifle Brigade were accordingly ordered back, and so actively did they ply their rifles, that in less than an hour the Ashantees were put to flight. Another attack was, however, made on the right and rear of Quarman, by one of the principal Ashantee generals, but the enemy was gallantly held in check by its small garrison until the arrival of a company of the Rifle Brigade.

In the meantime Amoaful had been taken by a gallant rush of the 42nd Highlanders, led by Major Cluny Macpherson, and here the major-general established his headquarters.

The action altogether had lasted twelve hours, extending along two and a half miles of road. During the greater part of the time the firing was incessant,—the loss suffered by the 42nd being proof of its severity, nearly every fourth man having been hit. The enemy must have lost upwards of 2000 men in killed and wounded.

In the action, besides Captain Buckle, there were two privates of the 42nd and one of Wood's regiment killed. Of wounded, there were 15 military officers, and 147 men; 6 officers of the Naval Brigade, and 26 men. As short a time as possible was spent at Amoaful, when the force again advanced on the 2nd of February.

The advance guard was under Colonel McLeod, the main body under Brigadier-General Sir Archibald Alison. The troops carried two days' rations in their haversacks, a similar quantity being conveyed by the spare hammock bearers. A fifth day's rations were to be brought forward to them.

Colonel McLeod, pushing on, found but little opposition. The force was now concentrated at a place called Aggemmamu, within fifteen miles of Coomassie.

Sir Garnet now announced his intention of making a dash on Coomassie. The soldiers were asked whether they would undertake to make their rations for four days last if necessary for six. The answer was, as may be supposed, "Most willingly." Leaving their baggage under the care of such men as were too weakly to march, the army advanced on the morning of the 3rd.

As usual, Lord Gifford with his scouts went ahead, followed by Russell's regiment under Colonel McLeod. In a short time the enemy was encountered. After a sharp and short action, however, he was driven back, but with some loss on the side of the British. The advance guard pushed on until within a short distance of Coomassie, when messengers arrived from the king again entreating for peace, at the same time stating that there were 10,000 men on the other side of the river, who would fight if the British advanced. Sir Garnet Wolseley returned word, "that unless the queen and prince royal should be put into his hands, the march would be continued."

The advance guard reached the river Ordah at 2:10 p.m. It was found to be fifty feet wide and waist deep. Russell's regiment at once passed over, forming a covering party to the Engineers, who immediately set to work to throw a bridge across for the passage of the European troops, while clearings were made on the south bank, and rush huts thrown up in which the British soldiers bivouacked. At first some apprehensions were entertained that a night-attack would be made, but a heavy thunderstorm coming on, during which the flintlocks of the enemy would have been useless, rendered that improbable.

By daybreak on the 4th, the bridge over the Ordah was completed, Major Home, of the Engineers, having worked at it all night throughout the whole of the tornado and drenching rain.

As no hostages had arrived, it was expected that another battle would have to be fought.

At an early hour the advance guard pushed on, the Naval Brigade being left at the bridge to guard the passage until the baggage had crossed. Directly the troops advanced, the enemy opened fire. The native troops on this occasion firing wildly, Colonel McLeod ordered a company of the Rifle Brigade and the 7-pounder gun under Lieutenant Saunders to the front.

The enemy pressing the advance, a vigorous flank fire being also opened on the troops under Sir Archibald Alison, reinforcements were ordered up. Colonel McLeod continued steadily to advance, Lieutenant Saunders' gun clearing the road, when the Rifles again pushed forward, until the village of Ordahsu was carried and a lodgement effected there.

In this skirmish Lieutenant Eyre was mortally wounded, and several of the men were severely hurt, although the enemy did not fight with the same obstinacy as at Amoaful. As the village was approached, a tremendously heavy fire was opened on both flanks of the British force. The Rifle Brigade and the Fusiliers, with two of Rait's guns, having now got up to the village, under Sir Archibald Alison's command, the force was ordered to move on.

At that moment the enemy commenced a vigorous attack on the village, so that the Rifle Brigade and Fusiliers had to be thrown into the bush to check them. According to the brigadier's request, the 42nd were pushed forward, the object being to break through the enemy who appeared in force in front. The Highlanders were quickly sent on, and the major-general with the headquarters entered the village immediately after them. A short halt, however, was required, to allow the baggage to arrive.

During this time the enemy pressed boldly up to the village, firing volleys of slugs, one of which struck the major-general on the helmet, fortunately at a part where the leather band prevented it entering.

About noon, the 42nd, with Rait's artillery, led the attack on the enemy's front, for the purpose of breaking through and pushing on direct for Coomassie, followed by the Rifle Brigade. They had not got far before a tremendous fire was opened on the head of the column from a strong ambuscade behind a fallen tree, and several men were knocked over, but the flank companies working steadily through the bush, the leading company sprang forward with a cheer. The pipes struck up, and the ambuscade was carried. Then, without stop or stay, the 42nd rushing on cheering, their pipes playing, officers to the front, ambuscade after ambuscade was successfully carried, and village after village won in succession, until the whole of the Ashantee army broke and fled in the wildest disorder down the pathway towards Coomassie. The ground was covered with traces of their flight. Umbrellas, war chairs of their chiefs, drums, muskets, killed and wounded, strewed the way. No pause took place until a village about four miles from Coomassie was reached, when the absolute exhaustion of the men rendered a short halt necessary.

Meanwhile the attack on the village continued, and the enemy were allowed to close around the rear, Ordahsu, however, being strongly guarded.

On the arrival of the major-general, he ordered an advance of the whole force on Coomassie. It was nearly five o'clock before the troops again moved forward. The village of Karsi, the nearest to Coomassie, was passed without opposition. When close upon the city, a flag of truce was received by the brigadier, who forwarded it with a letter to Sir Garnet Wolseley, whose only reply was, "Push on." On this the brigadier immediately advanced, and, passing the Soubang swamp which surrounds the city, entered the great market-place of Coomassie, without opposition, about 5:30. The major-general himself arrived at 6:15, when the troops formed on parade, and, at his command, gave three cheers for Her Majesty the Queen.

The town was full of armed men, but not a shot was fired. The brigadier had so placed the artillery that it could sweep the streets leading to the market-place, and had thrown out the necessary pickets. A party was sent down to the palace, under the guidance of an Englishman who had long been a resident at Coomassie; but the king, queen-mother, and prince, with all other persons of distinction, had fled. Due arrangements were made to preserve order. The major-general issued a proclamation, threatening with the punishment of death any person caught plundering. The troops were exposed to much danger, flames bursting out in several directions, the work of the Fanti prisoners who had been released. The great palace of the king was entered,—a building far superior to the ordinary habitations of the natives,—and was found to contain treasures of all sorts, and evidence also of the fearful atrocities committed within it; while close to it was seen the dreadful pit into which the bodies of those slaughtered almost daily by the king's command were thrown.

In vain Sir Garnet Wolseley waited for the king to fulfil his promise; neither any part of the sum demanded, nor the hostages, had been delivered. To remain longer at Coomassie was hazardous in the extreme. The rains had already commenced, and the rivers, which had been crossed with ease, were now much swollen.

For the sake of the health of the troops, the major-general resolved, therefore, having destroyed the town and palace, to retreat. That the enemy might not be aware of his intentions, a report was circulated that the army would advance in pursuit of the king, and that any Ashantee found in the town after six o'clock would be shot. This effectually cleared out the natives.

Prize agents were appointed to take charge of the riches in the palace. Arrangements were made for destroying it on the following morning, and setting the whole town on fire.

Early the next morning the return march began. The rear company of the 42nd Highlanders remained at the south end of the market-place while the guard was removed from the palace. The city was then set on fire, and the mines for the destruction of the palace exploded,—the dense columns of smoke which curled up in the sky showing the King of Ashantee and all his subjects that the white man had not failed to keep his word. Gallant Colonel McLeod remained until the last of the engineers and sappers had passed to the front; he then waved his hand as a signal for the rear company to march, and Coomassie was abandoned to the flames.

The troops on their return march, although they encountered some difficulties, were not molested, so thoroughly and completely had the Ashantees been defeated. As a further proof of this, ambassadors from the king overtook the army on the 12th, bringing upwards of 1000 ounces of gold, as part of the indemnity of the 50,000 ounces demanded, and returned with a treaty of peace for the black monarch to sign. The forts which had been constructed were destroyed, the sick and wounded, with the stores, sent on, and the major-general and his staff reached Cape Coast Castle on the 19th of February.

The Naval Brigade, consisting of 265 men and 17 officers, rendered valuable service throughout the campaign, and fought on all occasions with most dashing courage. Though only one was killed, 63 were wounded in action, while several others were killed and wounded during the operations which took place along the coast, to punish several of the petty chiefs who had sided with the Ashantees.

One of the most gallant performances of the campaign was the ride across the country, from the eastward, by Captain Sartorious, who with 20 followers passed through Coomassie five days after the army had quitted it, and, though fired on twice by the enemy, safely arrived at Prahsu. The following day, Captain Glover, R.N., having marched from the Volta, entered the city at the head of 4600 native allies. Here King Coffee sent him a token of submission by the hands of an ambassador, in the shape of a plateful of gold, which he returned, and then proceeded southward with his forces into friendly territory, having performed an exploit which, for daring, intrepidity, judgment, and the perseverance with which it was carried out, stands almost unrivalled.

Most of the officers engaged in the expedition were promoted, but on two only—Lord Gifford and Sergeant McGaw of the 42nd—was the Victoria Cross bestowed,—an honour which, by the unanimous voice of all who witnessed their behaviour, they richly deserved.

The Commander-in-Chief also recommended Captain A.F. Kidston of the 42nd, Private George Cameron, and Private George Ritchie, for the same honour.

The officers killed in action were Lieutenant E. Wilmot, R.A., Lieutenant Eyre, 90th Regiment, Captain Nicol, Hants Militia, Captain Buckle, R.E.; while three died from the effects of the climate,—Lieutenant the Honourable A. Charteris, A.D.C., Captain Huyshe, D.A.Q.M.G., Lieutenant E. Townshend, 16th Regiment; while seven others were wounded.

The Afghan War
1878–79

The Afghan War
1878-1879

For many years previous to the war, the relations between England and Afghanistan had been unsatisfactory. Shere Ali, the ruler of the latter country, received an annual subsidy from us, and had, besides, been presented with large quantities of arms and other warlike weapons. The events which led to the war have been debated with great acrimony, and are viewed in opposite manners by persons of different political opinions, and it is enough here to say that the approach of Russia to the northern frontier of Afghanistan caused considerable uneasiness to the Ameer, and that, unable to obtain from us any positive assurances of support in case of attack from the north, he appears to have determined that his best course would be to throw himself into the arms of Russia, even at the risk of breaking with us.

For some time all communications with the Ameer had ceased, and it was from a native news-writer that the intelligence that a Russian general with a mission had arrived in Cabul, and had been honourably received, came to the ears of our authorities.

Upon the news being made public, the Viceroy of India wrote to Shere Ali, requesting him to receive also an English mission. The answer of the Ameer was evasive, and Major Cavaignari, an officer of great experience in Afghanistan, was sent up with an escort as a precursor of a larger and more important mission to follow. Upon the 21st September he arrived at Ali-Musjid, an Afghan fort in the Khyber Pass, and

...ere stopped by an officer of the Ameer with a large ...e. A long parley took place; but the officer refused to al-...w him to pass, and Major Cavaignari, not having a sufficient number of men with him to force his way up, retired, with an intimation that the Ameer would be held responsible for the conduct of his officer.

As it was clearly impossible that the Indian Government could put up with this insult, and that, moreover, England could not submit to see Russian envoys received by a country upon her border which refused to admit her own officers, preparations were at once made for war. It was decided to invade Afghanistan in three columns, one starting from Jumrood, at the north of the Khyber Pass, the second to advance through Tull by the Kuram Valley, and the third to move *via* the Bolan Pass upon Candahar. The first of these was to be commanded by General Sir S. Browne, the second by General Roberts, the third by General Biddulph. The preparations for the concentration of these columns occupied considerable time, as India had been for some time in a state of profound peace, and the commissariat and transport service had to be entirely organised. The greatest efforts were, however, made, and the troops were rapidly got into place.

On the 26th of October a defiant reply to the Viceroy's letter was received from the Ameer, and an ultimatum was in consequence sent to him, to the effect that unless the British demands were complied with, the troops would advance across the frontier. No reply having been received from him up to the night of the 20th November, orders were given to the troops to advance, and upon the following morning Generals Roberts and Browne advanced across the frontier with their respective columns.

The division of General Browne was divided into four brigades. The first, under General Macpherson, consisted of the fourth battalion of the Rifle Brigade, the 20th Bengal Infantry, and the 4th Ghurkas, with a mountain battery. These were to go round by a mountain road, to make a long circuit, and to come down into the pass at a village lying a mile or two beyond Ali-Musjid. The second brigade, under Colonel Tytler, consisting of the first battalion of the 17th Foot, the Infantry of the Guides, the 1st Sikhs, and a mountain battery, were to take a hill opposite to Ali-Musjid, and capture some batteries which the Afghans had erected there; while the third and fourth brigades were to advance direct up the valley. The former of these brigades consisted of the 81st, the 14th Sikhs, and the 24th Native Infantry. The fourth brigade was composed of the 51st Foot, the 6th Native Infantry, and the 45th Sikhs. With them was a mountain battery, and a battery of Horse Artillery.

The fort of Ali-Musjid is situated on a rock standing out in the valley, at a distance of some six miles from the frontier. It is a most commanding position, and, flanked as it was by batteries on the hillsides, was a most formidable place to capture. The advancing column marched forward until from a rise in the valley they could see Ali-Musjid at a distance of a mile and a half. The fort at once opened fire. The gunners there had been practising for some weeks, and had got the range with great accuracy. The column was therefore halted, and the men allowed to eat their dinners, as it was desired that the flanking columns should get into position before the front attack began. The guns of the battery answered those upon the fort, and a battery of 40-pounders coming up and opening fire, their effect upon the fort was at once visible.

The Sikhs were now thrown out upon the hillside, and these began a heavy musketry fire against the Afghans in the batteries there. Presently a general advance was ordered. The 81st and 24th Native Infantry advanced on the right-hand slopes of the valley, while the 51st and 6th Native Infantry and the Sikhs worked along on the left.

The scene is described as one of the most picturesque ever seen in warfare. From the fortress standing on the perpendicular rock in the centre of the valley, the flashes of the great guns came fast and steadily, while the edges of the rocks and forts were fringed with tiny puffs of musketry. On the British side the heavy 40-pounders and the batteries of Horse and Royal Artillery kept up a steady fire, while both sides of the steep hill-slopes were alive with British infantry, the quick flash of the rifles breaking from every rock and bush.

Gradually our skirmishers advanced until they were nearly abreast of the fort; but, so far, there was no sign that Macpherson's brigade had accomplished its task and carried the hill, or that Tytler had worked round to the village in the rear. Some attacks, however, were made upon the Afghan entrenchments. These, however, were unsuccessful, and some valuable lives were lost. Major Birch and Lieutenant Fitzgerald, both of the 27th Native Infantry, were killed; Captain Maclean, of the 14th Sikhs, was wounded; and between thirty and forty rank and file killed and wounded.

As the fort and its defences could not have been carried without vast loss of life, it was now determined to halt, in order to give the flanking columns time to get in their places. These, who had met with enormous obstacles on their march, arrived in the night at their respective destinations, and the defenders of Ali-Musjid, taken by alarm at the news that forces were advancing which would cut off their retreat, precipitately abandoned their posts and fled. A great number were taken prisoners, and in the morning the troops occupied Ali—Musjid without resistance. So completely taken by surprise were the Afghans at the easy capture of a fort which they believed to be absolutely impregnable, that they fled without further resistance; and the British, moving quietly up the valley, occupied place after place with scarcely a shot fired until they reached Jellalabad.

In the meantime, General Roberts was advancing up the Kuram Valley. The tribes here greeted our advance with pleasure, for they were tributary to Cabul, and viewed the Afghan rule with aversion. It was upon the Peiwar Khotal, a steep and extremely strong position, that the Afghans determined to take their stand.

On the 30th of November the forces approached this position. The Afghans remained silent, and preparations were made for encamping at the commencement of the pass. The enemy, however, were nearer and more active than had been supposed, and scarcely had the troops taken up their position, when a heavy fire was opened upon them from above, and the force had to retire hastily out of range. Some of the infantry were pushed forward, and for a time brisk firing took place. The troops then encamped for the night out of range of shot. The next day was passed in endeavouring to feel the position of the enemy, who occupied the line upon the top of the crest, and it was not until the 2nd that an attack was delivered.

After thoroughly reconnoitring the ground, it was found that the position of the Afghans was too strong to be attacked in front, and it was determined to turn it by a long and very difficult night-march of nine miles, up a path leading to the extreme left of the enemy's position. The 72nd Highlanders, the 5th Ghurkas, and the 29th Native Infantry were told off for the service, and started after nightfall. At daybreak they came upon the enemy's pickets, and a fierce fight took place, the Afghans defending themselves desperately. Captain Kelso brought up his battery of mountain guns, and did good service in aiding the infantry, who were all fiercely engaged. He himself, however, was shot dead.

After three hours' hard fighting the enemy's left wing was beaten, and the British, pressing forward, drove them in confusion upon the centre. The 2nd Punjaub Infantry, the 23rd Pioneers, and four artillery guns on elephants now arrived on the scene. It was well that they did so, for the enemy were again found in a strong position in a thick wood, and an obstinate fight ensued. It was some hours before they were dislodged from this point, as they continually brought up fresh troops. So severe was their resistance that it was found impossible to force them back by a direct attack, and General Roberts now directed his men to advance in such a direction as to still further turn their position and threaten their line of retreat. This had the desired effect. The Afghans, as usual, lost heart as soon as it appeared that their retreat was menaced, and, leaving the strong positions on the Peiwar itself, fled hastily.

While this fight had been going on, the second battalion of the 8th Foot had advanced direct from the camp below. Hitherto they had made no great progress, but had succeeded in attracting the attention of the enemy and keeping a large body of men in their entrenchments, and so aided the main attack on the right. The moment the Afghans yielded, the 8th pushed forward and occupied the enemy's position.

The total loss on our side was 2 officers killed, 2 wounded, and 90 rank and file (Europeans and natives) killed and wounded. The troops were too much fatigued with their hard marching and fighting to be able to pursue the enemy. But no ill effect was caused by this, as the Afghans had completely lost heart, and in their retreat threw away arms and abandoned baggage of all kinds, most of their guns being left behind, and one battery falling into the hands of the British when they advanced to the Shaturgurdan Pass. General Roberts with a small party went on to this point, which they found abandoned, and from whence they commanded a view across the heart of Afghanistan almost to Cabul. It was considered unnecessary to occupy this position, as the winter was now at hand, during which time the pass is absolutely closed by snow. There was, then, no fear of the Afghans taking the offensive from this quarter.

Thus in two engagements the military strength which Shere Ali had been building up for many years, and which he considered sufficient to defend his country against the attacks of the British, fell absolutely to pieces; and a few days later he himself left Cabul, and started, a fugitive, for the northern frontier with the intention of passing into Russia. It was necessary, however, that letters should be sent asking permission for him to take this step, and during the delay which ensued the Ameer was seized by fever, and expired.

General Roberts determined to leave a force to garrison the Peiwar, and to take up his headquarters in the lower valley, there to winter. On the way down he followed a route hitherto unknown, leading through the defile of the Chappri. It turned out to be extremely wild and difficult, and the people of this part, a tribe called Mongols, attacked the baggage, which was proceeding under a small escort only, the troops having passed through ahead. The attack was sudden and unexpected; but the men of the baggage guard stood their way well. Captain Goad, assistant-superintendent of transport, was shot through the legs, and fell while fighting bravely. The natives made a rush towards him, but four soldiers of the 72nd stood over him and gallantly defended him against a crowd of enemies until the 5th Ghurkas, under Major Fitzhugh, came up from the rear. Heavy as the fire was, singularly enough, only one of these gallant fellows was wounded.

The Mongols stood boldly, and, taking to the rocks, kept up a very rapid fire, while the Ghurkas repeatedly charged home with the bayonet, using their terrible knives with great effect, and finally putting them to flight, three of the 5th being killed and 13 wounded. Farther up the defile the Mongols made another rush upon the train, but were here more easily beaten back. The attack was made with the hope of plunder only, and from no political animosity.

The population in the valley, although not hostile to British rule, were eager to plunder British wagons, and constant outrages of this kind took place, many soldiers and camp followers being killed. The marauders were in some cases taken and executed upon the spot.

Early in January, General Roberts started with a force up the valley of the Khost. The General reached Khost without much opposition. The villages round sent in their submission, and all appeared likely to terminate quietly. But upon the day after their arrival at the fort, the natives from around mustered in great numbers, and advanced to an attack upon the camp, occupying a number of steep hills around it, and massing in the villages themselves. A troop of the 5th Punjaub Cavalry advanced to attack them, with orders, if possible, to tempt them out on to the plain. This was well managed. The enemy, seeing the smallness of the force, poured out of the villages, when Major Bulkeley with the 10th Hussars swept down upon them, and the Afghans fled and took post on the hills.

They again advanced on all sides, and attacked the camp, and for four hours the 72nd, with two guns to assist them, could get but little advantage of them. Then, unable to withstand the fire of our breechloaders and the effect of our shell, they fell back to the hills. Near the villages on the south side Major Stewart with thirty men of the 5th Punjaub Cavalry made a notable charge. A body fully a thousand strong of the enemy was making from the hills, when, with his handful of men, he dashed down upon them, scattering them in all directions, cutting down twenty, and wounding a large number.

When the enemy had retired to the hills, the villages were searched; and as the inhabitants of these had taken part in the fight, and large numbers of arms were found concealed there, these were burnt, the inhabitants being expelled, and those whom their wounds showed to have taken part in the fight—over 100 in number—brought as prisoners. The loss on our side was but two killed and eight wounded, showing that the Afghans, courageous as they are, are contemptible as marksmen.

This brought the fighting to a close. General Roberts, finding his force too small to hold the Kuram and Khost valleys, evacuated the latter, and the force went into winter quarters.

This step had already been taken in the Khyber. It had not been intended from the first to push the advance as far as Cabul before the winter came on, as the difficulties in the way of so doing would have been enormous, and the troops would have had great difficulty in maintaining their position, even should they capture Cabul before the snow set in. The flight of the Ameer, too, and the accession to power as his father's representative of Yakoob Khan, his eldest son, who had for many years been kept by his father as a prisoner, naturally arrested the course of affairs. It was hoped that Yakoob would at once treat with us, and that our objects would be attained without further advance. These anticipations were to some extent verified. Negotiations were opened, and upon the 3rd of March Yakoob offered to negotiate terms of peace.

Nothing has been said as yet of the doings of the third column of invasion under General Stewart, who had taken the command originally assigned to General Biddulph. The difficulties in the way of advance of this column were immense. First, a sandy desert almost destitute of water, extending between the Indus and the foot of the mountains, had to be crossed; then the ascent of the Bolan Pass had to be made, a work of the most tremendous difficulty. This pass, whose ascent occupies three days, is in fact the mere bed of a stream, full of boulders and stones of all sizes, in which the baggage and artillery horses sank fetlock deep. In making this passage vast quantities of camels and other animals died, and a long delay took place in assembling the force at Quettah, a post occupied by us at the top of the pass. The arrangements were completed at last, and General Stewart advanced upon Candahar, which he captured on the 8th of January, having met with, a small amount of resistance only.

The negotiations with Yakoob, who had now succeeded to the dignity of Ameer, continued for some time; and upon the 8th of May he arrived at the British camp at Gundamuck, where he was received by General Sir S. Browne and staff. Three or four days were spent in visits and negotiations, Yakoob assenting to the British terms, and expressing the strongest hopes that a permanent friendship would be established between England and Afghanistan.

Previous to this a sad accident had occurred, which cast a gloom over the British camp. Upon the 1st of April a squadron of the 10th Hussars, following a squadron of the 11th Bengal Lancers, had, in crossing the river after nightfall, missed the ford, and had been carried off by the current. Lieutenant Harford and no less than fifty men were drowned. This was an accident almost without precedent.

The treaty made at Gundamuck had for its chief object the representation of the British Government at the court of Yakoob Khan; and in accordance with the terms of the treaty, and of a direct invitation on the part of the Ameer, Sir Louis Cavaignari, accompanied by Mr. William Jenkyns, of the Indian Civil Service, as secretary, and by 25 cavalry and 50 infantry of the Guides under Lieutenant Hamilton, went up to Cabul, where they arrived on the 24th of July. Doctor Kelly, surgeon of the Guides, accompanied the mission as medical officer. Some doubt had been entertained as to the prudence of sending this mission, but the Ameer's promises of protection had been given with such solemnity, that it was deemed advisable to carry out the provisions of the treaty.

For some time all went well at Cabul. But the arrival of some regiments from Herat altered the complexion of affairs. From the date, August 5th, when these regiments arrived, turbulent outbreaks commenced in the town. These regiments had not, like those of Cabul, suffered defeat at our hands, and they taunted the Cabul people with cowardice. The position of the Embassy became full of danger. Sir Louis Cavaignari, a man of most extraordinary courage, was aware of the threatening danger, but determined to remain at his post and do his duty. When told by the native *rissaldar* of one of our cavalry regiments, who was spending his furlough at a village near Cabul, that the Afghan soldiers would be likely to break into open mutiny, and that the danger was very real, he replied quietly, "They can only kill the three or four of us here, and our death will be avenged." It appears, however, that Cavaignari to the last believed that the Ameer's authority would be sufficient to protect the little British force.

On the night of the 2nd of September the Heratee troops attacked the Embassy. The party were lodged in a wooden building in the Bala Hissar. Although numbering but fifty fighting men, headed by four British officers, the little band for hours held out heroically against thousands of the enemy. These at last brought cannon to bear upon the place. Yakoob Khan, in his palace close by, heard the roar of the battle, but made no movement. Some of his councillors urged upon him to call out the loyal regiments at Bala Hissar, and to suppress and punish the mutiny. But the Ameer remained vacillating and sullen until the terrible night was over, and the last of the defenders, after performing prodigies of valour, and killing many more times than their own number of the enemy, succumbed to the attack, the British officers rushing out and dying sword in hand.

Twenty-four hours later, natives from Cabul brought the news over the Shaturgurdan Pass into the Kuram Valley. Thence it was telegraphed to Simla. The terrible news created a shock throughout all India. But no time was lost in taking measures to avenge the massacre. On the 5th orders were sent to Brigadier-General Massy, commanding at that time the Kuram field forces, to move the 23rd Pioneers, the 5th Ghurkas, and mountain train to the crest of the Shaturgurdan, and to entrench themselves there. The 72nd Highlanders and 5th Punjaub Infantry followed in a few days to secure the road between Ali Kheyl and the pass. On the 13th, General Baker took command of the troops at the Shaturgurdan, where the 23rd Pioneers and 5th Ghurkas had been strengthened by the arrival of the 72nd Highlanders.

General Roberts now set about the work of collecting transport. As usual, the moment the first campaign had terminated, the transport had been scattered, with the view of saving expense, and had now, at a great outlay, to be renewed. All the available animals in Peshawar and near the frontier were ordered to be sent up. But the drain had told heavily, and only 2000 mules, 700 camels, and 600 bullocks could be collected. The tribes in the valley, however, furnished many animals for local transport.

The Ameer at this time wrote to General Roberts, saying that he was trying to restore order and put down the mutineers, and to punish them for their conduct. But it was clear that he had lost all authority. On 26th September, General Roberts joined the troops at Ali Kheyl. On the way up from this point to the Shaturgurdan, two or three attacks were made upon baggage convoys by the natives; but these were all repulsed.

The advance now commenced. It consisted of the 12th and 14th Bengal Cavalry, two guns of the Royal Horse Artillery, two companies of the 72nd Highlanders, and the 5th Punjaub Native Infantry. These moved out as far as the Zerghun Shahr; and here the Ameer, with some of his principal nobles, came into camp, declaring that they could not control the soldiery of Cabul, but that he had come to show his friendship to the English. The brigades of Generals Baker and Macpherson joined the advance at Zerghun; and on the 29th a *durbar* was held. Yakoob, although received with all honour, was strongly suspected of treachery, and his conduct at the rising in Cabul had forfeited for him all claim upon our friendship. All matters were, however, deferred until after the arrival at Cabul. Before the force moved forward, a proclamation was issued and sent forward among the people, stating that all loyal subjects of the Ameer would be well treated, and that the object of the expedition was only to punish those concerned in the rising at Cabul.

Owing to the shortness of transport, some difficulty was experienced in moving forward, and the force was obliged to advance in two divisions. On the 3rd of October Macpherson's brigade, with the cavalry, reached Suffed Sang. There they halted, while the baggage animals went back to bring up Baker's brigade. Upon this day an attack was made by the villagers upon the rearguard; but these were driven off, and several of them captured.

The next march was a short one to Charasia. Beyond this place the enemy had taken up their position. Here a mass of hills shuts in the wild valley, and this narrows to a mere defile.

Upon both sides of this the enemy had placed guns in position, and lined the whole circle of the hills. In the afternoon a cavalry reconnaissance was made; but they did not succeed in getting the enemy to show themselves in force.

At daybreak on the 6th a working party was sent forward to improve the road through the defile. But they had scarcely started when the cavalry patrol announced that the enemy were in great strength on the hills, and had guns in position commanding the road.

Sir Frederick Roberts determined to attack at once without waiting for the division in the rear, as he feared that any inaction before the mutinous troops now facing them would lead to a general rising, and that in another twenty-four hours there might be not only the regulars, but the whole tribal force of the country to contend with.

The following were the troops who, under the command of Brigadier-General Baker, marched out at eleven o'clock to attack the position:—Four guns Number 2 mountain battery, two Gatling guns, the 7th company of Sappers and Miners, the 72nd Highlanders, six companies of the 5th Ghurkas, 200 men of the 5th Punjaub Infantry, and 450 of the 23rd Pioneers. On the right, the attack was to be made under the command of Major White of the 72nd Highlanders, who had three guns Royal Artillery, two squadrons of cavalry, a wing of the 72nd, and 100 men of the 23rd Pioneers. It was determined to attack the enemy by both flanks, as their power of resisting a front attack was considerable, and flank attacks are always found the most certain against foes of this kind. A reserve was left in Charasia, as the temper of the villagers around was very uncertain, and these would have been sure to rise and attack the baggage left there if the least reverse happened to the advancing force.

The attack was completely successful, both columns effecting their objects and driving the enemy before them. The Afghans, however, fought with great courage, for it was an hour and a half before any advantage was gained. The enemy were armed with Sniders and Enfields, and their fire was rapid and continuous. They were, however, bad shots, and our loss was extremely small. The 72nd were in advance, and these, after some hard fighting, carried the first position. The enemy rallied on some low hills about 600 yards to the rear. But the mountain guns and Gatlings opened upon them, the 72nd fired volleys into them, and a general advance being made, the enemy were driven back.

Major White, in the meantime, on the right had been doing excellent service with his column. It was but a weak one, and the operation had been intended as a feint rather than a real attack. However, they pushed forward, drove the enemy from their position, and captured 20 guns; and having done the work allotted to him, Major White was able to send a portion of his force to co-operate with General Baker's brigade.

Unfortunately our cavalry were in the rear; the road through the pass was difficult; and before they could get through, the masses of Afghans had fallen back into strong villages on the plain, and could not be attacked by cavalry. The enemy had altogether from 9,000 to 10,000 on the ridges, including 13 regiments of regular troops. They left 300 dead on the field; but their losses in killed and wounded must have been much greater. Upon our side 20 were killed and 67 wounded. Among the latter were three officers.

This defeat, by a small portion only of the British force, of the whole of their troops placed in a position considered well-nigh impregnable, struck a complete panic into the Afghans, and no further resistance was offered. In the night a great portion of the Afghan troops scattered and fled. The cavalry under General Massy swept round Cabul, and came upon the Sherpur entrenched camp, where 75 guns were captured. Unfortunately considerable delay took place in the operations of our infantry; and in the face of the troops, who could easily have crushed them, the regiments which had taken the principal part in the massacre of Major Cavaignari marched off unmolested. The villagers were to a man hostile, and seized every opportunity of firing upon bodies of our troops. It was necessary to show considerable severity, and all captured with arms in their hands in such cases were shot at once.

Cabul was now open to us; and upon the 11th October, Sir Frederick Roberts and his staff entered the Bala Hissar, and visited the ruins of the Embassy. The Bala Hissar is a large enclosure containing many important buildings, and situate on the hill above Cabul, which town its guns command. Even had the Afghans made a stand here, the place could not have resisted the British guns, as the walls were old and ruinous.

On the 12th of October formal possession was taken of Cabul, the troops occupying the Bala Hissar. Delay had taken place in this operation, as it was feared that the Afghans might explode large quantities of ammunition known to be stored there. A *durbar* was held after we had entered the Bala Hissar. The whole of the *sirdars* and principal men of Cabul and its neighbourhood attended. Of these the leaders, who had been more than suspected of heading the plot against us, were at once seized and held as prisoners. A proclamation was issued by Sir Frederick Roberts, warning the people that any attempt against our authority would be severely punished; forbidding the carrying of weapons within the streets of Cabul, or within a distance of five miles from the city gates; and commanding that all arms issued to, or seized by, the Afghan troops should be given up, a small reward being given for the delivery of each. A reward also was offered for the surrender of any person, whether soldier or civilian, concerned in the attack on the British Embassy.

For some time things went quietly. The people were clearly intensely hostile to us. But except in the case of the women, no open insults were ventured upon. But it was unsafe in the extreme for small parties to ride about the country. On the 16th the camp was startled by a tremendous explosion at the Bala Hissar, where the 67th Foot were encamped, and where a body of Engineers, under Captain Shafto, were examining the various small buildings in which powder was stored.

The southern wall of the arsenal was blown down, and great damage was done; but, singularly enough, no soldiers of the British regiment were killed, but of the Ghurkas, who were on guard at the arsenal at the time, twelve were killed and seven wounded. Captain Shafto was unfortunately killed. No examination could for a time be made, as some of the buildings were on fire, and explosions continued frequent. In the afternoon another tremendous explosion occurred; four Afghans were killed and several soldiers hurt at a distance of 300 or 400 yards from the spot. Although it was never proved, it was believed that these explosions were caused by the Afghans; and as large quantities of powder still remained in the Bala Hissar, it was determined that, for the present, the place should remain unoccupied.

The little force at Cabul was now isolated. Between that place and the Shaturgurdan the natives were in a restless and excited state. Two attacks by 3000 men had been made on the garrison holding the crest of the Shaturgurdan, 300 in number. These bravely sallied out, attacked the enemy in the open, and killed large numbers of them. General Gough, with the 5th Punjaub Cavalry and 5th Punjaub Infantry and four guns, was therefore sent from Cabul to bring down from the Shaturgurdan all the stores accumulated there and the garrison, and then to desert the place, which would shortly be closed by snow.

Several executions now took place at Cabul, of men who had shared in the attack on the Embassy. Many of the villagers were also hung for shooting at bodies of our troops; and the position of the British force at Cabul was that of a body holding only the ground they occupied in the midst of a bitterly hostile country. The Ameer was powerless, and, indeed, his goodwill was more than doubtful. He was regarded as a prisoner, although treated with all courtesy; and feeling his own impotence, and being viewed with hostility by both parties, he resigned his position as Ameer, and asked to be sent into India, which was done. The abdication of the Ameer really took place on October the 12th, but it was not publicly known until the 28th.

On the 4th of November, Brigadier-General Gough returned with the garrison of Shaturgurdan, which he had safely brought off just as their position was becoming almost untenable, so large was the body of men assembling round them. The roads were now carefully examined upon the way down to Jellalabad, and communication was opened with the force occupying that valley. Some of the cavalry were sent down to the valley, as it was clear that with all the efforts the commissariat could make, sufficient quantities of forage could not be collected for their support during the winter. Up the Khyber Pass troops were slowly coming, destined in the spring to join the force at Cabul, should it be necessary to carry on further operations.

The Sherpur cantonments were now occupied, and were made the headquarters of the force. These cantonments consisted of barracks surrounded on three sides by a lofty wall, steep hills rising at the back. They had been built by the Ameer for his own troops, but had never been used for the purpose. The winter was now setting in. Snow began to fall on the hills around, and ice formed in the pools every night. Several expeditionary columns were sent out round the country to bring in provisions and grain, and these were attended with great success. The enemy were, however, collecting in several places, specially at Kohdaman and Maidan, and had stopped the influx of provisions, which the natives were ready enough to sell for sums which to them were handsome indeed.

Two columns were told off to march out and attack these parties of the enemy. But the movement was an unfortunate one. The force under General Macpherson found Mahommed Jan near Chardeh, and pushed on the 14th Bengal Lancers, who came across several thousand men on their way to join Mahommed Jan. A sharp fight ensued. The guns shelled the enemy, but the water-courses prevented our cavalry from being of any service. Mahommed Jan had with him 10,000 men, and, passing General Macpherson, placed himself between him and Cabul, and there watched the movements of our troops.

Shortly afterwards, four Horse Artillery guns, under Major Smith Wyndham, moved along the Argandeh road to join the infantry. Brigadier Massy, with a squadron of the 9th Lancers, and 44 men of the 14th Bengal Lancers, escorted the guns. After a four-mile march, the advanced troop reported the enemy to be in sight. It was apparent that the Afghans had thrown themselves between the infantry and the guns; but as only 2,000 or 3,000 appeared, it was thought that they were fugitives, flying either from General Macpherson or General Baker.

As they came streaming down the hill, General Massy got his guns into action. After a few shells had been fired, the enemy advanced in full force. Four thousand men were extended in the shape of a crescent, marching in good order, and in rear was an irregular body numbering 6,000. The four guns pitched their shell rapidly into the thick of the enemy; but no effect was produced in the way of breaking the line of advance. It never wavered, but came steadily on; and as General Massy had no infantry with him, he was obliged to retire. The guns fell back a little, and again opened fire. The enemy's bullets were now dropping fast among the cavalry and guns. Thirty of the 9th Lancers dismounted and opened fire with their Martini carbines, but the enemy were too numerous to be checked by so small a body of men.

While the artillery were in action, Sir F. Roberts with his staff joined General Massy. General Roberts ordered him to send the Lancers at the enemy at a charge. Colonel Cleland led his squadron of 126 Lancers of the 9th full at the advancing mass, the 14th Bengal Lancers, 44 in number, following in his wake. On the right, Captain Gough, with his troop of the 9th, also took his men into action at the enemy's left flank. Two hundred and twenty men, however, against 10,000 could scarcely be expected to conquer. The three bodies of cavalry disappeared in a cloud of dust. They were received with a terrific fire, which killed many horses and men, and, charging bravely on into the midst of the enemy's infantry, were surrounded, and their progress blocked by sheer weight of numbers. The *mêlée* was a desperate one. Many of the soldiers were struck from their horses. Some were dragged up again by their comrades, others were killed upon the ground. The chaplain of the force, the Reverend Mr. Adams, had accompanied the troopers in the charge, and extricated one man from the midst of the enemy under a heavy fire, for which he was recommended for the Victoria Cross.

When the dust cleared away, it was seen that the cavalry charge had made no impression upon the enemy, who were still steadily advancing across the fields. The Lancers had fallen back, having suffered terribly. Two of their officers, Lieutenants Hersee and Ricardo, had been left on the ground dead, with sixteen of their men. The colonel and Lieutenant Mackenzie were both wounded, as were seven of the troopers. This squadron rallied upon Captain Gough's troop, which had kept better together, and still held its post between the guns and the enemy. A second charge was ordered; but it was not pushed home, the country being of extraordinary difficulty for cavalry, owing to the water-courses which cut it up. As Major Smith Wyndham was falling back with his two guns, which had been advanced after the first charge, he found one of the other guns stuck in a water-course. The greatest efforts of the remaining horses were insufficient to draw it from the mire in which it was bogged. Lieutenant Hardy was killed by a shot through the head, and the gun was abandoned. The other three guns were taken back 400 or 500 yards farther. They were then stopped by a channel, deeper and steeper than any which had been before met, and here they became hopelessly bogged. They were spiked and left in the water, and the drivers and gunners moved off with the cavalry just as the long line of the enemy came upon them.

General Macpherson's troops, which had been sent for by General Roberts, were now showing down the Chardeh Valley. At their sight the enemy turned off from the Sherpur road and made direct for the city. General Roberts sent a message to Brigadier Gough, commanding at Sherpur, ordering 200 men of the 72nd Highlanders to go out to the gorge at a double. The cavalry retired steadily, keeping up a fire with their carbines, and checking the advance of the enemy. But they could not have stemmed the rush had not Colonel Brownlow, with 200 rifles of the 72nd, arrived at the nick of time. These opened fire instantly upon the enemy, who charged down upon the village. The steady fire of the Highlanders checked the rush, and after half an hour's persistent fire the enemy were forced back, their entrance to Cabul having been frustrated. They occupied, however, a position on the heights to the south of the Balar Hissar region.

General Macpherson had broken up a large body of Afghans higher up the valley, and pursued them towards Argandeh. As he came back, he came upon the scene of the charge, and recovered the bodies of Lieutenants Hersee and Ricardo, and the troopers who had been killed. The guns had already been carried off by Colonel Macgregor, who, with a small scratch lot of Lancers and artillerymen whom he had collected, worked round into the village, which had been left by the main body of the enemy, and, putting down the opposition of the villagers, carried off the guns.

The next day a body of 560 men, composed of portions of the 67th Foot, the 72nd Highlanders, the 3rd Sikhs, and 5th Ghurkas, made an attack upon the enemy, who had established themselves on a lofty peak south of Cabul. The enemy occupied the crest in strength, and away on the south, hidden from our view, had 5000 or 6000 men waiting for our attack to develop. After several hours of fighting, the little British force drove the Afghans from the low hill, but were unable to carry the position above. No more troops could be spared, and ammunition ran short. It was determined, therefore, to put off the attack until morning. At eight o'clock General Baker left Sherpur with a strong force, and attacked the enemy's position. After desperate fighting, he stormed the ridge. Great masses of the enemy in the meantime were moving round, so as to threaten the road to Sherpur. The 9th Lancers charged with great gallantry among them, and defeated them. Captain Butson, who commanded the Lancers, was, however, killed, and two other officers wounded. Several other brilliant charges were made, and the plain was kept clear of the enemy.

Our position, however, although actually victorious in the field, was getting more and more serious. The city was now in open revolt. Large numbers of natives continued to arrive and reinforce the enemy; and it was rapidly becoming clear that the British force, although strong enough to hold the Sherpur cantonments or the Bala Hissar, would not be able to maintain itself in both. Upon the next day, the 15th, desperate fighting again took place. General Baker, with 1200 bayonets and 8 guns, left the cantonments to make another attempt to clear the hills, and in this he succeeded, but only after the greatest efforts. Several officers were killed or wounded, but the enemy were driven from their first position. Just as they had done this, a body of from 15,000 to 20,000 of the enemy marched out upon the plain, and made towards the position captured by General Baker.

Steadily they advanced, and the shells which our mountain guns sent among them, and the volleys poured down from the hills, did not suffice to cause the slightest faltering in their advance. Steadily they came forward, and desperate fighting took place. A position held by the 5th Punjaub Infantry was carried by their attack; two guns were lost; but the rest of the positions were held. There were now 40,000 men, at least, gathered round the British forces, and General Macpherson was ordered to fall back to Sherpur with all his force. General Baker was to hold the village he had occupied since the morning, until all the troops from the heights were within the walls. The movement was well carried out, and although some loss took place as the troops fell back, by nightfall all the British forces were gathered in the cantonments of Sherpur.

For some days fighting was suspended, the Afghans being busy in plundering the Hindoo portions of the city, and in preparing for an attack. The British forces in Sherpur were now fairly besieged, and it was considered certain that nothing could be done until the arrival of troops from Jugdulluck and Gundamuck, down in the Jellalabad Valley.

Unfortunately the position had been considered as so secure from attack, that no steps had been taken to demolish the old forts and villages standing round Sherpur, and these were now occupied by the enemy, who kept up a steady fire upon the cantonments. Upon the 18th the enemy made an attack upon the place, but this, although hotly kept up, was repulsed without much difficulty.

On the 19th, General Baker made an assault upon a small fort situate at a few hundred yards from the cantonment, from which the enemy had greatly annoyed us. A portion of the place was blown up, the Afghans being driven from it after severe fighting. Skirmishing went on each day; but the Afghans could not bring themselves to make another attack until the night of the 22nd, when 20,000 men advanced to storm the British position.

The garrison had received warning, and at four in the morning signal fires were seen burning, and the fire of the enemy's skirmishers began. The enemy crept quietly up, and at six o'clock, with a shout, the whole body rushed out from the villages and orchards round the place, and charged upon the walls. They opened fire with a tremendous roar, but this was drowned by the roll of musketry which broke out from the whole circuit of the walls, where the men had been lying for the last three hours, rifle in hand, awaiting the attack. Some of the enemy pushed forward to within eighty yards of our rifles, but beyond this even the bravest could not advance. For a few hours they skirmished round the place; but finally fell back, and the attack was abandoned.

With the morning came the welcome news that General Gough had reached the Cabul plain, and the cloud of dust arising in the distance showed that the enemy had also heard of our reinforcement, and was marching out to attack him. The garrison of Sherpur at once sallied out and attacked the Afghans, creating a diversion, and killing large numbers of the enemy. By nightfall the whole of the Afghans were driven into Cabul. Upon the following day General Cough's force arrived, and the British were again masters of the country. The whole of the Afghans engaged in the attack fled during the night, and the British marched into Cabul without resistance. This was virtually the end of the fighting at this point.

The time now passed quietly, and it was not until the month of May that any serious fighting took place. Then the tribesmen again began to muster. General Stewart was on his way from Candahar, and the tribes, feeling that if any hostile movement against us was to be successful it must be undertaken before the arrival of the reinforcements, assembled in great numbers. General Macpherson moved out against them, and another battle took place at Charasia, and after some very severe fighting the enemy were scattered.

Sir Donald Stewart's march had been uneventful as far as Shahjui, the limit of the Candahar province. Here the Teraki country begins, and the Mollahs had been actively preaching a holy war, and had collected several thousand men. As we advanced the villages were deserted. Upon arriving at Ahmed Khel, the enemy were found to have taken up a position in front. Our baggage stretched far in the rear, and it was all-important to prevent the column being outflanked. General Stewart therefore determined to attack at once. The two batteries of artillery opened fire upon the enemy, who numbered from 12,000 to 15,000, and who, at a signal, rushed headlong down from their position, and charged upon General Stewart's force.

This charge was executed by some 3000 or 4000 Ghazees, as they were called—that is to say, fanatics sworn to give their lives to carry out their object of exterminating the hated infidel. These men were armed, some with rifles and matchlocks, some with heavy swords, knives, and pistols, others with pikes made of bayonets or pieces of sharpened iron fastened upon long sticks. Some were on foot; some on horseback. So sudden and unexpected was the attack, so swiftly did they cross the four or five hundred yards of intervening ground, that they came upon the British before preparations could be made for their reception.

Cavalry were moving in front of the infantry, and these, before they could be got into line for a charge, were surrounded by the enemy. In an instant they were lost to sight in the cloud of dust and smoke caused by the battle; and in the confusion a troop charged to the right in rear of our infantry line, and burst into the 19th Punjaub Native Infantry, in rear of the General and his staff. All was for a moment confusion. The ammunition mules were stampeded, riderless horses dashed hither and thither, and behind the cavalry came in the Ghazees with a furious rush, and a hand-to-hand fight took place.

So impetuous were they, that on the left they swept round in the rear of our infantry; and the results would have been most terrible, had not Colonel Lister, V.C., commanding the 3rd Ghurkas, formed his men rapidly into company squares, and poured a tremendous fire into the fanatics. All along the line the attack raged, and so hurriedly had the affair come on that many of the men had not even fixed bayonets. Desperate was the hand-to-hand fighting; and valour more conspicuous than that of the Ghazees was never shown. But the three regiments, British, Sikh, and Ghurkha, to whom they were exposed, held their own, and poured rolling volleys into the ranks of the enemy. So fiercely did these charge that they came up to within thirty yards of the muzzles of Major Waters' guns, which were firing case and reversed shrapnel, and mowed them down in hundreds. The 2nd Punjaub Cavalry charged again and again in the most gallant manner, and protected the guns from the Ghazees' attacks. The General, surrounded by his escort, was in the midst of the fight, the enemy having burst in between the guns and the 59th Foot, and officers and troopers had alike to fight for their lives, several of the escort being killed. At last, however, the Ghazees fell back before the terrific fire, and the 1st Punjaub Cavalry, coming up from the rear, took up the pursuit.

The fighting had lasted but an hour; but of the enemy 1,000 dead lay upon the field, besides those bodies which had been carried off, and their wounded must have been even more numerous. Among our troops 17 were killed and 126 wounded. Our native allies, the Hazaras, seeing the Afghans defeated, took up the pursuit, and the rout of the enemy was complete.

Ghuznee fell without opposition, the fighting men having been engaged in the battle of Ahmed Khel, and having had enough of hostilities. A force was sent out from Ghuznee on the 23rd of April, under Brigadier-General Palliser; and this had a severe engagement with the natives near the village of Shalez, where they fought with a desperation equal to that shown by the fanatics in the previous battle. Our men, however, were this time prepared, and were able to inflict very heavy losses upon the enemy, without allowing them to get to such close quarters as before. This was the end of the Afghan resistance, and General Stewart moved on to Cabul, and effected a junction with General Roberts. This brought the second period of the Afghan war to a close.

For some months the forces remained quiet at Cabul. Negotiations were now going on. Abdul Rahman was advancing upon Cabul. This chief had long been a resident among the Russians, and had assumed the Ameership, and had been received cordially in the north of Afghanistan. As no other competitor appeared to have equal chances with him, and as the British Government were most desirous to retire from the country, his authority was recognised by us, and upon his approach to Cabul the British force was ordered to retire.

Just at this moment, however, news came which showed that the work was not yet over.

When General Stewart left Candahar in his march towards Cabul, a strong British force had been left at that city. A protégé of the British, named Wali Shere Ali, had been appointed by us Governor of Candahar. His native army was not, however, regarded as reliable; and when the news came that Ayoub, a brother of Yakoob, was moving down from Herat, of which town he was the governor, with a large force, a body of British troops advanced with the Wali's army towards Girishk on the river Helmund.

On July the 14th the conspiracy which had been going on among the Wali's troops came to a head. The whole of them deserted, and the small British brigade found itself alone on the Helmund. General Burrows had with him but 1500 infantry, 500 cavalry, and 6 guns, a force clearly inadequate to meet the large body with which Ayoub was advancing, and which would be swelled by the addition of the Wali's late troops. General Primrose, who commanded at Candahar, decided that no more troops could be sent forward to strengthen this brigade.

Ayoub was advancing steadily, and, after deliberation, General Burrows fell back from Girishk to a point upon the road near Maiwand. Ayoub had crossed the Helmund higher up, and was moving in a parallel line to that taken by the British; and the object of the English commander was to take up a position which would at once bar the road to Candahar and would prevent Ayoub striking by a more northern road, by which he would place himself north of the city and on the road to Cabul. The camping-ground was a village called Khussk-i-Nakhud. Reconnaissances were made by General Nuttal's cavalry in the direction of the enemy; but General Burrows had but bad information, and had no idea of the real strength of the force with which Ayoub was advancing.

It was not until the 26th that the forces came into collision. It was known then that Ayoub was trying to reach Maiwand without fighting, and General Burrows at once marched from Khussk-i-Nakhud to Maiwand to anticipate this movement. At half-past six the troops marched, the general belief being that it was only Ayoub's cavalry with which he should have to deal. Upon arriving near Maiwand, however, our spies brought in the news that the whole of Ayoub's force was in front.

The morning was thick, and but little could be seen of Ayoub's army. The cavalry were indeed found moving about in large masses, but these fell back on our advance. Lieutenant Maclean, with two Horse Artillery guns and a small cavalry escort, galloped out on the extreme left, and got his guns into action on the Afghan cavalry. The position was considered a dangerous one, and the guns were withdrawn. Large numbers of the enemy, led by Ghazees, were now seen swarming down over the low hills.

The British infantry were formed in the following order:— On the right were the 66th Regiment, the Bombay Grenadiers formed the centre, and Jacob's Rifles the left. Two guns were placed in position to support the 66th on the right, the remaining ten—for the six British guns had been increased to twelve by a battery captured from the Wali's mutineers—between the Grenadiers and the main body of Jacob's Rifles. There was no reserve, nor, indeed, with so small a force could there have been any. The cavalry, the 3rd Scinde Horse and 3rd Bombay Cavalry, formed up in the rear of the left centre.

Our guns shelled the enemy as they advanced, and it was fully an hour before his artillery opened in reply, when five batteries unmasked and opened fire. Under cover of this artillery fire, the enemy's irregulars advanced. When within 600 or 700 yards of the 66th, the Martini fire of the latter checked them, and in this quarter for a moment the attack ceased.

Unfortunately our position was in every way a bad one. Deep ravines ran both to the right and left of our force. By these the enemy could advance until within a short distance of us. The position, too, was dominated by the hills on either side, and after an artillery duel lasting for some time, the enemy's guns were moved on to the hills and a terrible fire opened upon our infantry. At about two o'clock the smooth-bore guns began to run short of ammunition, and as only sixty rounds had been captured with them and there was no reserve, these were abandoned. The enemy's battery now came boldly up, their cavalry manoeuvred on the left flank of the brigade, large numbers of their infantry and irregulars got into the villages behind us, and the position became more and more serious.

Half an hour later the two companies of Jacob's Rifles on the extreme left began to waver. The retirement from the smooth-bore guns demoralised them, and they broke their ranks and fell into utter confusion, breaking in upon the Grenadiers, who had up to that time fought steadily. The Ghazees swept down in great masses, and the Grenadiers likewise gave way. The remaining companies of Jacob's Rifles shared in the panic. The enemy now swept in in all directions, their guns from the heights poured volleys of shell into the ranks of the crowded British, and the 66th, borne in upon by the rush of native troops on the one side, pressed by the Ghazees on the other, and cut down by the artillery fire, began to fall back also.

The confusion became hopeless. The artillery fired until the Ghazees were within a few yards of them, and two of the guns were lost. The cavalry were ordered to charge; but they had already been much demoralised by the artillery fire, and could not be persuaded to charge home. In the walled enclosures behind, the 66th and the Grenadiers rallied, and fought nobly. Here Colonel Galbraith was killed and nine other officers of the 66th. Some bodies of troops, entirely cut off from the rest, fought desperately to the end, and, dying, surrounded themselves with a ring of slaughtered enemies. But at length the surviving troops were extricated from the villages, and the retreat commenced.

Fortunately the pursuit lasted only two or three miles, the enemy having themselves suffered terribly, and being, moreover, anxious to take part in the loot of the camp. The retreat was a terrible one. Fifty miles had to be passed, and no water was obtainable on the way. Along the whole line the villagers rose upon the fugitives, and the loss was terrible.

Had the cavalry remained, as was their duty, behind the infantry, protected the retreat, and so given time to the fugitives to rally, the result would have been different. But the conduct of the native cavalry regiments was the reverse of creditable.

Fortunately Ayoub's army had been to a great extent demoralised by the tremendous losses which it had incurred in the defeat of this handful of British troops, and some days elapsed before it could continue its advance. This gave time to the garrison at Candahar to put all in readiness. The doubtful portion of the population was cleared out of the city, provisions collected, and all put in readiness for a siege.

The news of Maiwand aroused tremendous excitement throughout India, and orders were at once issued for the carrying out of relieving operations. General Roberts was to march from Cabul with a strong division, consisting of tried troops, while General Phayre, with another force, was to move from Quettah. Unfortunately the same false economy which had so delayed the advance after the massacre of Cavaignari, by the instant break-up of the transport trains, again operated to delay General Phayre; and although every possible effort was made, the force advancing from the Bolan could not reach Candahar until after that coming down from Cabul, although the latter had many times the distance to march.

The forces which took part in the memorable march of General Roberts were the 92nd Highlanders, 23rd Pioneers, 24th Punjaub Infantry, 2nd Ghurkas, 72nd Highlanders, 2nd Sikhs, 3rd Sikhs, 5th Ghurkas, 2nd, 60th, 15th Sikhs, 25th Punjaub Infantry, and the 4th Ghurkas. There were three batteries of artillery, and four cavalry regiments—the 9th Lancers, the 3rd Bengal Cavalry, the 3rd Punjaub Cavalry, and the Central India Horse. This gave a total of about 10,000 men. The march would be between three and four weeks. There would, in addition, be 8,000 followers to feed, 2,000 horses, and some 8,000 transport and artillery mules and ponies.

The new Ameer did his best, by sending orders that all should be done to assist the march. But the operation was in any case a dangerous one, and it was questionable whether the force would be able to subsist upon the road. However, it started, and marching steadily day by day, passed through Ghuznee and down to Khelat-i-Ghilzai, where Colonel Tanner had been besieged. No difficulties were met with, and scarce a shot was fired on the way down. In seven days Ghuznee was reached, in fifteen Khelat-i-Ghilzai, the marching being no less than 15.7 miles per day,—not an extraordinary distance for a single regiment to perform, but a wonderful feat for a force containing some 18,000 persons, and 9,000 baggage animals, marching through mountainous valleys.

Candahar had held out during the advance of General Roberts. Indeed, Ayoub's forces had never ventured upon anything like a formidable attack upon it, believing that they would be able to starve out the garrison in time. A sortie had been made, but with disastrous effects, and the garrison were now standing strictly on the defensive.

As the relieving force advanced, Ayoub drew off and took ground on some hills near the town. On the 27th of August the cavalry established heliographic communication, this being the nineteenth day of their march from Cabul. On the 31st the entry was made into Candahar. There was little delay here. Ayoub's army had taken up its position on the Baba Wali Hills. On the south-west his right was protected by the Pir-Paimal Hill. This, however, was liable to be turned. A reconnaissance was at once made by the cavalry, and the enemy unmasked five guns and opened upon them. The Afghans poured out to the attack of the 15th Sikhs. But these retired steadily, as there was no wish to bring on an engagement. General Macpherson's brigade, with those of Generals Baker and Macgregor, were to take part in the fray, the latter being in reserve.

The men breakfasted at eight o'clock, and at nine were ready for the advance. The attack commenced by General Macpherson's brigade carrying a village which the Afghans had occupied in advance of the range. Without maps, it is difficult in the extreme to describe battles; but it may be briefly said that Generals Macpherson and Baker advanced round the end of the Pir-Paimal, carried village after village, in some of which a desperate defence was made by the enemy, and so at last, winning every foot of the ground by hard fighting, they swept round the hill, and turned the enemy's left. Many of the men were killed by Ghazees, who shut themselves up in the houses of the villages and sold their lives dearly, firing upon our troops until house after house was carried by storm. The whole ground was orchard and enclosed fields, and each of these was the scene of a conflict. Behind the northern hill, where the country is cut up by water-courses and canals between the river and the slopes, the Afghans made their last stand. A deep water-cut, twelve feet broad, with banks two or three feet high, and with cultivated fields in front, served them as an excellent defence. The banks had been ingeniously loopholed for rifle fire, and two camps lay in rear of it. The Highlanders, however, carried the place with a rush, losing upwards of 40 men as they did so. The rest of the enemy, numbering from 8000 to 10,000, who had been gathered in the orchards, were driven round the rear of the line of hills. Wherever they tried to rally, the British were upon them, and at last the fugitives reaching their camp, the whole body of Ayoub's army took to flight, although his regular regiments had never been engaged during the day, the whole fighting having been done by the irregulars.

In four hours from the time the fight began, the Afghan army was driven from the position it had taken up, its camp and all its appurtenances falling into our hands, as well as thirty-one guns and two Horse Artillery guns, which had been captured at Maiwand. They had made certain of victory, for not a tent was struck, nor a single mule-load of baggage off.

This action, which completely crushed the force of Ayoub, concluded the campaign.

The battle cost the lives of three officers—Lieutenant-Colonel Brownlow, commanding 72nd Highlanders, Captain Frome, 72nd Highlanders, and Captain Straton, 2nd battalion 22nd Foot. Eleven officers were wounded, 46 men were killed and 202 wounded. The enemy's loss was about 1,200 in killed alone. Their work was over; and as General Stewart, with the army of Cabul, had retired from beyond the borders of Afghanistan on the one side, so General Roberts, with his relieving force, fell back on the other, and the Afghan Campaign came to a close.

The Zulu War
1879

RORKE'S DRIFT

The Zulu War
1879

Towards the end of the year 1878, serious disputes arose between the British authorities of Natal and Cetewayo, the King of the Zulus, a savage monarch possessing a large army of warriors, composed of men well-trained according to the savage idea of warfare, and possessed of extreme bravery.

The ill-feeling had commenced at the time that the British took over the Transvaal. Between the Boers and the Zulus great hostility prevailed, the Boers constantly encroaching upon the Zulus' ground, driving off cattle, and acting with extreme lawlessness. The Zulus had long been preparing for retributive warfare; and as the Boers had proved themselves shortly before unable to conquer Secoceni, a chief whose power was as nothing in comparison with that of Cetewayo, the Zulus deemed that they would have an easy conquest of the Transvaal. The occupation of that country by the English baulked them of their expected hopes of conquest and plunder, and a very sore feeling was engendered. This was heightened by the interference of the English with the tribal usages. Wholesale massacres had been of constant occurrence in Zululand, the slightest opposition to the king's will being punished not only by the death of the offender himself, but by the destruction of all the villages of the tribe to which he belonged. Every fighting man was in the army, and the young men were not permitted to marry until the king gave permission, such permission being never granted until after the regiment to which the man belonged had distinguished itself in fight. Hence it happened that frequently the men were kept single until they reached middle age, and this privation naturally caused among the whole of the younger population an intense desire for war.

The British Government, seeing the danger of such an organisation, and feeling that unless it was broken up war would shortly break out, called upon Cetewayo to abolish this institution. At the same time the Government was acting as arbitrator between the Zulus and the Boers on a question of frontier, and there was also a minor dispute concerning some chiefs who had crossed the Tugela, the frontier river, and carried off some captives.

In December a *durbar* was held, in which the Government gave the decision on the frontier question in favour of the Zulus, ordered the persons who had violated the frontier to be given up, and at the same time gave in an ultimatum to the Zulu king respecting the dissolution of his army. It was not known what answer the king would give; but it was believed that it would be unsatisfactory. Accordingly every effort was made to place a strong force upon the frontier. Three columns were assembled, one near the mouth of the Tugela, which was to march along the coast; another was to cross the river at Rorke's Drift; a third was to enter Zululand from the Transvaal. The first of these was to be commanded by Colonel Pearson; the second would be commanded by Colonel Glyn, and accompanied by the General, Lord Chelmsford, himself; and the force acting from the Transvaal would be commanded by Colonel Evelyn Wood.

On the 31st December, Cetewayo returned an answer, expressing his willingness to give up some of the persons whose surrender was demanded, and to pay the fine imposed upon him. As to the other points, however, his answer was purely evasive, and preparations were made to cross the frontier at once. On the 3rd, General Lord Chelmsford left Capetown for the front, and the time given to Cetewayo to return a favourable answer was extended to the 11th. On the 12th, no further reply having been received, the British troops crossed the Tugela River. Lord Chelmsford's column moved slowly forward, and occupied no less than ten days in getting to Isandula, a place little more than ten miles from the frontier. On the morning of the 22nd, Lord Chelmsford, taking with him the main body of the column, advanced to reconnoitre the country beyond,—five companies of the 1st battalion of the 24th, one company of the 2nd battalion of the 24th, two guns, two rocket tubes, 104 men of one of the frontier corps, and 800 natives remaining behind to guard the camp. These were further reinforced in the course of the day by the arrival of Colonel Durnford with a body of frontier troops. The Zulus were presently seen advancing towards the camp. This was situate in a valley. At the back of the camp was a very high and steep hill, which, had time been given, could have been occupied and held against overwhelming forces. Unfortunately, however, no steps had been taken to occupy this point of vantage, or in any way to strengthen the camp. Had the force been pitched in Salisbury Plain, it could not have acted as if in more perfect security.

Upon the Zulus making their appearance, advancing in their usual formation,—namely, that of a great crescent,—two companies of the 24th advanced to meet them, and Colonel Durnford, with his horse, went out to skirmish. The Zulus, however, were so numerous and came on with such determination, that even the rapid fire of the infantry rifles scarcely sufficed to check them for an instant. The cavalry were forced to fall back; the infantry, after resisting to the last moment, also retired hastily. In the meantime the wing of the Zulu force had swept round, and came down upon the baggage wagons in the rear of the camp. Then the whole body fell upon the little force of British.

So sudden and determined was the attack, so unexpected in its character, that the British force had scarcely time to prepare in any way for it. For a few minutes they fought fiercely, and then the Zulus, with a tremendous rush, were upon them. Then, in a moment, all was confusion and disorder. Some stood in groups and fought desperately, back to back. Others broke and fled. But to all, whether they fought or fled, the same fate came. A few, and a few only, of the mounted frontiers succeeded in cutting their way through the enemy and making for the river but the footmen were, to a man, killed.

The loss was over 1000, and scarce 50 of those engaged effected their escape. Among the dead were Colonel Durnford and Lieutenant Macdonald, Royal Engineers; Captain Russell and Captain Stewart Smith, Royal Artillery; Colonel Pulleine, Major White, Captains Degacher, Warden, Mostyn, and Younghusband; Lieutenants Hobson, Caveye, Atkinson, Davey, Anstie, Dyson, Porteous, Melville, Coghill; and Quartermaster Pullen of the 1st battalion 24th Regiment; and Lieutenants Pope, Austin, Dyer, Griffith, and Quartermaster Bloomfield, together with Surgeon-Major Shepheard, of the 2nd battalion 24th Regiment. A large number of British officers commanding the native contingents were also killed.

Among those who had ridden off while the fight was raging were Lieutenants Melville and Coghill. These were both mounted, and Melville bore the colours of the regiment. Cutting their way through the surrounding Zulus, they rode for the river, hotly pursued by the enemy. Lieutenant Coghill swam safely across; but upon reaching the other side, perceived that his comrade was helpless in the river, his horse having thrown him, and he clinging to a rock. The gallant young officer at once returned and rescued his friend; but the delay was fatal. The Zulus were upon them, and, after a desperate resistance, the young officers were both killed.

In the meantime, by some extraordinary neglect, the column under Lord Chelmsford was marching on without having any idea of what was happening in its rear, no communication whatever being kept up between the two bodies. At last, late in the afternoon, just as it was preparing to halt, the news was brought of the attack upon the camp. The column marched back with all speed; but only arrived at the camp late at night, to find it deserted by the enemy, and strewn with the bodies of those they had left in high health and spirits in the morning, and with the remains of wagons and stores of all descriptions.

That night the force lay on their arms on the scene of the encounter, and next morning marched back to the Tugela, and crossed at Rorke's Drift.

Here another conflict had taken place upon the previous day; and had it not been for the gallantry and presence of mind of two young officers, not only would the depots here have fallen into the hands of the Zulus, but the retreat of the column would have been cut off, and in all probability it would have shared the fate of those at Isandula.

At Rorke's Drift was a depot of provisions and stores. This was guarded by a little force of some 80 men of the 24th Regiment, under the command of Lieutenant Bromhead; Lieutenant Chard, Royal Engineers, being senior officer.

In the afternoon the news reached them that the enemy were approaching in force; and without a moment's loss of time the young officers set their men to work to form an entrenchment with the grain bags and boxes, to connect a house used as an hospital with the storehouse. Scarcely were the preparations complete, when the Zulus, several thousand strong, crossed the river and advanced to the attack. The little garrison defended themselves with heroic bravery. Fortunately, among the stores was a large quantity of ammunition, and they were therefore enabled to keep up a steady and incessant fire all round, without fear of running short. Several times the Zulus charged up to the breastwork and endeavoured to climb over; but each time these efforts were repulsed. The little force, however, was unable successfully to defend the hospital, which, after desperate fighting, was carried by the Zulus and burnt, the garrison then being concentrated in the storehouse and a small piece of ground enclosed by meal-bags in front. For twelve hours the fight continued, and then the Zulus, after suffering a loss which they themselves admit to exceed 1000, fell back, and the all-important station was retained.

Upon the 23rd, as Colonel Pearson's column was advancing from the lower Tugela Drift, they were attacked by the enemy at the Ebroi River, and a fierce fight ensued. The Zulus, however, were kept at bay by the fire of the rifles, artillery, and rockets, and were unable to come to close quarters. After making several efforts to charge, they fell back with a loss of 300 killed. The force pushed on as far as Ekowe, and there receiving the news of the defeat at Isandula, Colonel Pearson set to work to entrench the position, sent back his mounted men and the native contingents, and determined to hold the place to the last.

When the news of the disaster at Isandula reached England, the effect was immense, and preparations were instantly made to send reinforcements to the Cape, to the extent of six battalions of infantry, two regiments of cavalry, and two batteries of artillery. The 88th Regiment, which was at the Cape, was at once hurried round, and every available man who could be spared landed from the men-of-war. For a few days a panic pervaded the colony, as it was feared that the Zulus, inflamed by victory, would cross the river and invade Natal; and had this bold policy been carried out, there can be no doubt that wholesale devastation could have been caused by them. Fortunately, however, the Zulus, satisfied with their victory and to a certain extent appalled by the tremendous loss which had been inflicted upon them, both at Isandula before they overwhelmed the 24th, and at Rorke's Drift, where they failed in their attack, fell back from the frontier and allowed the British preparations to be made without interruption.

The column of Colonel Evelyn Wood was attacked two days after the battle of Isandula; but having received news of that disaster, they were well prepared, and repulsed the enemy with much loss. They then fell back to the frontier, and, like the other columns, stood on the defensive.

The troops on the way from England made rapid passages, and arrived at Durban earlier than could have been expected. About the same time Prince Napoleon, who had gone out from England with the permission of Government as a spectator in the war, also arrived there, and was permitted to accompany the British column. Upon the arrival of the first troopship at Natal all fear of an invasion passed away, and as vessel after vessel arrived with its load, the hopes of the British, that the defeat of Isandula would speedily be wiped out, rose high. There was, however, considerable delay in obtaining the wagons and mules required for transport.

The first operation to be undertaken was the relief of Ekowe. This position had been attacked, and had not only defended itself successfully, but the little garrison had sallied out, and burned various kraals in the neighbourhood. Considerable anxiety, however, was felt as to them, for they were entirely cut off from news. A few runners only had managed to make their way through, and these had now ceased, the Zulu watch being too strict to allow any of them to pass. Fortunately the Engineers were able to establish communication by means of flashing signals, and from that time news was received daily, giving an account of the camp, and acquainting those there of the preparations which were being pushed forward for their relief.

On the 12th of March, 100 men of the 80th Regiment, under the command of Captain Moriarty, when marching from Durban to Luneberg, on the north-western frontier of Zululand, were attacked in the night by the enemy; Captain Moriarty and half the force being killed, while the remainder of the party, who were encamped upon the other side of the river Intombi, succeeded in making their escape.

On the 29th of March the column of relief advanced from the Tugela. It consisted of the 99th, 91st, 57th, 3rd, 60th, several companies of the Buffs, the Naval Brigade, 200 cavalry, and two battalions of the native contingent. The Naval Brigade, consisting of the men of the *Shah* and *Tenedos*, with two 9-

pounders and three Gatling guns, led the advance. No enemy was met with during the first day's march, and they encamped on the Ioyuni, nine miles north of the Tugela, where they threw up entrenchments at once. The next day they marched to Matacoola, and thence on the following day seven miles farther, to Gingihlovo.

This camp was situated on slightly rising ground, and the tower of Ekowe was distinctly visible from it. From this Colonel Pearson flashed signals that a large force of the enemy was on the march. Entrenchments were thrown up, and the force remained in readiness for an attack. At half-past five in the morning large masses of the enemy were sighted. They crossed the river Inyanzi, and advanced in their usual crescent-shaped formation. The camp was formed in a square; the 60th Rifles were holding the face first threatened by the enemy. For half an hour the 60th were hard at work; but their steady fire beat back the enemy at this point. Sweeping round to the right, they then made a determined effort to force their way in on that side, but were met and checked by a tremendous fire from the 57th and 91st.

Nothing could be finer than the way in which the natives advanced to the attack upon the line of entrenchments, and, notwithstanding the tremendous musketry fire which they encountered, they pressed forward so closely that for some time it appeared as if they would force their way to the entrenchments, and bring the matter to a hand-to-hand fight. The fire, however, proved too much for them, and they wavered and began to fall back. Then the little body of cavalry sallied out from the camp, and fell upon them, and the native contingent followed and took up the pursuit hotly. The Zulu army was composed of some of the picked men of the best regiments of the king, and the result showed conclusively that British troops, if only properly led, can resist an attack of any number, even of the most gallant savages. The loss of the Zulus was estimated at 1500.

The relieving force now pushed on to Ekowe, where they found the gallant garrison in great straits from want of food and from disease, brought on by living so long in confinement. During the siege 4 officers and 26 men had succumbed. Ekowe was evacuated, a force was left at Gingihlovo, and the column then returned to the Tugela.

On the 28th of March, the day before the relief column started for Ekowe, very heavy fighting had taken place in the north-west of Zululand. Colonel Wood had, during the whole of the time of inactivity, harassed the enemy with great success. A chief by the name of Umbelini, however, had made repeated attacks, and it was now determined to punish him by an attack on the strong plateau of Mhlobani, on which Umbelini kept the greater part of his herds. On the morning of the 28th, Colonel Buller, with all the mounted forces, started, gained the plateau without much difficulty, collected great herds of cattle, and prepared for the return.

When, however, they were on the point of leaving the plateau, vast bodies of Zulus were seen approaching from the plains. These were an army which had been sent by Cetewayo to the assistance of Umbelini. The cavalry, scattered among the herds, and unable to act from the rocky nature of the ground, were now in a bad position, and suffered most heavily. Captain Barton's Volunteer Horse and Colonel Weatherley's troop suffered most heavily, losing no less than 86 men and 12 officers. Among these were Colonel Weatherley himself, Captain Hamilton of the Connaught Rangers, and Captains Campbell and Burton of the Coldstream Guards. The rest of the force succeeded in getting away, and, hotly pursued, fell back upon the camp at Kambula.

The following day the Zulus were seen approaching in great force. Colonels Buller and Russell, with the cavalry, went out and skirmished, but were speedily driven in. The enemy came on in great force until within 300 yards of the entrenchment, when a heavy fire was opened upon them by the men of the 13th Regiment. This checked their advance upon the front, and they then threatened the cattle laager, hard by, by a flanking movement. Major Hackett of the 90th, with two companies, moved to this, and for three hours a desperate fight raged round the whole circuit of the camp. At the end of this time the Zulus, having suffered terribly from the fire of our breechloaders, began to fall back, when our cavalry under Colonel Buller at once sallied out and fell upon them, and for seven miles pursued and cut them up. Our loss was comparatively small. Lieutenant Nicholson, R.A., and Lieutenant Bright of the 90th were killed, Major Hackett and several other officers being severely wounded.

Many weeks now passed without striking events, and the greatest discontent was caused by the long inactivity. Kambula and Gingihlovo had shown how British troops, when steady, could defeat great masses of the enemy; and it was inexplicable to all why a British force of some 15,000 men could remain for weeks inactive within but four days' march of the stronghold of the enemy. So great had the discontent become, both in England and Natal, at the extraordinary inaction of the British troops, that the greatest satisfaction was diffused when, on the 26th of May, Sir Garnet Wolseley was appointed to the chief command at the Cape.

On the 1st of June an occurrence took place which cast a gloom over the whole country. The Prince Imperial started with Lieutenant Carey of the 98th, and six men of Bettington's Horse, on a reconnoitring expedition, and reached a kraal some ten miles from the camp. Here they unsaddled their horses and rested for an hour. As they were in the act of re-saddling, a party of Zulus suddenly sprang out. All leaped to their horses and rode off, unhappily headed by the officer, who should have been the last in the retreat. The Prince Imperial was unable to mount his horse, and was overtaken by the Zulus within 300 yards of the kraal, and, being deserted and alone, was killed by the Zulus, making a noble resistance to the last. There is no blacker episode in the history of the British army than this.

Another month was passed in tedious delays and crawling movements. General Sir Garnet Wolseley reached the Cape in the last week in June, and the news of his approach appears to have quickened the faculties of the officer until then commanding the British troops, who accordingly advanced, and upon the 4th of July fought the battle of Ulundi. The British were formed in square, and upon their approach to the king's head village, were attacked by the Zulus. The fight was never for an instant in doubt. From the four sides of the square a tremendous fire from our breechloaders, aided by guns and Gatlings placed at the angles, mowed down the Zulus, who advanced bravely, but were wholly unable to stand the withering fire. The conflict lasted but a very few minutes, at the end of which the Zulus were in flight, and the war in Zululand was virtually at an end.

After this there was no more actual fighting. Scattered bands were dispersed and places occupied; but the Zulus lost all heart, and went off at once to their villages. A hot pursuit was kept up after the king, and he was finally captured and sent a prisoner to the Cape. The troops were sent back to England as speedily as possible.

After the pacification of Zululand, Sir Garnet Wolseley carried out a very dashing little expedition against Secoceni, who had long defied the strength of the Boers and the authority of the English. His stronghold was captured after sharp fighting, and for a time the South of Africa was pacified.

The Egyptian War
1882

TEL EL KEBIR

The Egyptian War
1882

In the spring of 1882 a movement, in which the military were the principal actors and Arabi Pasha the guiding spirit, took place in Egypt; and although Tewfik, the Khedive, was not absolutely deposed, his authority was set at naught. He had, from the commencement of his reign, acted under English advice, and as there was a strong anti-foreign element in the movement, considerable apprehensions were excited lest the safety of the Suez Canal would be threatened, should the revolution be carried to a successful end. The support given by the English to the Khedive excited against us a strong feeling of hostility on the part of Arabi's party, and the position grew so threatening that an English and French fleet was sent to Alexandria to give a moral support to the Khedive, and to protect the European inhabitants. The situation was further aggravated by a serious riot in Alexandria on 11th June, arising primarily from a quarrel between the natives and the lower class of Greeks and Levantines. The riots spread, and a considerable number of Europeans were killed and wounded.

Preparations were at once made for war, but before the troops could arrive upon the scene a crisis occurred. Arabi's troops commenced throwing up fresh batteries, in positions menacing the English fleet. Admiral Seymour requested that the work should be discontinued; but as it still went on, he sent in an ultimatum. This was not attended to, and at the expiration of the time given, the British fleet opened fire upon the Egyptian forts and batteries. The firing continued all day, and by the afternoon the Egyptian batteries were all silenced.

The next day the enemy exhibited a flag of truce, and negotiations were kept up until evening. That night the Egyptian troops evacuated the town; but before leaving, they, with the fanatical portion of the populace, set fire to the greater portion of the European quarter, which was almost entirely destroyed. Little loss of life, however, took place, as the greater part of the European inhabitants had gone on board ship previous to the commencement of the bombardment.

The next day 600 marines and seamen landed, and took possession of the town. The troops now began to arrive from Malta and Gibraltar, and a position was taken up outside the town at Ramleh, facing the army of Arabi. Several small skirmishes took place at the outposts, a body of twenty mounted infantry, under Lieutenant Pigott of the 60th Rifles, particularly distinguishing themselves. The troops arrived fast, General Sir Archibald Alison took the command, and reconnaissances of the enemy's position were made by the troops and by an armour-clad train manned by sailors.

On the 6th of August a reconnaissance in force was made. Six companies of the 60th Rifles, four companies of the 38th, and four of the 64th marched out from the lines at Ramleh, accompanied by seven companies of the marines with the iron-clad train. The 38th and 46th moved forward with one gun, on the left bank of the Mahmoudieh Canal; the 60th, also with a gun, moving on the right bank, while the marines advanced on the railway embankment. The enemy were seen in large numbers in front of the Rifles, and these advanced in skirmishing order. The enemy lined a ditch which ran across the country with a dense jungle on its rear, and opened a heavy fire from the cover upon the Rifles. A hot fire was kept up on both sides, the English gradually pressing forward towards their invisible foe. When the Rifles reached within 100 yards of the ditch, the Egyptians began to steal away through the jungle, and the 60th charged down upon the ditch with a cheer, when the enemy at once took to their heels. The marines were equally successful along the line of the railway embankment. The enemy made a bold stand at the point where the canal and railway approach each other, and, strong reinforcements coming to their assistance, the British fell back in good order, the Egyptians declining to pursue.

At the commencement of the fight, the mounted infantry under Captain Barr and Lieutenants Pigott and Vyse were in advance of the 38th. The officers with six men went forward to reconnoitre, and suddenly found themselves in front of a large body of the enemy; the infantry dismounted and returned the fire opened upon them, expecting support from the rear. Orders, however, came for them to retire. In the meantime two of the little band were struck dead, and two were wounded. Lieutenant Vyse, a great favourite with his men, was struck high in the leg, and, the arteries being severed, bled to death. His comrades would not desert his body, but carried it off under a tremendous fire, the two wounded men, who were still able to use their rifles, covering the retreat with their fire.

Sir Garnet Wolseley arrived at Alexandria on the 15th of August, and on the 19th, the whole of the troops from England having arrived, the fleet with a large number of transports sailed from Alexandria, leaving a division under the command of General Sir Evelyn Wood to defend the town. Arriving at Port Said, the fleet sailed up the Suez Canal to Ismailia, which they occupied without resistance, and the troops at once began to land.

On the 24th an advance was made on Ismailia, and at a distance of seven miles the enemy was encountered. The force was not sufficient to attack the enemy, but an artillery fire was kept up hotly all day. In the evening British reinforcements came up, and the Egyptians in the morning retired without fighting. They made a stand, however, farther back; but the cavalry under General Drury Lowe pushed forward on their flank, and after a short resistance the Egyptians fled, a great number of them making their escape in the railway trains. Seven Krupp guns, an immense quantity of rifles and ammunition, and seventy-five railway wagons, loaded with provisions, fell into our hands. The troops now advanced as far as Kassassin, where the advanced troops were under the command of General Graham.

On the 29th of August the enemy were seen in considerable force near this post, and the cavalry at Mahsameh, four miles in the rear, rode out to assist the force there. The enemy, however, made no attack, and in the afternoon the cavalry returned. Scarcely had they reached camp when a heavy and continuous roar was heard; the Egyptians, with a force of 13,000 men, had advanced with the intention of crushing the small bodies of British troops in their isolated posts. The garrison of Kassassin consisted only of a battalion of Marine Artillery, the 46th and 84th Regiments. The enemy came on in overwhelming numbers, and with great resolution. The British infantry turned out to defend the positions, manning the slight earthwork which had been thrown up round the camp. The Egyptians advanced in a storm of bullets, their artillery playing heavily on the camp. The Egyptians suffered heavily, but advanced with considerable courage, and the position of the British was becoming serious.

At this moment, however, the British cavalry, consisting of the Horse and Life Guards and the 7th Dragoon Guards, with the Horse Artillery,—who had remounted and advanced when the recommencement of the cannonade told that the attack had begun in earnest,—came into action. Instead of advancing direct upon Kassassin, General Lowe took his men by a long detour by the right, and so came round in the darkness upon the enemy's rear. It was not until they arrived within a mile that the enemy saw the black mass advancing in the moonlight over the sandy plain. A battery of nine guns at once opened upon them, and the Horse Artillery replied immediately to the enemy's fire. Bullets as well as shell were now falling fast around the cavalry, and General Lowe gave the order to charge the guns. Led by Colonel Sir Baker Russell, the cavalry rode straight at the enemy's battery. Fortunately, in their haste the Egyptian gunners fired high, and with a few casualties the cavalry reached the guns. The Egyptian gunners were cut down, and then the horsemen dashed into the infantry behind, who were already turning to fly.

The opening of the British guns in their rear at once checked the advance of the assailants of the garrison of Kassassin. The cavalry charge completed the confusion of the enemy, and in a short time the plain was covered with bodies of the flying Egyptians making their way back to Tel-el-Kebir, from which they had started in the morning, confident in their power to annihilate the little British force at Kassassin. Large numbers were killed, and the rout would have been even more complete had not the horses of the cavalry been too much exhausted with their long day's work under a broiling sun, to permit the pursuit being vigorously continued.

The British advance had been terribly hindered from the difficulties of transport, but at last all was in readiness, and the division which had come from India having been brought round from Suez to Ismailia, all was prepared for the advance against the strong Egyptian position at Tel-el-Kebir.

On 9th September the enemy again advanced in great numbers, many of them having been brought up by train from Tel-el-Kebir. The videttes of the Bengal Lancers, who were now at the front, brought in the news of their approach, and the infantry and guns moved out to check them. The enemy had, however, already reached positions whence their fire commanded the camp, and opened fire with thirty guns upon the camp and moving column. The English artillery returned the enemy's fire, but the numbers were so great that for a time the position of the force appeared critical. General Lowe with his cavalry rode out from camp, and repeated his manoeuvre of the previous engagement. The enemy's flank movement was checked, and their cavalry fell back, and for half an hour the two bodies of cavalry manoeuvred to outflank each other, halting occasionally while the light artillery on both sides opened fire. In the meantime the Egyptian infantry had advanced on either side of the canal and railway, and down the slopes of the sand-hills, until within 800 yards, when they opened a continuous rifle fire. The 60th Rifles and the marines advanced to meet the enemy coming by the canal and railway line, when the 84th pressed forward against those on the high ground. For a time a tremendous fire was kept up on both sides; then the fire of the Egyptian guns began to slacken under the superior aim of the British artillery.

The order was given to advance, and the three regiments, supported by two others in reserve, went at the enemy, who at once broke and fled, abandoning three of their guns. The English pursued them until within four miles of Tel-el-Kebir. The cavalry, on their side, had not only driven in the cavalry of the enemy, but 5000 of their infantry, who were advancing from Salahieh to outflank our position. So completely demoralised were the enemy by their defeat, that there can be little doubt the force engaged would have been sufficient to have carried Tel-el-Kebir at a rush. Sir Garnet Wolseley, however, ordered a halt, as he had no wish to attack their position until able to deliver a crushing blow with his whole force, which was now close at hand.

On the 12th the whole expeditionary force was assembled at Kassassin, and in the evening the camp was struck, and the army, 14,000 strong, moved out, and, piling their arms, lay down on the sand until one o'clock; then they again fell into rank and advanced. Scarcely a word was spoken, and the dark columns moved off almost noiselessly, their footfalls being deadened by the sand. On the right was Graham's Brigade, which had already done such good service by twice repelling the assaults of the enemy; next to them came the brigade of Guards, which was, when the action began, to act as their support; next to these moved 42 guns of the Royal Artillery, and on the line of railway the Naval Brigade advanced with the 40-pounder on a truck; beside them came the Highland

Brigade,—the Cameronians, 74th, Gordon Highlanders, and Black Watch,—the 46th and 60th forming their support. It was upon these that the brunt of the action fell. So silent was the advance in the darkness, that the enemy did not perceive the advancing column until they were within 300 yards. The Highlanders were advancing to attack the face of the works nearest to the line of march, and consequently arrived at their destination some time before Graham's Brigade, which had to make a sweep round. Suddenly a terrific fire broke from the Egyptian entrenchment upon the Highlanders. Not a shot was fired in reply, but with a wild cheer the Highland regiments dashed at the enemy's line.

Against so fierce and rapid an onslaught the Egyptians could make but little stand, and the Highlanders dashed over the line of earthworks. Scarcely, however, had they won that position when the Egyptians opened a tremendous fire from an entrenchment farther back. The Highlanders for a minute or two replied, and then again advanced at a charge. The Egyptians fought stoutly, and for a time a hand-to-hand struggle went on; then some of the Highlanders penetrated by an opening between the Egyptian entrenchments, and opened fire upon their flank. This was too much for them, and they almost immediately broke and fled.

In the meantime fighting had begun on the other flank. Warned by the roar of conflict with the Highlanders, the Egyptians were here prepared, and for a time kept up a steady fire upon our troops. The 18th Royal Irish were sent to turn the enemy's left, and dashed at the trenches, carrying them at the bayonet's point. Next to the 18th came the 87th and 84th, with the Guards close behind. For a short time the enemy clung to the line of entrenchments, but their fire was very ineffective. By this time the Highland division was already in their camp, and soon losing heart they too fled, and the whole Egyptian army were in full rout. With hardly a moment's delay, the cavalry were pushed on in pursuit, and, riding forward with scarcely a halt, reached Cairo in twenty-four hours. Although there was a strong garrison here, it at once surrendered, and Arabi Pasha gave himself up to the English. The instant the news reached the Egyptian army facing Alexandria, it dispersed in all directions, and the war in Egypt came to an abrupt termination.

On every occasion throughout this war, when the British came in contact with the enemy they behaved with great valour; but the nature of the conflict, and the poor fighting power of the Egyptian troops, afforded comparatively few opportunities for the display of deeds of individual heroism.

England, however, has every reason to be proud of the conduct of her soldiers and sailors during the Egyptian Campaign, which was accomplished with a dash and rapidity, and with a smallness of loss, in comparison with the number of the enemy's troops and the strength of their artillery, altogether unprecedented in the annals of modern warfare.

Campaigns Against
the Mahdi
1883-85

Campaigns Against the Mahdi
1883-1885

Although the defeat of Arabi was complete, another and much more serious danger to Egyptian civilisation soon after arose in the Soudan. An Arab of Dongola, a Moslem fanatic, who had been accepted by many of the Arabs as the Mahdi or prophet, the expected Messiah of Islam, had, as far back as 1881, resisted and defeated the Egyptian forces, and during 1882, by repeated successes, had largely increased his power and the number of his adherents. In 1883 serious preparations were made by the Egyptian Government for a campaign against these rebels; and in August an army of over 10,000 men of all arms was collected and despatched against the Mahdi under the command of Colonel Hicks, a retired Indian officer, and at this time a Pasha in the Egyptian service; and with him were many other English officers. For some weeks nothing was heard in lower Egypt of the expedition, but at last news reached Khartoum that the whole force had become entangled in a defile in which an ambuscade had been prepared by the enemy, and that after three days' fighting, the ammunition being exhausted, the army had been annihilated by the superior numbers of the Mahdi's followers. In this awful slaughter there fell with Hicks Pasha, the Governor of the Soudan, and more than 1000 officers; while all the guns, munitions of war, and transport animals fell into the hands of the Mahdi.

This and other victories of the Mahdi and his lieutenants added greatly to his prestige as prophet, and to the number of his fanatic followers, who now overran the whole of the

Soudan. The British Government urged upon the Egyptian Ministry the necessity of relieving the various invested garrisons, and withdrawing from the country without delay. To this plan the Egyptians reluctantly agreed, but they found themselves unable to accomplish it. The British Government then applied to General Gordon, who had formerly acted as Governor-General of the Soudan, and who had more influence over the Arabs than any other European, to undertake the task of the evacuation of Khartoum, the civil population of which was about 11,000, an operation which, as they could only hope to retire by the Nile, would require months of preparation. General Gordon set out at once for his post, and, reaching Cairo on the 24th January 1884, left for Khartoum on the 26th, with General Stewart as his sole companion. Travelling up the Nile, these two reached Korosko on 1st February, and then mounting camels rode for six days across the desert, and eventually reached Khartoum on 16th February, where they were hailed with the greatest enthusiasm by the people. At first all seemed well, the country was fairly quiet, and Gordon hoped to be able to send the garrison back, and indeed did send in safety some 2500 widows and children to Korosko, but events soon occurred which destroyed all hopes of a peaceful retreat.

After the defeat of Hicks Pasha, Baker Pasha, another quondam British officer, had been collecting a force of Egyptians at Suakin, and while Gordon was still on the road to Khartoum came into contact with the Mahdi's men. Baker's force consisted of some 3000 or 4000 Egyptians, who proved of such miserable quality that at the first attack of the enemy they were seized by wild panic, and notwithstanding the heroic effort and example of their European officers, could not be prevailed upon to stand, but broke and fled in all directions, followed by the relentless Mahdists, who massacred them without pity, 2300 men being slaughtered like sheep, and with no more show of resistance, in fifteen minutes. Nearly all the European officers were killed fighting, and only a few, among whom was Colonel Baker, succeeded in cutting their way through, and returning to Suakin. Soon after this disaster Sincat fell; its gallant garrison, under Tewfik Pasha, refusing to surrender, blew up the forts, and then marched out and fell fighting to the last; and Tokar also fell into the Mahdists' hands, its garrison agreeing to terms of surrender, thus leaving Osman Digna, the Mahdist leader, free to attack Suakin itself.

Battle of El-Teb
1884

As it was now clear that no reliance could be put upon Egyptian troops, even when led by British officers, it became necessary for Great Britain to intervene if Suakin was not to fall into the hands of the Mahdi. This had to be prevented at all costs, and by the end of February a British force consisting of about 3500 troops was assembled at Suakin under General Graham. The Arabs had taken up a strong position at the village of Teb, a few miles inland of Trinkitat, at the scene of the defeat of Baker's army, and it was decided to drive them from this position.

Early on the morning of 29th February the British column set out, marching in the form of a hollow square, with the transport animals carrying reserve ammunition and hospital equipment in the middle. The force consisted of 3000 infantry selected from the Gordon Highlanders and Black Watch, the Royal Irish Fusiliers, King's Royal Rifles, York and Lancaster Regiment, Royal Marines, and some Engineers, 115 of the Naval Brigade, six machine guns and eight Royal Artillery 7-pounders, and some 750 mounted troops.

The Arabs were found in carefully made entrenchments, on which were mounted the guns recently taken from Baker Pasha's force, but their rear was unprotected; the attack was therefore made on this side. After the village had been shelled by 7-pounders for some time, the square marched against the rear of the Arab lines, the storm of bullets and shell by which they had been greeted having by this time ceased. As the column reached the lines the Arabs, who were concealed on all sides, suddenly sprang up, and with the reckless courage which the British soldier was often to witness in the near future, rushed upon the square, upon three sides at once; they had now, however, a foe of a quality widely different from that of Baker's force to deal with, and a continuous and well-directed hail of bullets swept them down by hundreds, while all who reached the square fell by the bayonet on its outside, the square meantime steadily advancing. As the village was approached the formation could no longer be kept so regular, and there was fierce hand-to-hand fighting.

When the fort was reached, a company of the Black Watch charged, with them being Colonel Burnaby and some bluejackets. The enemy stood their ground, and fought like heroes; in the *mêlée* Colonel Burnaby was wounded, and also Captain Wilson, R.N., of the *Hecla*. The latter, seeing a marine in difficulties with five or six of the enemy round him, went to his assistance, and after breaking his sword set to with his fists, doing terrible work with the hilt. The enemy were at length driven out at the point of the bayonet, and though they stubbornly contested every inch of the ground for three hours and a half, at length gave way in all directions. The cavalry were now called into action to pursue the scattered ranks of the Mahdists and prevent their re-forming. The enemy again met the attack with great bravery, and it was at this stage of the action that the principal British losses occurred, for the Arabs lying concealed in holes in the sand and behind hillocks, drove their spears into the horses and men as they passed over them, the sword proving a very inefficient weapon in the encounter, a fact which led to the general use of the lance on future similar occasions.

The Mahdists suffered a crushing and, as it seemed at the time, a complete defeat, and the troops meeting with no further opposition advanced to Tokar, and after destroying the fort returned to Suakin. On our side Major Slade, Lieutenants Freeman and Probyn, and Quartermaster Williams, and 26 non-commissioned officers and men were killed, and 142 officers and men wounded; whilst of the enemy 2500 were found dead upon the field, and probably as many more were wounded.

BATTLE OF TAMANIEB
1884

It was naturally hoped that after so thorough a beating the Arabs round Suakin would make their submission, and a proclamation was issued calling upon the Sheikhs to do so. This, however, only provoked defiance, and it soon became known that the Mahdists were collecting in force at Tamai, about 16 miles to the south-west of Suakin, and accordingly another fight, which proved to be a very severe one, became necessary.

This took place on March 13th, the troops having bivouacked on the previous night a mile or two from the enemy's position. The force consisted of two brigades under General Sir Redvers Buller and General Davis respectively, the first consisting of men from the Gordon Highlanders, Royal Irish Fusiliers, and King's Royal Rifles; and the second of some of the Black Watch, York and Lancaster Regiment, and marines, with a force of 10th and 19th Hussars, and mounted infantry under General Stewart.

The Hussars and mounted infantry first came into touch with the enemy, dismounting and firing by volleys and independently, the nature of the ground not being suitable for charging; the enemy faced their fire with great courage, and retired in good order and slowly, as though unwillingly; the loss on our side being only two killed and eight wounded, a number quite out of proportion to the services rendered and loss inflicted on the enemy.

The second brigade, which was leading, had a very severe fight, and suffered heavy loss, which was mainly owing to the open formation of the square at a critical moment. On this account it was not strong enough to resist the sudden rush of the Arabs, who had lain concealed about fifty yards away. The charge being delivered at such close quarters and so suddenly, enabled the enemy to get to close quarters before the guns of the Naval Brigade could be got into position. A charge was ordered, but the Arabs swept round each line as it charged, burst through it, and pressed it back, and a terrible hand-to-hand fight followed. The Black Watch lost many men, being attacked both from front and rear. Three times the naval officers commanding the guns, which they would not leave, were surrounded; at last all of them and many of their men were killed, and for a few minutes the guns were in the hands of the enemy.

The York and Lancaster Regiment were also hard-pressed. Seeing the serious position of the brigade, General Stewart sounded a charge, and 700 flashing sabres swept down upon the enemy,—an awe-inspiring sight, which even the courage of the Mahdists could not endure, and after a moment's hesitation they retreated. Upon this Colonel Wood, commanding the Hussars, ordered his men to halt, dismount, and fire upon the enemy; at the same time General Buller's brigade poured in a heavy fire, thus affording the second brigade time to re-form, and in a few minutes the victory was complete. The guns were retaken, and the whole force advanced and took possession of the enemy's position, and destroyed the village and tents, all opposition having entirely ceased.

There fell in this action 120 British officers and men, the heaviest losses being among the Black Watch. Lieutenant Montresor, R.N., Lieutenant Almach, R.N., and Lieutenant

Houston, R.N., with seven of their men, were killed at their guns. The enemy's force was estimated at 15,000 and their loss at over 5,000.

THE EXPEDITION TO KHARTOUM
1884 AND 1885

The fighting around Suakin in 1884, though successful as to its immediate result, namely, the defeat of local levies of the Mahdi, had no beneficial effect upon the position of Gordon in Khartoum; rather, it would appear, the contrary. The defeat and terrible slaughter of the Arabs at El-Teb and Tamai seem to have been taken as an earnest of the intention of the British to re-conquer the Soudan, and so to have decided many hitherto friendly, or at least neutral, Sheikhs to throw in their lot with the Mahdi. Whether this view is correct or not, the fact remains that up to March Khartoum was open, and by the end of the operations it was besieged. Our purpose being rather to relate achievements of "Our Soldiers" than a history of the events which preceded them, we will not attempt to state the cause which led to the seclusion of Khartoum and the isolation of the heroic Gordon and his companions, Colonel Stewart and Consul Power, nor the causes which rendered the splendid engagements at Suakin fruitless, and led to the fall of Berber. It is enough to say that at length the people of Great Britain could bear the spectacle no longer, and the force of public opinion compelled the Government to take steps in the summer of 1884 to achieve, if it were not too late, the relief of Khartoum. What was a possible task a few months before had now become an exceedingly difficult, if not impossible, one, and it was thought that, under the circumstances, the route which was the most feasible would be by the Nile.

In the early part of October news arrived that Colonel Stewart and Mr. Power, the special correspondent of the *Times*, who had also acted as Vice-Consul at Khartoum, had been murdered on their way to Dongola. They were proceeding down the Nile in one of Gordon's steamers in order to open communications with the British expedition under Lord Wolseley, which was then advancing up the river, and with them were some forty-five other people, including the French Consul at Khartoum. The steamer struck on a rock, and the whole party had to disembark. They were hospitably received by the Sheikh, who promised no harm should happen to them if they came unarmed. This they accordingly did; but no sooner had Colonel Stewart and the Consul entered the Arab's house than they were attacked, and having no weapons but their fists, were eventually overcome and killed. General Gordon was now absolutely alone, and still holding Khartoum against the Mahdi, and no time was to be lost if he was to be released. Strenuous efforts were made to push on the expedition, and by the middle of December a strong force had assembled at Korti, on the Nile, 1400 miles by the Nile from the sea.

Here Lord Wolseley arrived on the 16th of December. The latest news from General Gordon was dated 14th November, saying that his steamers awaited the expedition at Metammeh, and that he could hold out for forty days, but that after that the defence would be difficult. Upon this news Lord Wolseley decided to send a flying column as soon as possible across the desert to Metammeh, with instructions to send a detachment by the steamers up to Khartoum. The desert route to Metammeh direct from Korti is 176 miles, but the distance is very much greater by the river, which between these two places makes a bend of three parts of a circle. The command of the force selected was given to General Sir Herbert Stewart, with Sir Charles Wilson as second in command. A strong depot having previously been established at the wells of Jakdul, about 100 miles towards Metammeh, the expedition started on the 8th January. It consisted of 5 naval officers and 53 bluejackets under Lord Charles Beresford (sent for service on the steamers), a battery of artillery, 9 officers and 120 men of the 19th

Hussars under Colonel Barron, the Guards Camel Regiment under Colonel Boscawen, the Heavy Camel Regiment, consisting of Household troops and cavalry, under Major Gough, infantry mounted also on camels, 400 men of the Royal Sussex, some transport engineers and hospital details—in all 114 officers and 1687 men, with 153 horses and 2888 camels, and some 350 native drivers, etcetera.

THE BATTLE OF ABU KLEA

Nothing of importance took place until the 17th of January, when the wells of Abu Klea were approached and found to be held in great force by the enemy. Leaving a few men of the Sussex and mounted infantry to hold the camp, the General advanced the remainder of his force to seize the wells, the possession of which was, of course, a matter of supreme importance. The British as usual advanced in the form of a hollow square, the troops being disposed as in the diagram.

As the square approached the enemy's position, the attack was delivered in the shape of a well-ordered charge, commencing with a wheel to the left and falling upon the left front and rear of the square. It was a matter of wonder to our men how such a regular formation was preserved over a space of 300 yards in face of a continuous and withering rifle fire. When the enemy got well within 100 yards, the fire of the mounted infantry and Guards began to tell, and the Arabs fell in heaps.

The rear left was not so fortunate, for either from the rear not closing rapidly enough, owing to the fact that the Heavies were not trained to infantry work, or from its opening out in order to bring the Gardner gun into action, the square at the left rear corner was not able to bear the force of the charge, and was driven in by sheer weight of numbers, and several of the Arabs got inside. The Gardner gun had become jammed at the tenth round, and so became a source of weakness to the solidity of the square, a fact of which the enemy was quick to take advantage. At this point Colonel Burnaby, who had joined the expedition as a volunteer, was killed while gallantly facing the crowd. The Naval Brigade, as usual refusing to retire from their gun, suffered heavily, and lost all their officers except Lord C. Beresford, who was knocked down in the *mêlée*. For a few moments the Arabs were in the square and among the camels, and many of the officers had narrow escapes, while Major Gough and others were killed. For five minutes it was a hand-to-hand fight, but after the first wild rush no more of the enemy could pierce the ranks of the Heavies, and all who had entered the square were killed; and the enemy retreated, while the column marched down to and occupied the wells, and rejoiced in abundance of sweet if muddy water. The square had another fight of the same nature before the Nile was reached, but on this occasion the enemy failed to penetrate the zone of fire, and left all their leaders and many of their men lying dead on its front. In the early part of the day General Stewart received a wound which subsequently proved fatal.

It is sad here to relate that all this gallantry of the men, the loss of valuable lives, and the slaughter of thousands of Arabs, which had become necessary by delaying operations until the Mahdi had gathered so much strength, failed in its object, namely, the relief of Khartoum and the rescue of its heroic defenders. For when Colonel Wilson and his party, having found Gordon's steamer, reached the city, they found it in the possession of the Mahdi, and subsequently learned that Gordon had been killed, and the garrison put to the sword, but two days before their arrival; but, in the words of Lord Wolseley's despatch—

> It was not through any lack of zeal or want of energy that the steamers only reached Khartoum two days after it had fallen. There is no hesitation in saying that all ranks worked as hard as human beings could, hoping to render the earliest possible assistance to their heroic comrade who was besieged in Khartoum.

FIGHTING ROUND SUAKIN
1885

In addition to the operations undertaken for the relief of Khartoum by way of the Nile and across the desert, the British Government had placed General Sir G. Graham in command of a strong force collected at Suakin, with instructions to destroy the power of Osman Digna, and to occupy the Hadendowa territory in order to enable a railroad to be built between Suakin and Berber, for which purpose vast quantities and stores had been despatched from England. Among the components of this force were not only Indian troops, both the cavalry and infantry, but for the first time in history a well-equipped body of Volunteer Horse, some 800 strong, despatched at the expense of the Colony of New South Wales, who joined the force on March 8th, and proved to be of great assistance and well worthy of a place among the Soldiers of the Queen.

The Arabs had been in no way disheartened by the defeats inflicted upon them by Sir G. Graham in the preceding year, and from the very first offered a fierce resistance to the advance of the expedition, so that skirmishes of more or less importance took place daily. The first serious battle took place on March 20th near the village of Hasheen, upon which the British column was advancing. About nine a.m. the Berkshire Regiment, supported by some marines, advanced upon the Dhilibat Hill, which was held by swarms of the enemy, who were soon driven down the opposite slope. In pursuing these the 9th Bengal Cavalry were ordered to dismount and fire volleys, but as this most unfortunately took place in thick bush, they were placed at a great disadvantage when the Arabs turned upon them, and they in turn were pursued, and many who were unable to mount in time lost their lives. This pursuit, however, cost the Arabs very dear, for it brought them right down to the square of the Guards, who were in reserve below the hill, before they were aware of them. With their usual bravery the Arabs charged the square, but so heavy and well-sustained was the fire that none got within fifteen yards of the rifles. The hills for the time were cleared, but the Arabs did not retire far, and hung in around the troops in the dense bush, full of fight and as undaunted as ever. The estimate of the enemy's losses was about 250, while the British loss was 22 killed and 43 wounded; and, in the words of the official despatches:

> The conduct of the force was satisfactory in all respects. The Dhilibat Hill was carried by the Berkshire Regiment with the greatest spirit, and the behaviour of the Guards' square under a heavy fire from an unseen enemy was marked by extreme steadiness.

McNeill's Zareba

Two days later, on Sunday, March 22nd, a second engagement took place, very much more serious than the first, and much more important in its result. General Graham had decided to form a *zareba* eight miles out on the road to Tamai, in order to make a depot for water and stores,—more especially the former,—preparatory to an advance in force on that place; it was intended to leave troops in this *zareba*, and on the return of the main body to form and occupy a smaller *zareba* between it and Suakin.

The force selected for the purpose of effecting this object consisted of one squadron 5th Lancers, Naval Brigade with four Gardner guns, detachments of Royal Engineers, Berkshire Regiment, Royal Marines, and company of sailors with four Gatlings, some Royal Engineers, Madras Sappers, 15th Sikhs, 17th Bengal Native Infantry, and 28th Bombay Native Infantry, and one squadron of Hussars, and was under the command of General Sir John McNeill; General Hudson of the Indian force being second in command. The convoy which these troops had to protect consisted of about 1000 camels carrying water and supplies, as well as a large number of mules and horses—no easy task in a country covered with dense bush, which afforded concealment to an enemy who were absolutely fearless.

The column started at 6:30, and its troubles soon began, for no sooner was it fairly within the bush than the difficulty of keeping the transport together became apparent, and the rate of progress was necessarily so slow that Sir J. McNeill saw that it would be impossible to carry out the programme of building and occupying the two *zarebas* before night, and therefore decided to form one only on an open space that the troops had reached about 10:30 a.m. Up to this time no sign of the enemy had been seen, but all precautions were taken to prevent a surprise.

The force was drawn up as follows: the Indian troops occupied three sides of a hollow square, the open side being towards the bush through which the column had just come; outposts of infantry, and beyond them of cavalry, were placed in advance on the three sides; and the road to Suakin in the rear was patrolled by the Lancers, and all the convoy was drawn up in the square. All hands at once proceeded to form the *zareba*. The idea was to form a *zareba* with its north-east corner pointing to Suakin, and its south-west to Tamai, and at each of these corners to form a minor *zareba* or redoubt to contain two Gardner guns apiece, and to leave these garrisoned by the Berks, the marines, and the bluejackets, who would thus be able to guard the main *zareba*, all sides of which could be swept by their fire. The work proceeded merrily, and by three o'clock was nearly finished. At that time the marines had got inside the north-east *zareba*, and half the Berkshire were having their dinner outside, behind the camels, which, by this time having unloaded, were filing out of the square at the rear of the open side; the other half of the Berkshire were busy cutting bush, leaving their arms piled in the south-west *zareba*, with half the bluejackets and the two Gardner guns, and the central *zareba* was nearly completed.

Suddenly a yell was heard, some cavalry videttes came galloping in, and in a moment 5000 Arabs were rushing upon the unclosed square.

The outposts got together and stood back to back, forming rallying squares which the enemy could not break; the Berkshire men who were cutting bush rushed back to the *zareba* where the small naval brigade was suffering severely, for the guns not being in position the enemy got into the square, but so quickly did the Berks men follow them and recover their weapons, that, though 124 Arabs got into the square no Arab came out again. The other half of that regiment formed square, and with a steady fire kept the Arabs at bay, and eventually gained the north-east *zareba* without losing a man. But amongst the transport animals the state of affairs was very different. The 17th Native Infantry fell back before the rush, and the enemy, following their retreat, dashed into the central *zareba* among the transport animals, cutting and slashing in every direction, and in a few moments a general stampede ensued; camels, mules, and horses made one wild rush for Suakin followed by triumphant Arabs, who in their turn were met and routed by the Bengal Cavalry and 5th Lancers. At the first rush a number of the enemy succeeded in getting into the north-east *zareba*, the east side of which was at the moment undefended, and for a few minutes the marines were in a dangerous position, but while the front rank continued to fire on the enemy on their side, the rear rank faced about, and, fighting back to back, soon cleared the *zareba* of the enemy and lined the open side. After about twenty minutes the bugle sounded "Cease fire," and as the smoke cleared away, the enemy were seen streaming away. Thus ended the fight. It was indeed a soldiers' battle, and but for the steadiness and heroism of the individuals it would have proved another Isandlana. The enemy's loss was very heavy, and the power of Osman Digna utterly crushed; but the cost to the British was heavy, for the losses of British and Indian troops was 600 in killed and wounded, and a large proportion of the transport train was destroyed.

The Chitral Campaign
1885

The Chitral Campaign 1885

In January 1895 the reigning Mehtar of Chitral was murdered by his brother, whom, in breach of a time-honoured custom of Chitralis, he had neglected to murder or exile upon his own accession. Umra Khan, the chief of Jandol, who had long had designs upon Chitral, made this occasion a pretext for invading the territory off which he had been repeatedly warned by the British Government as the Suzerain of Chitral, and laid siege to Kila Drosh. On February 1st, Dr. Robertson, the British resident at Mastuj, arrived in Chitral, and at once ordered Umra Khan to retire. Umra Khan, however, who had in the meantime taken Kila Drosh, retorted by calling upon Dr. Robertson to retire, and to recognise Sher Afzul as Mehtar. This, of course, the British resident refused to do; and called a *durbar*, at which Soojah-ul-Moolk was declared Mehtar of Chitral, on 1st of March. The position of the British resident and his small party, which by way of precaution had occupied the fort some time previous, now became very serious. On 2nd of March, Sher Afzul had advanced upon them, and Chitral was very soon invested on all sides, and indeed, as will be seen, the actual siege commenced on 3rd of March.

The siege and defence of Chitral

With Dr. Robertson were Captains Colin Campbell and Townshend of the Central India Horse, Lieutenant Harley of the 14th Sikhs, Surgeon—Captain Whitchurch, Captain Baird of the 24th Punjaub Infantry, and Lieutenant Gurdon, who was acting as political officer before Dr. Robertson's arrival;

the troops consisted entirely of natives, there being eventually shut up in the fort, in addition to those named, 543 persons, of whom 460 were combatants, namely 361 Kashmirs and 99 Sikhs. On the 3rd of March, Captain Campbell with 200 men was sent out to make a reconnaissance in the direction of Sher Afzul's position, and with him were Captains Townshend and Baird, and Surgeon-Captain Whitchurch, joined afterwards by Dr. Robertson and Lieutenant Gurdon.

They were at once attacked by the enemy in strong force, and were met with a very hot fire, and eventually had to retire to the fort, fighting every inch of the ground, with the enemy on the front and both flanks, and firing from the cover of garden walls. Captain Campbell being wounded, the command devolved upon Captain Townshend, who fought his way back with his wounded to a small hamlet where Dr. Robertson was rallying the men; meantime a message had brought out from the fort Lieutenant Harley and 50 Sikhs, a reinforcement which enabled the party to retire steadily into the fort, which they reached at eight o'clock.

At the same time a detachment of 50 men under Captain Baird and Lieutenant Gurdon were hotly engaged in another part of the ground. Captain Baird was wounded early in the action, and under the care of Surgeon-Captain Whitchurch, while Lieutenant Gurdon conducted the retreat to the fort. With Whitchurch were a few Kashmir sepoys and some hospital bearers, but the two parties soon got separated in the *mêlée*, and Whitchurch and his men had to fight their way back inch by inch, carrying their wounded officer.

Every now and then they had to stop and make bayonet-charges to clear the enemy out of the shelter of stone walls around them, and when at length they reached the fort nearly half the party had been left dead on the field, yet not a man had left the party. Poor Captain Baird was hit three times in the retreat, and died next day; while, strange to say, his gallant rescuer, Whitchurch, escaped untouched. Many heroic acts are done by our men in war and peace, but none can be greater heroes than these few sepoys, who were able so long to bear the strain of an apparently hopeless retreat and retire orderly, resisting all temptation to a *sauve qui peut*, when a speedy retreat without encumbrance of the wounded and bearers must at times have seemed the only chance for life. For his gallant conduct on this occasion, Surgeon—Captain Whitchurch received the Victoria Cross.

The total loss on this day was very heavy, and in addition to Captain Baird, General Baj Singh and Major Bhikam of the Kashmirs, and about 60 men, were killed; an ominous outset for the defence, which at first had a very depressing effect upon the troops, the majority of whom, it must be remembered, were of newly raised regiments, and without any British troops to give them confidence. Everything therefore depended upon the vigilance and calmness of the few British officers, one of whom unfortunately, Captain Campbell, was severely wounded in the knee, the command in consequence falling upon Captain Townshend.

From this day the siege commenced, and the fort was cut off from the outer world. On taking stock of their resources the garrison found that, everyone being on half rations, there was supply until about the middle of June, by which time, if they could hold out, they might expect relief; while there was a supply of about 300 rounds of ammunition per man. Of water there was no lack, as fortunately when first the fort was occupied a covered way had been made down to the river, and this covered way was all through the siege one of the principal objects of the enemy's attacks, and had to be held day and night by a strong guard.

The fort itself was 80 yards square, the walls being 25 feet high, and made of stone held together by a frame-work of wood, and 8 feet thick at each angle was a tower, while a fifth guarded the way to the water. Outside the walls were gardens and out-buildings, which afforded shelter to the enemy; these, owing to the rapidity with which the siege had developed, there had been no time to destroy, and this necessary work had therefore now to be done under fire. The enemy all through fought very well, and made every use of the cover afforded to their riflemen, who were excellent shots; and they built *sangars* on the rising ground above, commanding the fort, so that it was necessary for the besieged to build sheltering galleries to protect the men going from post to post.

Hardly a night passed without an attack of some sort, and three times the enemy succeeded in setting the towers on fire, only to be extinguished with great difficulty by the use of earth and water. The enemy employed every device to get into the fort, and succeeded in mining close up to the walls, adding thus the labour of making counter-mines to the other tasks of the garrison.

The principal fight took place on the 17th April. The enemy had been for some days previous in the apparently innocent amusement of making a noise with drums and pipes in a summer-house not far from the walls. One of the men suggested that the noise was made to cover the sound of mining—a not uncommon trick of Umra Khan's. Accordingly men were told off to listen, and the sound of mining was heard close to a tower, so close indeed that no time was to be lost in blowing it up.

This dangerous duty was successfully performed by Lieutenant Harley, who rushed the summer-house with 100 men. There was a fierce hand-to-hand fight, and some 30 Chitralis were killed, and the mine successfully destroyed; Harley and his men regaining the fort in an hour and twenty minutes. From the start 22 of the brave 100 were hit, of whom 9 were killed. Nothing of importance occurred after this, for the enemy had heard of the close approach of Colonel Kelly, and by the 19th of April had disappeared.

Thus ended a defence as gallant as any recorded in this book. For forty-six days this little band of sepoys, with five English leaders, held the fort, with inadequate defences and no artillery, against a superior force; the sepoys suffering greatly from want of food, for their caste forbade their eating horseflesh—their *ghee* or melted butter, which is as meat to the native, had run out, and all they had left was half rations of flour. To the want of food must be added the mental effect, first of the disastrous day at the opening, then of the absolute ignorance of the measures taken to relieve, and the apparent hopelessness of their position, if we are to take due measure of the pluck and determination of the garrison.

THE DEFENCE OF RESHUN

On the 5th of March, Lieutenants Edwardes and Fowler left Mastuj with orders to join the British agent at Chitral, and they had with them 20 Bengal Sappers and 40 men of the Kashmir Rifles, conveying sixty boxes of ammunition and seven days' rations. The day on which they arrived at Reshun they heard rumours of opposition ahead of them, and therefore entrenched themselves as well as possible near the river. The next day they were attacked by the tribes, and finding the position too exposed, they carried the houses of the village close by with the bayonet, and hastily made them defensible, and succeeded by nightfall in getting in all their ammunition and supplies and all the wounded. Here the little force, now reduced to about 50 men, was regularly besieged. The first great difficulty was the want of water, as the enemy had diverted the rivulet, thus making it necessary for the garrison to go some distance under fire to bring in sufficient for their daily wants. Food was fortunately plentiful, as, in addition to the rations, eggs and fowls and flour were found in the village. The enemy, after several attempts to take the place by assault, contented themselves with besieging the village, doing as much damage as possible by a continuous fire from the cover of houses and trees, and at length succeeded in occupying a house not more than a few feet from the wall.

On the 13th the enemy hoisted a white flag, and informed the officers that there had been some fighting at Chitral but that now peace was made, and offering to let the garrison go either to Chitral or to Mastuj. Lieutenant Edwardes upon this agreed to a three days' armistice, and sent letters to Chitral and Mastuj; meantime the garrison were well treated and supplies sent in to them. On the 14th the enemy proposed a game of polo, and invited the officers to come and see it. This invitation was unfortunately, as it turned out, accepted, for, although under the fire of their own men, the two officers were suddenly seized from behind and bound, and a sudden attack was made upon the house occupied by the troops. This was taken by assault, most of the sepoys being killed.

On March 16th, the officers were taken to Chitral, where they found about a dozen of the sepoys who had been taken prisoners; after being kept here some time, they were sent to Drosh to Umra Khan. He treated them very well, and even offered to let them join the force in Chitral, but as he would not let their men accompany them they declined. They were afterwards taken with Umra Khan on his return to Jandol, and though strictly guarded were treated with every respect and courtesy, and finally sent in safety to Sir R. Low's camp. The sepoys also were allowed to go unharmed—an act of forbearance on the part of Umra Khan almost without precedent among Pathans.

The affair of Reshun, which cost the lives of so many brave men, was the indirect cause of the loss of many more at the same time. For as soon as the British officers discovered the state of things at Reshun, they sent back word to Mastuj, and Captain Ross and Lieutenant Jones with 93 Sikhs at once set out to their assistance. Thirty-three men were left at Buni, and the remaining 60, with the two officers, pushed forward towards Reshun. On the way they had to pass through a narrow ravine with precipitous cliffs on either side. Here they were suddenly attacked by the enemy in great force from the cliffs above. Soon the enemy closed the end of the pass, and retreat or advance was equally impossible. For a time shelter was found in a cave, and an attempt was made to rush out of the defile in the night; but the enemy were found on the alert, and though the rifle fire could be faced, it was impossible to pass several stone shoots which were in the possession of the enemy, who could annihilate with avalanches of rocks any troops passing below.

The cave was again occupied for a day, but without food, and therefore it was necessary to make one desperate effort if the men were to escape starvation. Accordingly, in the middle of the night a sudden rush was made, and after a desperate fight the *sangars* held by the enemy were taken, but with heavy loss, Captain Ross being among the first killed. Eventually, after desperate fighting, and a great number having been killed in crossing the stone shoots, a small remnant reached the end of the ravine; here a stand was made, and at length Lieutenant Jones with 17 men, of whom 9 and himself were wounded, returned to Buni, where the enemy did not attack them; and on the 17th reliefs arrived from Mastuj, to which the whole party returned. Here they were besieged, and would in all probability have in time been reduced by famine had not Colonel Kelly's force arrived.

COLONEL KELLY'S MARCH

While these stirring events were taking place on the frontier, the Indian Government had not been inactive, for in the month of March an army of 14,000 men was mobilised, under the command of Major-General Sir R. Low, the intention being originally that this expedition should be sent to Chitral through Swat and Bajour, starting in April. On receipt of the news of the disaster at Karagh it became necessary to not only advance the troops as early as possible, but also to take immediate steps for the relief of Chitral at the earliest possible moment, as it was known that that place was only supplied till the end of April. It was impossible to send troops from India to Gilgit for this purpose, as the passes would not be open till June. Most fortunately a force of the 32nd Pioneers, under Colonel Kelly, were at this time road-making at Bunji, on the

Indus, only 38 miles from Gilgit; it was therefore determined to send Colonel Kelly with all the men he could collect to march as rapidly as possible to Chitral. On the 21st of March Colonel Kelly received orders by telegraph to march, and he set off the same afternoon. And a famous march it was!

On the 23rd of March the expedition set out from Gilgit. It consisted at starting of 400 men of the Pioneers, two guns of Number 1 Kashmir Mountain Battery, and 100 Hunza and Puniali Levies under their own chiefs; the officers with Colonel Kelly being Captain Borrodaile, Surgeon-Captain Browning-Smith, and Lieutenants Beynon, Bethune, Cobbe, Paterson, and Cooke; and these were joined at Gupis by Lieutenant Stewart, R.A., who took charge of the guns, and Lieutenant Oldham, R.E., with 40 Kashmir Sappers, and Lieutenant Gough with 100 Kashmir Rifles. It will be noticed that again the troops and non-commissioned officers were entirely native.

On April the 1st, in spite of five days' snow, the column set out from Ghizr to attempt the Shandur Pass. The first difficulty was a stampede of the impressed native bearers, who had bolted in the night and were not collected again till late in the afternoon. After a few miles the guns stuck in the deep snow, and it was found impossible to get them along. Captain Borrodaile, with Lieutenant Oldham and 140 men, with the Hunza Levies, remained at Teru with provision for ten days. The rest of the column with the guns had reluctantly to return to Ghizr.

The snow continuing, it was impossible to attempt the pass; but the Kashmirs set to work to dig a road from Teru through the snow to Langar, the camping-ground on their side of the pass, and on the next day the guns were got along to Teru and thence to Langar, but this was only effected by *carrying* the guns, carriages, and ammunition. These were divided amongst squads of four men, relieved every fifty yards, so that the progress did not exceed a mile an hour, the men being often up to their middle in snow in a bitter wind and a glaring sun. The camping-ground at Langar, some 13 miles from Teru, was not reached till near midnight, and the guns had to be left by their exhausted bearers a mile or so outside the camp. This was indeed a great achievement, but there remained still the pass. First there was a very stiff climb for about a mile, then a more gradual ascent up to 12,300 feet above sea-level, then five miles of fairly level plain, a sheet of glaring snow swept by a bitter wind.

The distance from Langar to Laspur on the other side of the pass is only ten miles, but though Borrodaile's party of Pioneers and Levies started early next day, they did not reach Laspur till evening. The villagers were as surprised as though the party had dropped from the moon, and thought it expedient to be friendly. The enemy had so implicitly relied upon the impossibility of getting through the pass in such extreme weather that no preparation to block our movements had been made.

The next day the village was put into a state of defence, and supplies were collected, and with the aid of the villagers the guns were brought down. Both men and officers suffered severely; most had blue spectacles, but by the time the whole column had got over there were 68 cases of snow-blindness and 43 of frost. The opposition shown by the enemy as the column proceeded was overcome by the gunfire, which the Chitrali seemed quite unable to stand; and Mastuj, from which the enemy had retired on the same day in the direction of Chitral, was reached on the afternoon of the 9th of April.

The march was continued the next day, and after a sharp fight on the 13th, in which Colonel Kelly lost eight men, Chitral was entered on the 20th. In this wonderful march the column had gone 350 miles in 35 days over a very difficult country, climbed a difficult pass, carrying the guns through the snow and in the face of an enemy. The men carried each two days' rations; and only seven days' rations being provided, after that the force had entirely to depend upon what the country afforded, which was very little.

THE CAPTURE OF THE MALAKAND PASS

We have now to return to the actions of the army, which, as we have seen, had been ordered to assemble under General Sir R. Low in March. The first Army Corps, consisting of 14,000 men, was mobilised at Nowshera and Hoti Mardan, with General Sir Bindon Blood, Chief of the Staff, and Lieutenant—Colonel H.S. Craigie, Assistant Adjutant-General; the three brigades being commanded by Generals Kinloch, Waterfield, and Gatacre. When the news arrived of the danger at Chitral the preparations were pressed forward, and on the 1st of April the troops were moved forward, marching without tents, and water supplies for only three weeks; and on the 2nd of April the second and third brigades were at Dargai, a village at the foot of the Malakand Pass. There are three passes into the Swat valley, namely, Malakand, Shakhot, and Morah; all of these were held by the enemy, but as it had been given out that the British intended to cross by the Shakhot Pass, to which the first brigade had been sent, the enemy were not in such force at Malakand as they should have been.

The fact was that when Sir R. Low learned that the greater part of the enemy were at the Shakhot and Morah Passes he determined to mislead them into staying there by acting as though he intended to attack the Shakhot Pass, and for this purpose marched the first brigade in that direction with orders to rejoin him if possible at Dargai by a forced night-march; intending that the three brigades should meet on the 2nd of April at 8 a.m. and carry the pass before the enemy had discovered their intention. The weather frustrated the carrying out of this plan, the night-march had to be abandoned and the attack postponed until the 3rd, but the plan of deceiving the enemy was quite successful, for the enemy had not time to get across the hills to help their comrades in the Malakand Pass. And this was fortunate, for the pass was so obstinately defended as it was that all three brigades, with the exception of one regiment held in reserve, were engaged in the attack.

The pass is through a valley gradually narrowing for about two miles from Dargai, and at this point it bends for about a mile and a half to a point where the hills drop precipitately into the pass. From this bend the pass was strongly defended, the whole range on the west side being held by the enemy. The 4th Sikhs were sent along the heights to guard the left flank of the advance, and climbing up the sides cleared many *sangars* of the enemy with great gallantry. The Guides Infantry had an equally arduous task on the hills. Meanwhile the force advanced up the valley. To quote from the General's despatch:

When the infantry advance was ordered it soon became apparent that if the assault was delayed till the position was turned by the Guides the action would be unduly delayed and the Guides themselves seriously out-numbered. At this time I ascertained that though the pass appeared to lie in the valley itself, and to round the corner of the western hill where it dropped into the valley, yet beyond this point there was no path or roadway whatever, the valley being blocked with huge blocks and boulders; and that the crossing of the pass lay to the left, over the heights to our left which were so strongly held by the enemy. Action was at once therefore taken to carry the hill to the left, which from this point was about 1000 feet high. The Gordon Highlanders were directed up the end of the western hill from the point where it touched the valley, and the King's Own Scottish Borderers were directed up the centre spur; the 60th Rifles were directed up the slopes from farther back on the line, while the Bedfordshire Regiment and the 37th Dogras pushed on and rounded the point from which the Gordon Highlanders commenced the ascent, and, turning to the left, ascended the hill from the northern side—the 15th Sikhs being held in reserve. As the infantry ascended it was seen how well the defence of the hill had been organised. The Gordon Highlanders and

King's Own Scottish Borderers, ascending as they did on a direct attack, met with the greatest resistance and suffered most. *Sangar* after *sangar* was obstinately held; each *sangar* as it was rushed coming at once under fire of the one above it. And here I may note the admirable service done by the artillery and Maxim guns. Several attempts were made by the enemy to concentrate from above and hold the lower *sangars* and positions, but all such attempts were frustrated by the admirable practice of the Mountain Batteries and Maxim guns over the head of our advancing infantry. Although at several points *sangars* were only carried by hand—to—hand fighting, the enemy were gradually driven from position to position, and eventually fled down the other slopes of the western hill as the heads of the attacking columns reached the top when the pass was captured and the fighting over, though they were pursued down the other side as soon as the men got together.

The action commenced at 8 o'clock and lasted six hours. The force of the enemy was estimated at 12,000 men, of whom perhaps 4000 or 5000 had firearms. The loss on the British side was only 11 men killed, and 8 officers and 39 men wounded.

The Terah Expedition
1897

The Terah Expedition
1897

In 1897 a general rising of the tribes took place along the north-west frontier, which, in addition to minor expeditions, was the cause of the despatch of an expedition through the Terah country, under Sir William Lockhart. It is impossible here to detail the innumerable acts of gallantry called forth by almost daily skirmishes with fierce and numerous bands of hardy mountaineers, but we must content ourselves with referring only to the most stirring incidents of the campaign.

The first Action of Dargai

It had become necessary to clear the enemy out of the commanding position at Dargai, from which a harassing fire had been kept up upon our men, and on 18th October this was achieved. The village lies on the north of a small plateau, which ends in a steep cliff approached by a sloping ridge; this ridge is well within range of the cliff, but by keeping on the south side troops can approach under cover; but connecting the ridge with the cliff is a narrow neck 100 yards long by 30 broad, completely open to fire from the cliffs, which must be crossed in order to get to the path up to the heights. The enemy were in force on the top of the cliff, under cover of rocks and boulders. On this occasion the attack was made by the 3rd Ghurkhas and the King's Own Scottish Borderers, and the Northampton Regiment in reserve. Every point from which rifle or artillery fire could be brought to bear on the enemy was occupied, and at noon a rush of Ghurkhas and Borderers was made across the ridge. A tremendous fire burst out from the heights, but so sudden was the rush that only twenty-two men were hit, of whom only three were killed. The enemy did not stay long when once the ridge was crossed and the heights were occupied. It was not, however, thought advisable to retain the position, and satisfied with having cleared the enemy out, Sir William Lockhart recalled the troops. As they retired the rearmost regiments were pressed by the tribesmen, who in consequence lost heavily; but several men of the Gordon Highlanders were wounded, and Major Jennings Bromley killed, in the fighting that ensued.

SECOND ACTION OF DARGAI

On 20th October the enemy were again in force on the heights, and in much greater numbers, and a second attack became necessary. The troops upon whom this duty fell were the 2nd Ghurkhas, the 1st Dorset and the Derbyshire, with the Gordon Highlanders in reserve. The first to cross were the gallant Ghurkhas, led by Colonel Travers, Captains McIntyre, Bower, and Norie, and Lieutenant Tillard; these succeeded in crossing unhurt, but with the loss of 30 men, and Major Judge and Captain Robinson. The bullets now swept the ridge, and in attempting to follow many a brave Dorset and Derby was killed, officers and men, and but few reached the Ghurkhas. To quote from the despatch of Sir William Lockhart:

> By 11:30 the force was in formation under cover in readiness to capture the heights, but when the 2nd Ghurkas, accompanied by the Ghurka scouts of the first battalion 3rd Ghurkas, made their first rush across the open, they were met by such a hot and well-aimed fire

that all they could do was to hold on to the position they had reached without being able to advance farther. At 2 p.m. the Dorsetshire Regiment was ordered to storm the enemy's entrenchments, but though a few men were able to get across the fire-swept zone, an advance beyond the line held by the 2nd Ghurkas was reported by the commanding officer to be impracticable owing to the large number of tribesmen lining the edge of the Dargai plateau, and the steepness of the slope leading up to it. The General officer commanding the second division accordingly ordered Brigadier-General Kempster to move up the Gordon Highlanders and the 3rd Sikhs, the former regiment being replaced on the lower spur which it had hitherto occupied by the Jhind Imperial Service Infantry.

The Gordon Highlanders went straight up the hill without check or hesitation. Headed by their pipers, and led by Lieutenant-Colonel Mathias, C.B., with Major Macbean on his right and Lieutenant A.F. Gordon on his left, this splendid battalion marched across the open. It dashed through a murderous fire, and in forty minutes had won the heights, leaving 3 officers and 30 men killed or wounded on its way. The first rush of the Gordon Highlanders was deserving of the highest praise, for they had just undergone a very severe climb and had reached a point beyond which other troops had been unable to advance for over three hours.

The first rush was followed at short intervals by a second and a third, each led by officers, and as the leading companies went up the path for the final assault the remainder of the troops, among whom the 3rd Sikhs were conspicuous, streamed on in support. But few of the enemy waited for the bayonet, many of them being shot down as they fled in confusion. The position was won at 3:15.

Amongst the losses of this day were—

Dorsetshire.—Nine men killed; Captain Arnold, Lieutenant Hewitt, and thirty-nine men wounded.

Gordon Highlanders.—Lieutenant Lamont and two men killed; Colonel Mathias, Major Macbean, Captain Uniacke, Lieutenants Dingwall, Meiklejohn, Craufurd, and thirty-five men wounded.

Derbyshire.—Captain Smith and three men killed, eight wounded.

The Victoria Cross was awarded to Lieutenant Pennell, who endeavoured under fire to bring in Captain Smith; to Piper Findlater, who though wounded in both legs still continued to blow his pipes; to Private Lawson for carrying Lieutenant Dingwall out of fire and returning to bring in another, being himself twice wounded; to Private Vickery and Colonel Mathias.

The Re-conquest
of the Sudan
1898

The Re-conquest of the Sudan 1898

Once more our attention is directed to the doings of our soldiers in Egypt. All the toil, all the bloodshed, and all the treasure expended against Mahdism had been in vain. General Gordon nobly holding out at Khartoum waiting for the relief which the vacillating and divided counsels of the British Cabinet had delayed until it was too late, had been slain, and the inhabitants of Khartoum despoiled and massacred by the savage followers of the Mahdi. Berber, Dongola, and Tokar had shared the same fate; and the Anglo-Egyptian army, leaving the Sudan to its fate, had fallen back to Wady Haifa, at which the southern frontier of Egypt was fixed, and which became a barrier against which the tide of Mahdism was to rush in vain.

Suakin was also strongly held, and the Mahdi's forces came no farther south; but the whole of the immense territory from the Second Cataract to the Equatorial Lakes was overrun by his fanatic hordes, who carried "fire, the sword, and desolation" far and wide over that unhappy land. It is not to the British administrators in Egypt that the blame of all this failure, and of the purposeless bloodshed of the two expeditions from Suakin, is to be laid, nor can it be said that after the fall of Khartoum any other course could have been adopted than to retire for a time; but it is to the British administrators in Egypt, and not to the Home Government, that belongs the credit of years of patient perseverance, of restoring the finances and resources of Egypt, and of instilling so much character into an oppressed race that at length the poor fellaheen were able to hold their own against the Sudanese, and to wipe out the disgrace of the defeat at El-Teb and the slaughter of the army of Hicks Pasha in 1883. And it may be said that it was these same English rulers in Egypt—administrators, engineers, military officers, and drill sergeants—that made it possible for the English to march in triumph through Khartoum and to avenge the death of Gordon, to some extent to wipe out the humiliations and blunders of past years.

The original Mahdi died within six months of General Gordon, and was succeeded by the chief Khalifa, Abdullah. Abdullah was an ignorant and wholly abominable person, and by his unspeakable cruelty and rapacity soon alienated vast numbers of the followers of his predecessor, and by 1889 Mahdism could no longer be looked upon as an aggressive but as a decaying force; yet, though dwindling, it still existed as a strong military power, with its headquarters at Omdurman.

Meantime the English had been making soldiers of the fellaheen, to whom successful skirmishes under their English officers and drill instructors were yearly giving confidence and self-reliance; and in addition to the fellaheen regiments, Sudanese regiments were formed of the very men who fought so bravely against our squares at Abu Klea, the "Fuzzywuzzy" of Kipling, "a first-class fighting man." Whilst the British campaigns in the Sudan, though affording many a brilliant fight, and many an example of the heroism and endurance of the British soldiers, were fruitless in result, the Egyptian campaigns were from 1885 onwards one continual success,—the fruit of steady effort and perseverance directed to one end through every kind of difficulty and disappointment, but which nothing could turn aside from its object, never faltering or swerving for fourteen years, the credit of which is wholly due to Sir Evelyn Baring (now Lord Cromer), Sir H. Kitchener (Lord Kitchener), Sir F. Grenfell, Colonel Wingate, Colonel H.A. Macdonald, and many others; and their subordinates, among whom must be remembered the English drill sergeants.

In 1888 Osman Digna again threatened Suakin, and threw up trenches against the town, but was defeated by Sir F. Grenfell, the *Sirdar* or Commander-in-Chief of the Egyptian forces, on December 20th. Next, Wad-en-Nejunii, the great Emir who had defeated Hicks Pasha, came south in 1889, attempting to get to the Nile at Toski behind Wady Haifa, the garrison of which, under Sir F. Grenfell, attacked him at Toski, with the result that he was killed and his army annihilated, and Egypt freed from fear of invasion.

After this Egypt began to advance; Sarras, beyond Wady Haifa, was reoccupied, and a railway laid between the two places. In February 1891 Colonel Holled Smith, commanding the Egyptian garrison at Suakin, marched out against Osman Digna's men with only Egyptian and Sudanese troops, and defeated them after a good fight and occupied Tokar. In this action Captain Barrow was killed, and of the enemy a large number of Emirs; but Osman as usual got away. The effect of this battle was to clear away the dervishes from the Eastern Sudan and re-establish Egyptian government there.

In 1892 the dervishes again gave trouble both on the Nile and in the Eastern Sudan, and there were many skirmishes. A serious attempt was made in January 1893 to cut the railway between Wady Haifa and Sarras, but without success; in the fight Captain Pyne, commanding the Egyptian force, was killed. Osman Digna again turned up near Suakin, but had no success except in his usual flight.

In this year Sir Horatio Kitchener, who had had a long experience both of Egypt and the Sudan, having been on active service in one or the other since 1882, became *Sirdar* in succession to Sir F. Grenfell, who was appointed to the command of the British forces in Egypt, and he set himself to the task of the re-conquest of the Sudan. He had not the British tax-payer to draw upon, but the very meagre Egyptian Treasury, and he had therefore to work with very limited means. His plan was not to raise a costly army for the purpose of winning victories glorious but fruitless, slaughtering Arabs by the thousand and then retiring till they gathered head and then slaughtering more, after the manner of the peace-loving Government of 1885, but to make sure of each stage of his progress as he went along, driving back the Mahdi and bringing confidence and commerce in his train, never retiring from ground once occupied, but never advancing till his course was clear; and his chief instrument for effecting his purpose was, as it will be seen, the railway.

The Advance to Dongola

During all these years, as has been said, the Egyptian army was in the making; and in 1896 it was decided to put it to the test, and to make an advance on Dongola. On March 21st the *Sirdar* left Cairo for Wady Haifa, taking with him a British regiment, the 1st Staffordshire, to join the Egyptians already at the front; Indian troops having taken the place of the Egyptian garrisons of Tokar and Suakin. Meantime, railway making had been pushed on apace, and the line reached Kosheh, a distance of 76 miles, by the end of April; but rapid as this was, it was as nothing to the achievements of the following year. On June 7th a considerable force of dervishes was attacked and utterly defeated by the Egyptian army, whose conduct delighted their officers and gave them all confidence in the future. A further advance was made in September, and Dongola was occupied. The campaign had been entirely successful, the character of the Egyptian soldiery was established, the fertile province of Dongola rescued from the devastating rule of the Khalifa, and the frontier pushed back as far as Mirawi and Abu Dis—the steamboats could pass to this point up the Nile, and thus a great step was taken upon the road to Khartoum.

The *Sirdar* now conceived, and at once began to carry out, the bold idea of laying a railway from Wady Haifa across the desert to Abu Hamed, and thence to Berber and to Dakhala, and the junction of the Nile and the Atbara, a distance of nearly 400 miles. A bold idea indeed, for not only had every rail and every sleeper to be brought up to Wady Haifa, and thence along the rail itself as it disappeared into the trackless desert, but every mile the railway advanced the work was getting farther away from its base and penetrating deeper into the enemy's country, for at this time Abu Hamed was still held by the dervishes. Water was bored for and actually found along the route; and before the line arrived there Abu Hamed had been captured, and by the end of the year the railway reached the Nile again, at a point 234 miles from Haifa, and above the Third Cataract. General Hunter, after a sharp fight in which Major Sidney and Lieutenant Fitzclarence were killed, had seized Abu Hamed; and by the end of the campaign, Dongola, Debbet, Khorti, and Berber were held by Egypt, while the Nile was patrolled even up to Metammeh by the six steamers which, despite all difficulties, had been passed over the cataracts.

The railway making did not pause at Abu Hamed, but at once set out towards the junction of the Atbara with the Nile, a point 150 miles farther, and just south of the Fifth Cataract; the object being not only to provide for the rapid transport of provisions and stores, but also to get on to the Nile the three new steamers which had been brought from England in sections, so that they might be ready for the final advance.

THE ATBARA CAMPAIGN

At the beginning of 1897 the *Sirdar's* force at the front was in four brigades, three Egyptian and one British. The Egyptian division of three brigades was under Major-General Hunter; the first brigade, three regiments of black hoofs, Sudanese, and splendid soldiers, and one of Egyptian, was commanded by Lieutenant-Colonel H.A. Macdonald, and quartered at Berber. The second brigade, also consisting of three Sudanese and one Egyptian regiment, and under the command of Lieutenant—Colonel Maxwell, was about half-way between Berber and the Atbara River; while the third brigade, under Lieutenant-Colonel Lewis, consisting entirely of Egyptians, was at the Atbara. The British brigade, commanded by Major-General Gatacre, had its camp about a mile away from the second brigade, and consisted of the 1st Lincolnshire, Colonel Verner; the 1st Cameron Highlanders, Colonel Money; 1st Warwickshire, under Lieutenant-Colonel Onagle Jones, and was afterwards joined by the 1st Seaforth Highlanders, Colonel Murray. The whole force in the field, exclusive of the railway battalion and the crews of the gunboats, but including four batteries of artillery under Lieutenant-Colonel Long and eight squadrons of Egyptian cavalry under Lieutenant-Colonel Broadwood, amounted to about 14,000 men.

About the end of February it was known that Mahmoud was concentrating at Shendy, and preparing to make an attack upon Berber, which being held only by Egyptian troops he hoped to capture before the *Sirdar* could come to its relief. Nor was this by any means an impracticable plan, for Mahmoud's force consisted of some 20,000 horse and foot, with ample supplies of arms and ammunition, guns, and transport animals; but Mahmoud reckoned without the *Sirdar*.

On the 25th February the British brigade was ordered to proceed from Abu Dis, to which point they had recently advanced, to Debeker, a village 10 miles or so south of Berber. The men had but just returned from a 16-mile route march, but the start was made without delay. The railway, which was always being pushed ahead, was available for 17 miles out, and by the evening of the 27th the whole force was on the march; while by the evening of 3rd March they had reached their destination,—as good a performance as even the records of British Infantry can show. To quote the Special Army Order issued from the Horse Guards at the end of the campaign, "The march of the British Brigade to the Atbara, when in six days—for one of which it was halted—it covered 140 miles in a most trying climate, shows what British troops can do when called upon."

On the 20th of March the entire force marched to Ras-el-Hudi, a point on the bend of the river which Mahmoud would have to pass if he decided to attack Berber. But Mahmoud, finding now that he would have the British as well as Egyptians to deal with, changed his plans, and instead of advancing entrenched his position, hoping to receive assistance from the Khalifa. On the 26th a raid was made on Shendy by the steamboats, under command of Commander Keppel and Lieutenants Beatty and Hood, R.N.; the troops being commanded by Majors Hickman and Sitwell, Captain Sloman, and Lieutenant Graham. This was completely successful: the dervishes fled; Shendy, where was Mahmoud's reserve depot, was occupied, and the forts and depot destroyed, and a large number of female prisoners released. Attempts to draw Mahmoud out of his cover were unsuccessful, and the *Sirdar* decided to attack him.

On April 7th the force, with the British leading, made a night-march, and after a short rest took up a position about one and a half miles from the enemy's camp, and about 4:30 a.m. a general advance in attack formation was made. The British brigade was on the left, Macdonald's in the centre, Maxwell's on the right, and Lewis's Egyptians were held in reserve. The enemy were in a large irregular enclosure, with its rear on the now dry bed of the river. The position was defended by trenches, and in part by palisades; and was surrounded by a strong *zareba*, the inside being full of shelter trenches and pits. After a bombardment by 12 guns and the rocket detachment, at 7:10 the general advance was sounded, and with pipes and bands playing the infantry bore down upon the *zareba*. In front of the British were the Camerons in line, and behind them the Warwicks on the left, Seaforths in the centre, and Lincolns on the right; General Gatacre, the Staff, and Colonel Money in front. The *zareba* was soon reached and torn aside, and in a few minutes our men were in the enclosure. The enemy fought bravely, and, refusing quarter, died fighting. In every hut and trench the dervishes were hid, and slashed and fired at their enemy till bayoneted, or shot themselves. There were many hand-to-hand fights and many narrow escapes, but in forty minutes the firing was over and the dervish army scattered and annihilated. With the exception of Osman Digna, who with his usual luck escaped, and three others, all the important leaders were killed, and Mahmoud himself taken prisoner. He was found in a hole under his bed! a rare instance of cowardice among dervishes. Of the British, Captains Urquhart and Findlay of the Camerons, and Lieutenant Gore of the Seaforths, who had only recently joined, were killed leading their men over the trenches, besides 22 non-commissioned officers and men; and 10 officers and 82 non-commissioned officers and men wounded. The Egyptian army lost 57 officers and men, and 5 British and 16 native officers and 365 non-commissioned officers and men wounded. The dervish losses were estimated at over 3000 killed at and around the *zareba*; but of the whole dervish army but very few, and none of the wounded, could have escaped to Omdurman,—in fact the army was practically annihilated.

Among the many escapes from spear or bullet that occurred, none are more curious than those of Corporal Lawrie of the Seaforths, which he related in a letter home, afterwards published in a daily paper. A bullet took off the toe of his shoe, his bayonet was bent by a shot; a shot passed through his sleeve, his rifle was struck by a bullet; a dervish striking at him with a spear only split his haversack; a shot entered the lid of his ammunition pouch, passed into his coat pocket, smashing a penknife and two pencils, tore four holes in his shirt, made a surface wound on his left breast, and came out near his left shoulder through his coat and pouch braces.

THE ADVANCE TO KHARTOUM.

After the battle of the Atbara the troops returned to the Nile and went into summer quarters, waiting for the time of high Nile, when the advance would be made.

The British troops settled down for a time in camp as in times of peace, for there was no fear of any dervish force, and were made as comfortable as possible; and the men, who were all well seasoned and inured to the climate, spared as much as possible during the heat. But it was a very busy time with the Egyptians, and especially with the railway brigade, which, under the able direction of the director of railways, Major Gerouard, R.E., laboured incessantly to complete the track to Dakhala, which now became the base and depot of the autumn campaign.

The new gunboats were brought up by rail in sections, and put together, as well as the barges for transport, and launched at Abadieh on the Nile, a village between Berber and the Fifth Cataract. Camping-grounds were prepared, commissariat stores and ammunition forwarded to the front, wood cut and stacked for fuel, and every preparation made, so that there might be no delay or hitch at the critical moment.

From the 17th of July, everything being in readiness to receive them, reinforcements for the British command, now to be raised to a division and commanded by Major-General Gatacre, were moved up from Cairo; amongst these were Royal Artillery, Royal Engineers, Army Service Corps, Medical Corps, and the 21st Lancers under Colonel Martin, a regiment which had never yet been in action, and was therefore burning to distinguish itself, as indeed it did, as we shall presently see.

A second British brigade had been formed, under the command of Colonel Lyttleton; it was comprised of 1st Northumberland Fusiliers, Lieutenant—Colonel Money; 2nd Lancashire Fusiliers, Lieutenant-Colonel Collingwood, from the Army of Occupation at Cairo; 2nd Rifle Brigade, Colonel Howard; and 1st Grenadier Guards, Colonel Hatton; which last two regiments had come direct to the front from Malta and Gibraltar respectively. There was also a detachment of Royal Irish Fusiliers, with Maxims, making in all about 7,500 men.

The 21st Lancers numbered 500, the rest of the cavalry being Broadwood's Egyptians, about 1,000 sabres. There was also an addition to the artillery of the 32nd Field-Battery R.A., Major Williams; 37th Field-Battery with the new 5-inch howitzers firing Lyddite shells, and two siege-guns, besides some twenty or more Maxims.

The first British division was composed, as before, of the Camerons, Seaforths, Lincolns, and Warwicks; the last two having changed colonels, Lieutenant-Colonel Louth now leading the Lincolns, and Lieutenant-Colonel Forbes the Warwicks. The brigade was commanded by Colonel Wauchope; General Gatacre, as has been said, being now in command of the division.

The land forces numbered over 8,000 British troops and about 15,000 Egyptian; in addition to this the *Sirdar* had a river flotilla of eleven steamboats well armed, besides iron barges especially made for transport of troops, and innumerable native craft.

THE BATTLE OF OMDURMAN

On 15th August the final advance began, and on the 22nd the whole force was concentrated at Wad Hamed, some 50 miles from Omdurman, a brilliant achievement even for the *Sirdar*, for it meant that 23,000 men, with all impedimenta, stores, and ammunition, had been moved within ten days 150 miles across the desert into the enemy's country by means of marching and the use of the flotilla on the Nile.

The task before them is one of the most arduous that an army has ever been called upon to perform, being at a distance of something like 1,200 miles from the real base of operations, on the sea, in a climate the conditions of which are trying, and amidst deserts devoid of all resources—even of those few which existed in 1884 when the British forces under Lord Wolseley advanced to Metammeh, and which have since been utterly destroyed by the complete devastation of the villages on the banks of the Nile and the murder or despoliation of their inhabitants.—Field-Marshal Sir J. L. A. Simmons, in a letter to the *Times*.

On the 2nd September the army lay encamped at Agaiga on the Nile, a few miles only from Khartoum, having already come into touch with he Khalifa's outposts, the main body of whose army, some 40,000 or 50,000, had come out of Omdurman, and was entrenched between them and the city. The *Sirdar's* camp was in the form of a semicircle, with about one mile of the Nile for its diameter. On the extreme left was the 32nd Field-Battery R.A.; and next them, with their left on the Nile, and on the right of the guns, lay the second British brigade (Rifles, Lancashire, Northumberland, and Grenadier Guards); then the first British brigade (Wauchope's), Warwicks, Seaforths, Camerons, and Lincolns; then Maxwell's 2nd Egyptian; Macdonald's, and then Lewis with his right on the Nile. On the left, and extending close down to the lines, was a small hill, Gabel Surgham; and on the right, some way off, the rising ground of Kerrin. The camp was protected by a *zareba* and trench, with spaces at intervals, and all along the river were the flotilla of gunboats.

At an early hour the whole army was armed and everything in readiness for the advance, when the scouts and the pickets of the 21st Lancers came galloping in with the astounding but most welcome news that the Khalifa, instead of waiting to be attacked behind his entrenchments, as did Mahmoud at Atbara, was rapidly advancing with his whole army upon the *zareba*. Nothing could have been more fortunate for the *Sirdar* or more foolish on the part of the Khalifa; had he even remained in his position he would have caused his assailants heavy loss, while had he awaited our attack in Omdurman the siege might have presented many difficulties. As it was, over-confident in the fanatic courage of his followers, and their superior numbers, he threw his host upon our fire, verily *"Quem deus vult perdere prius dementat"* was true in his case.

The black flag of the Khalifa and the huge host of the Arabs was soon seen approaching, and at 6:30 a.m. the firing commenced. First the Maxims and 15-pounder field-guns, 2800 yards; then the Lee-Metford rifles. The air was full of shot and bullet, shrapnel and shell, mowing out great gaps in the charging masses, who never faltered in their movement. Thousands upon thousands fell, and were succeeded by thousands upon thousands who likewise fell; and of all that host never a man reached the *zareba*. Nothing could exceed the courage of the dervishes. Following their old tactics, they meant to rush the *zareba*, piercing, as they hoped, the line of fire by sheer force of numbers.

Stormed at by shot and shell
Bravely they fought and fell.

A large body of horse tried to break through the centre, and were annihilated. At length human endurance could do no more, and the shattered remnants of what had been but an hour before a mighty host, withdrew behind Gabel Surgham. So ended the first act, with a loss of a few hundred in killed and wounded; 10,000 dervishes were slain.

It was at first thought when the last dervish disappeared behind the high ground that the fight was over, and that Omdurman lay open; and after a delay occupied in removing the wounded to the steamers, and replenishing ammunition, the army, about 9:30, re-formed for marching, moved out of the camp. Lyttleton's and Wauchope's brigade, turning by the left, moved round the bottom of Gabel Surgham; Maxwell passing on their right, while Lewis and Macdonald moved away much farther on the right; and thus the brigades became at some distance apart.

And now took place one of the most stirring events of this eventful day. The 21st Lancers, trotting ahead a mile or more beyond Gabel, came upon a small body of dervishes hiding in a hollow; and Colonel Martin having decided to cut them off, the regiment charged in line, led by Colonel Martin. Within 200 yards of the enemy the horsemen saw the trap that had been laid for them; instead of 200 or 300 men in a hollow, 2,000 or more dervishes lay in wait for them in a narrow and rather deep ravine. Four hundred against 2,000 rode the Lancers, and somehow or another were into the ravine and out again, and with lance and sword and revolver had pushed and hacked their way through the dense mass of the enemy. Clean through and out on the other side; but not all of them, for any whose horse fell and could not recover at once was cut to pieces. There were many wonderful escapes, and many acts of bravery. The colonel rode through well in front without drawing sword or revolver; his horse fell in the midst of the *mêlée* but was up again, and both came through without a scratch. Perhaps 80 dervishes were knocked over, but the Lancers suffered severely.

Lieutenant Grenfell fell at the head of his troop, and ten of his men with him. As he was lying surrounded by a crowd of dervishes, Lieutenant de Montmorency, who had got through safely, returned to his assistance. He succeeded in driving off the enemy, and finding Lieutenant Grenfell dead he attempted to place the body across his horse. While he was doing this his horse bolted, and he was left to face the enemy. Captain Kenna and Corporal Swabrick came to his assistance, and fortunately caught the horse and were able to keep the enemy at a distance with their revolvers, while all three got safely through. Lieutenant De Montmorency received the Victoria Cross, and also Captain Kenna, who had also saved Major Windham, whose horse was bolting, by taking him up behind him on his own horse.

Meantime Macdonald's brigade, which had moved away to the right, had to bear a sudden attack of 15,000 dervishes who had rallied behind the high ground, and with reckless courage threw themselves upon the Egyptian ranks, who now found themselves attacked on three sides at once. In old times no Egyptian troops could have sustained the shock, but all was altered now. Admirably handled by their commander, both men and officers as cool as on parade, the brigade thrown practically into line, with the left and right thrown back, held their own, mowing down the enemy with a well-sustained fire. The guns soon came to the relief, and shot and shell fell from steamers on to the devoted host; and Wauchope's brigade coming up, the rout of the dervishes was soon complete.

Again the army advanced, and soon after four o'clock the *Sirdar* with the captured standard of the Khalifa entered Omdurman, arriving just after the Khalifa, with a small body of followers, had succeeded in slipping away.

A Victoria Cross was also given to Captain Nevill Smyth, who galloped forward and engaged in single combat with an Arab who was attacking camp followers, and killed him, being slightly wounded himself.

The Funeral of General Gordon. On Sunday, 4th September, the *Sirdar*, Generals, and Staff, with detachments from all branches of the army, steamed up the Blue Nile to the ruins of Khartoum, and on the summit of Gordon's old palace, the scene of his death, hoisted the Union Jack and the Egyptian flag. After this ceremony the bands played the Dead March, the chaplains—Presbyterian, Roman, Wesleyan, and Anglican—offered prayer, and hymns were sung on the very spot where the hero fell.

Among the numerous rewards given for services in this campaign, none was more popular than the peerage conferred upon the *Sirdar*, now Lord Kitchener of Khartoum.

LEONAUR

ALSO FROM LEONAUR
AVAILABLE IN SOFTCOVER OR HARDCOVER WITH DUST JACKET

THE COMPLEAT RIFLEMAN HARRIS *by Benjamin Harris as told to & transcribed by Captain Henry Curling*—The adventures of a soldier of the 95th (Rifles) during the Peninsular Campaign of the Napoleonic Wars

WITH WELLINGTON'S LIGHT CAVALRY *by William Tomkinson*—The Experiences of an officer of the 16th Light Dragoons in the Peninsular and Waterloo campaigns of the Napoleonic Wars.

SERGEANT BOURGOGNE *by Adrien Bourgogne*—With Napoleon's Imperial Guard in the Russian Campaign and on the Retreat from Moscow 1812 - 13.

SWORDS OF HONOUR *by Henry Newbolt & Stanley L. Wood*—The Careers of Six Outstanding Officers from the Napoleonic Wars, the Wars for India and the American Civil War, with dozens of illustrations by Stanley L. Wood.

SURTEES OF THE RIFLES *by William Surtees*—A Soldier of the 95th (Rifles) in the Peninsular campaign of the Napoleonic Wars.

ENSIGN BELL IN THE PENINSULAR WAR *by George Bell*—The Experiences of a young British Soldier of the 34th Regiment 'The Cumberland Gentlemen' in the Napoleonic wars.

HUSSAR IN WINTER *by Alexander Gordon*—A British Cavalry Officer during the retreat to Corunna in the Peninsular campaign of the Napoleonic Wars.

NAPOLEONIC WAR STORIES *by Sir Arthur Quiller-Couch*—Tales of soldiers, spies, battles & sieges from the Peninsular & Waterloo campaingns.

JOURNALS OF ROBERT ROGERS OF THE RANGERS *by Robert Rogers*—The exploits of Rogers & the Rangers in his own words during 1755-1761 in the French & Indian War.

KERSHAW'S BRIGADE VOLUME 1 *by D. Augustus Dickert*—Manassas, Seven Pines, Sharpsburg (Antietam), Fredricksburg, Chancellorsville, Gettysburg, Chickamauga, Chattanooga, Fort Sanders & Bean Station..

KERSHAW'S BRIGADE VOLUME 2 *by D. Augustus Dickert*—At the wilderness, Cold Harbour, Petersburg, The Shenandoah Valley and Cedar Creek.

A TIGER ON HORSEBACK *by L. March Phillips*—The Experiences of a Trooper & Officer of Rimington's Guides - The Tigers - during the Anglo-Boer war 1899 - 1902.

Lightning Source UK Ltd.
Milton Keynes UK
21 June 2010